F*CK THE SYSTEM

AND OTHER BAD IDEAS FOR THE FUTURE

Can Europe become a real superpower?

Jo Caudron

Lannoo Campus

MIX
Paper | Supporting responsible forestry
FSC® C004472
www.fsc.org

This book was originally published as *Fuck the system, en andere slechte ideeën voor de toekomst*, LannooCampus, 2025.

D/2026/45/309 – ISBN 9789059966185 – NUR 740

Cover and interior design: Atelier Steve Reynders

LannooCampus Publishers is a subsidiary of Lannoo Publishers, the book and multimedia division of Lannoo Publishers nv.

LannooCampus Publishers
Vaartkom 41 box 01.02
3000 Leuven
Belgium

P.O. Box 23202
1100 DS Amsterdam
The Netherlands

www.lannoocampus.com

Contents

Introduction

Is it still possible to be optimistic these days? It's a question I have been asking myself daily in recent years. It has even become my central theme: what drives me in all my consulting work, the presentations I give, and the books I write. In today's world, where new challenges keep seeming to knock the foundations out from under our certainties, is there still room for a positive vision? For faith in a better future? By nature, I am more of a pessimist than an optimist, with a hefty dose of cynicism on top as a defence mechanism. So I was not surprised when my colleagues gave me a T-shirt with the slogan: 'I'm not cynical, everything just sucks.' And yet I keep searching for solutions and ways to bend my pessimism towards hope, towards outcomes, towards optimism. Fortunately, my cynicism does not get in the way.

My wife calls me the most optimistic pessimist she knows – and in a way, she's right. Everything I do confronts me with the challenges people, companies, sectors and, by now, the entire world are facing. Time and time again, I go looking for insights, models and solutions to deal with those challenges. The restlessness of pessimism and the worries about tomorrow give me the energy to keep searching for outcomes, for ways to improve what we do. In that sense, my books are almost therapeutic. *Digital Transformation* (2014) helped me turn the disruptive potential of the emerging internet into a guide for managing business transformations positively. *The World is Round* (2020) was a way of mapping the growing polarisation and, from there, sketching a vision of the future in which we can once again live together in a positive way. *The Future Formula* (2023) started from major societal challenges in the fields of sustainability, living together, (geo)politics, financial pressure and AI upheavals, and went in search of a formula that would allow our economy to restart – with respect for both people and planet.

With each new book, each therapeutic cycle, it became harder to find the positive energy – to bend my pessimism towards optimism. By late 2024, I even felt that it might no longer be possible at all. And then 2025 arrived, with all its geopolitical madness and the global disorder that suddenly swept over us. At first, that seemed to confirm my fatalism. But gradually, the sentiment shifted. I immersed myself in how the world responded to that sudden change in the status quo, and I noticed ambition, energy, the will – and even the absolute necessity – to translate the challenges we face once again into solutions for the next era. Now I feel more hopeful than I have in a long time, and that has everything to do with Europe – that old, hardening continent at which the United States, Russia, India, China and so many others have looked with contempt in recent years. Only still good as a travel destination, otherwise meaningless on the world stage. But it is precisely that Europe that now has the chance to pull itself together and seize the momentum to reinvent itself. Recent global crises have taught us that Europe is at its strongest when the pressure increases. And that is exactly the case now.

That is also the central theme of this book: can we, *in Europe, take back control of our future, and can we do this in a positive way?* Can we come up with a story our children want to hear, that we want to build (preferably collectively), and that puts us back on the map? I believe we can. More than that: I can see this feeling is shared by many. The momentum is there; the challenge will be to seize it and let it grow into something tangible. With this book, I want to contribute to that – however small that contribution may be. Even so, this is a difficult, and even dangerous, book for me. More than ever, I have to talk about things that polarise people, and that is not without risk. I therefore expect that ideas will be framed and that I will face criticism: to some I will be too progressive (certainly in the part where I analyse the forces behind Trump), to others too conservative (where I talk about solutions and an approach). And all the while, with this book I mainly do not want to take a position. This story starts from the systemic crisis the world finds itself in, in which we need a radically new way of thinking and acting. In that context, concepts such as progressive versus conservative, left versus right, and so on are no longer adequate. A new central, pragmatic position is necessary to tackle the challenges ahead. The question is: with which set of values and norms do we want to do that? Do we want to let that be dictated by what the United States, Russia, China or the Middle East consider important? Or does something like a shared European moral compass exist, one that can guide us in the choices we are going to have to make?

Fuck the System

I am surrounded by an interesting mix of progressive and conservative friends, family, business contacts and (former) colleagues. The progressives are generally a legacy of my own younger years; the conservatives mostly come from more recent times. Although these people are understanding and open-minded with one another and with me, in recent years I have noticed a striking phenomenon that I think I also see more broadly in society: no one likes 'the system' anymore. It is often about moderate positions – thankfully I do not have too many extremists in my immediate circle – but in our conversations there is barely concealed criticism of almost everything that forms the foundation of our society. There are a number of themes everyone can immediately agree on: politics no longer works and politicians sit at the very bottom of the reliability ranking, just above a bad-tempered chihuahua; our democracy is indecisive, bureaucratic and lacks decisiveness; the economy is doing badly and either ordinary people or businesses are the victims of that; the legal system fails spectacularly; the education and healthcare systems are not fit for purpose; we pay too much tax; we are allowed to retire later and later; and Europe is, well: Europe ... In short, a long list of everything that is wrong with 'the system'.

If you dig deeper into this dissatisfaction, the left and right generally have a completely different interpretation of similar themes. Where one sees too much impunity, the other sees too little support and empathy. Where one sees too much tax, the other sees too much inequality. For every person who thinks we are doing too little about the climate, there are others who are angry because their old diesel car is no longer allowed into the city. We pay too little attention to equal opportunities and inclusion, while there are also calls for stricter policy on replacement incomes. The world is too sour, selfish and even racist, or else far too multicultural and permissive. Either way, there is little left that is right about our society. This contradiction is of course not new, but what strikes me is that it seems to be becoming ever more outspoken and that – despite all the differences – the conclusion of that shared dissatisfaction is the same: the system no longer works, *fuck the system!*

Many people seem to believe that the social model we live in has reached the end of the line and must be replaced by something else. People do not want a better system; they want a different system. Even though no one has a clear picture of what that other system should be, let alone a worked-out plan. Yet that does not stop them from arguing that we should, at the very least, simply get rid of the current system. So fuck the system. This is very dangerous. On both the (extremely) progressive side of the spectrum and the (extremely) conservative side, there seems to be a willingness to dismantle the system without any real alternative. Yes, there is no shortage of slogans and, as long as they are the length of a single tweet (sorry, I do not know what else to call it now that Twitter has become X), they can be very effective. For the left, it is: we have to dial back consumption and growth, redistribute prosperity, ditch capitalism, move away from globalisation, stop all emissions immediately, invest (even) less in defence ... For the right, it sounds like: a strong leader will sort it out, harsher sentences for everyone, abolish all those rules and bureaucracy, get rid of taxes, and of course send all those migrants back to their home countries. Okay, I am making a bit of a parody of it, but you get what I mean.

What stands out is that both sides of the spectrum are being tempted by the same tactic: demolition populism. We are always against something, and almost never for anything. The first time it really struck me how this can create unexpected alliances was during the demonstrations against COVID-19 measures that were organised in European cities. It was a colourful mix of participants of all kinds. Shoulder to shoulder stood anti-globalists with far-right skinheads, artists and hospitality workers without jobs, progressives with a fetish for a radical healthy lifestyle, ordinary concerned citizens who had spent a bit too much time on Facebook, and anti-vaxxers who believed in a global conspiracy. Nothing that connects them in real life, except that they were against the COVID-19 measures. And yet this shared idea of throwing the system out with the rubbish is a bad idea. We need to think constructively about our future, and about the future of Europe.

Structure of this book

In this book, in Part 1, I outline how the current world order is falling apart, which forces are behind it, and why they are doing so. What kind of new world do they have in mind, and what might the consequences be for Europe? I focus in particular on the Western forces behind this movement: the extreme ideologies that have been present in Europe for quite some time, and of course the major accelerant the United States has now become under Trump II. Although a thorough analysis of this problem deserves a book of its own, I still want to analyse certain forces behind Trump II, because they will continue to have an effect even if he eventually disappears from the political stage. It is important to understand them, because their impact on the future of Europe and the rest of the world can be fundamental, and today we will have to make a choice as to whether we allow these forces to gain the upper hand in Europe once again – with all the consequences that would have for our social order.

In Part 2, I explore what is now happening in Europe: from the initial disbelief at the way the United States seems to be breaking away from us, to the energy and willingness to emancipate ourselves as a continent and claim our own position in the new world order. The momentum for a new Europe seems to be there, but is Europe able to translate it into action, into the necessary leadership, into support among citizens, businesses and politicians? Can Europe claim a new, strong position vis-à-vis other world powers – with, not least, revisiting the relationship with the United States as a major challenge? Next, we dive into the underlying causes that led populists like Trump to be given the mandate to shape the world to their liking. Anyone who has read *The World is Round* will recognise echoes of the patterns I describe there in detail. In that book I sketch possible positive and negative outcomes, and unfortunately we now have to acknowledge that the world has chosen the negative path. We cannot avoid recognising that there are problems in the world, that many people feel insecure – which leads to unrest, frustration and even anger.

The entire digital development of social media echo chambers, combined with hyper-individualisation as the shadow side of our social emancipation, has resulted in an extremely explosive mixture of loud dissatisfaction. Voters therefore seem willing to hand the keys to their country and their future to dubious figures offering simple, but unrealistic, promises. We should not simply dismiss this as protest votes from people who do not know any better. They want real change and solutions to problems that feel closer to them than abstract challenges such as climate change. By that I do not mean to say that the climate crisis is no longer relevant – quite the opposite. We will have to do everything we can to take those people's concerns seriously, tackle their problems and restore trust.

The most important part of this book, Part 3, is about the recipes I see for helping Europe make its regained ambitions a reality. I analyse the opportunities we have to compete successfully with other regions, and what we need to invest in to strengthen our position on the world stage. Central concepts here are transitional industries, stimulating smart innovation, and copy-back of strategic platforms and technologies. Themes covered include AI, digital platforms and data centres, energy, new and traditional media, communication, mobility, food and agriculture, and, of course, defence. I explore how we can reshape our economy and business models to make these innovations a success, and which ecosystems and financial solutions are needed to do so. I end with critical questions that I know readers will ask. Ambition and concrete plans are one thing, but will Europe really be able to deliver? Do we have the structures, the resources and the people to turn this new momentum into a Europe with real clout? Will Europe, with its differences in languages, markets, cultures and views, ever be able to act as one strong player? Perhaps not everything needs to be organised perfectly, as long as we believe that it is possible to use the talent and resources that do exist to seize the momentum and choose a different course: a course towards an optimistic and at the same time realistic future, in which Europe can once again play its role.

Just as in my previous books, I want to add a disclaimer right away. I am not an economist, not a sociologist, not a historian, not a political scientist, not an anthropologist – not even an academic. I am a meta generalist. The only thing I can do is – like a ravenous sponge – absorb everything I see happening around me. More than thirty years of experience with innovation and transformation have taught me to recognise connections and patterns that allow me to get a feel for what this could mean for the future. For years, that quality has enabled me to spot disruptions quickly and understand them. Sometimes I can even predict, with a certain degree of accuracy, the kinds of transformations they may lead to. Of course, that is not truly predicting the future. So take these writings for what they are: my – admittedly thoroughly researched – personal view of what is happening in the world, and my advice on how we, as Europe, can deal with it by thinking differently. This book contains a number of concrete suggestions, simulations and calculations. To all critical readers who know more about a particular subject than I do, I ask you to feel free to work with the assumptions yourselves. The world can only become better for it.

Enjoy the read, and may it inspire you.

1. What do you mean, changes?

I have been talking and writing about innovation, change, disruptions, transformations and systemic shocks for years. At every session there is always someone in the audience whom I know is going to comment on it. You can tell pretty quickly from their posture and the way they look (including the eye-rolling). Then it is just a matter of waiting for a variation on these questions: 'Yes, but Jo, those changes are not new at all, are they? Haven't they always existed? So what are we getting so worked up about? Isn't this just scaremongering? It has always turned out fine, so why would it be different now?'

Usually that is followed by an argument that is, in itself, correct. Since the Second World War (WWII) we have had plenty of moments in history when things got pretty tense, when society and the economy were under serious pressure, and when we narrowly avoided catastrophes. The example that is invariably cited is, of course, the Cuban Missile Crisis in 1962, when the nuclear threat between the United States and Russia briefly brought us to the edge of the abyss. People also often refer to the oil crises of the 1970s, which knocked the global economy off its feet. Another example meant to show that things today are not all that different from back then is the broad social fear of the Cold War and the risk of a nuclear war – a fear that embedded itself firmly in mainstream culture in the 1980s, with films such as *The Day After* and music like *Two Tribes* by Frankie Goes to Hollywood, but also *Vamos A La Playa* and *The Final Countdown*. (The musical taste of those years is, of course, open to debate.) When it comes to the economy, people point to the 1980s of Thatcher and Reagan, the dotcom crisis of 2001 and the banking crisis of 2008.

I can only agree with those people. Change, and the tensions that come with it, have always been with us. Even in our recent history of relative carefree comfort there are countless examples. And yet the current situation feels completely different to me. We are seeing different threats emerge at the same time, and they seem to accelerate and reinforce one another. There is not only the climate crisis, but also the rise of AI with potentially far-reaching consequences for the economy and employment; the economic pressure that many people already feel; geopolitical developments that are shifting the world order and creating uncertainty; challenges around migration and living together; political polarisation and frustrations with 'the system' – and we could go on. On top of that, the nuclear threat is back with a vengeance. In the war between Russia and Ukraine, the use of nuclear weapons is threatened time and again. Former Russian president and firebrand Dmitry Medvedev has even made something of a hobby of it: whenever the West takes action, he threatens with World War III and the end of days.

In *The World is Round*, I gave that multitude of overlapping challenges a name: the metastorm. The perfect storm of perfect storms. There is not one big problem we have to solve – there are many, and they all seem to be happening at once, with one storm reinforcing or influencing another. What is more, we face external challenges that are so vast that, for many people, they feel impossible to solve. Is the climate crisis even fixable anymore? Does what we would have to sacrifice today outweigh the abstract, elusive result somewhere in a distant future? Do we really need to push through those difficult transitions – in energy, food, housing, mobility, and so on – already, when no one truly seems to realise what is coming our way and what the results of our current efforts will be? None of the earlier changes people so often refer to had the same urgency and, at the same time, were as intangible as the climate crisis.

On top of that, we now also face the challenge of artificial intelligence. Since the mid-1990s I have been working in the world of innovation, technology and transformation, and I have had a front-row seat as the internet, social media, mobile applications, VR and the metaverse, blockchain – you name it – were introduced. Over the past ten years I have followed developments in AI closely, and I can say only one thing: the potential of this technology is unprecedented. The current generation of generative AI has been available since 30 November 2022, and the speed at which this technology has developed – from 'possibly interesting' to 'disruptive to markets and society' – is something I have never seen before in my entire career.

One final difference I want to mention when we compare the seriousness of today's problems with those of past decades is the influence of both traditional and social media. We live in an era in which we receive near real-time reporting of everything happening in the world. That means every event, every victim, every disaster goes around the internet live. Our brains are programmed to assign greater importance to things we are exposed to frequently. As a result, we live, paradoxically, in a world in which progress is being made on many fronts – from fewer aviation accidents and falling crime in the United States, to increasing emancipation and declining global poverty – while the media constantly confront us with the exceptions: disasters, incidents, outliers. The result is a growing discrepancy between the real state of many things in the world and our perception of them. And that perception is often far more negative than what the data shows.

Now, that can be an argument for the critical person in my audience who then says: 'See, it is not worse than it used to be at all, we're just paying more attention.' That is partly true, for many things that are still evolving in a positive direction. Unfortunately, it is precisely that negative perception of reality that becomes the driver of pessimistic feelings for a large part of the population. The problem we are facing is interpersonal in nature: we are losing our faith in systems, structures and democratic institutions, which makes the willingness to act collectively and the support base for change disappear. And that is exactly what we need to get through the major transitions that are very real indeed – such as climate change and the impact of AI on people, the economy and society.

If we accept that there are more changes than before, that some of these challenges are immense and unprecedented, and that we, as a society, struggle to understand and manage them all together, then the question arises of how we can best deal with this. There is no off-the-shelf solution, but I would still like to propose a simple model that at least makes it easier to map the many changes and think about them. The model I use is so elementary and obvious, yet, strangely enough, too few organisations and individuals adopt this approach and use it structurally. In my two previous books I discussed the model in detail. Here I briefly revisit the main principles. The name of the model is SUPERchange – we had to call it something, and it sounds good in presentations and workshops. SUPER is an acronym for See, Understand, Plan, Enable and Run. As I said: pure logic, if only we did not apply it far too rarely in practice. In this book too, you will find the model's logic throughout.

1. **See** means that we must learn to look at all the (more or less) visible developments in the world. Precisely because there are so many of them, this is harder than it seems. It is therefore no coincidence that a growing group of people are starting to avoid the news: there is simply too much happening, and for most people our brains turn that into a chaotic mush of negative stimuli. One way to bring structure to that is to give every message its place. In the book *Digital Transformation* we did that with seven metaphors that gave the most important digital disruptions a place. In *The Future Formula* I introduce the 'wheel of disruption', in which about fifty forces of change come together in five major domains: sustainability, social tension, (geo)politics, global versus local, and digital revolution and AI. Whether you use these models or work with something else does not really matter. The goal is to give what you see or pick up a place, so that your brain calms down and you begin to see structure in the multitude of stimuli.
2. **Understand** is probably the most important step in the method. Simply looking

around and putting developments into imaginary boxes, as in the previous step, is good – but not enough. The question is what each of these stimuli means, and whether you are starting to see patterns. Especially in the United States' seemingly chaotic policy in the first months of 2025, understanding meaning and recognising connections is particularly instructive. The more often you do this, the better you understand the current picture, and the better you can anticipate what it might mean for the future.

3. **Plan**: based on your insights, you go looking for a vision, a strategy, for solutions. The real goal of this book is to think about such a vision and plan for the Europe of tomorrow. A plan we can genuinely believe in – one in which Europe has the capacity to stand stronger in its own right, and therefore in its relationships with other world powers.
4. **Enable** is about getting organisations and our society ready to deal with the challenges, goals and transformations coming our way. Because this is about Europe, and therefore about a multitude of actors, this is probably the biggest challenge: what, exactly, is needed to develop the clout we currently lack?
5. **Run** is logical, and yet so difficult. It means we are actually going to do it. That we truly implement the new ideas, models and activities – even if we have to struggle against the inertia of the legacy of our systems and structures. To make this happen, the right leadership combined with positive public support will be the most important levers. That will be quite a challenge.

I use the first two steps extensively in this book: I try to bring structure to the many challenges putting pressure on the old world order, but I also provide answers to the why question and to the meaning of those actions. I also devote attention in this book to the 4th and 5th steps, unfortunately with the greatest reservations. I want to conclude this chapter with one of my personal hobby horses: the importance of a strong vision of the future. To me, a strong vision is the 'why' of change, as Simon Sinek introduced in his Golden Circle model. Sinek describes that 'why' as the real legitimacy of our actions: the reason why companies do the things they do and how they do them. He confronted us with the striking insight that most organisations do not have the faintest idea why they do certain things. His simple observation that this 'why' is usually missing was an eye-opener for many in the business world, and a stepping stone towards more strategic thinking about their activities.

I also use that insight when it comes to societal transitions. In recent years we have been constantly confronted with the necessity – and often even the obligation – to change: eating less meat, driving less, no more polluting cars in the city centre, ripping up paving, a halt to concrete, and so on. The list of adjustments is long. For each of these measures there are very good reasons why we need to implement them, but we often fail to explain those reasons well. The result is that people get the feeling that nothing is allowed anymore and everything is compulsory, precisely because they are never truly told and shown why those actions are necessary. With the massive upheavals we now face, it becomes crucial to tell people why we have to do things differently. Not because we are reacting to what is being thrown at us, but because we have proactively developed our own vision of the world we want to live in in 2050.

If we manage to write a credible vision of the future – a story we can pass on and use to motivate people – then we will be able to frame the changes required as the step-by-step materialisation of that plan. If, on the other hand, we are not able to write such a compelling story, it becomes far harder to achieve our goals – assuming we can even define them at all. If we want Europe to become a strong power and play a prominent role in the new world order, then we must be able to describe what we mean by that. Not in difficult academic or bureaucratic papers, but in an aspirational story that can touch and inspire the minds and hearts of citizens, policymakers and entrepreneurs. Such a vision has to be honest and pragmatic. A (techno-)utopian story that ignores real challenges such as the climate crisis is naive and will do more harm than good. In our vision we must dare to name things as they are, while also keeping an open mind to possible solutions. Those will not always be painless – but that, too, is part of a realistic future.

If, with this book, I manage to prompt at least a handful of readers to contribute to such a vision, then I will have succeeded in what I set out to do.

Part 1
The world order is falling apart. Europe, brace yourself!

2. 2025, the year the old world order fell apart

Europe, the sick old man of the world

If Europe were a person, I would genuinely feel sorry for him. For years, our continent was looked at with pity. No one had anything good to say about it. Cynically enough, the criticism did not just come from outside Europe: Europeans themselves eagerly joined in the round of Euro-bashing, even though they could and should have changed something about it themselves.

Yes, Europe has a problem with demographic ageing, and therefore with a shortage of labour. That puts social security under pressure and weighs on the continent's productivity. But countries such as China, Russia, Japan, South Korea, the United States and many others are in a very similar situation. Only Africa, India and certain Asian countries largely escape this phenomenon for now, although it is expected that, in the longer term, they will probably follow the same demographic trends. What is more, countries with very young populations have little impact on the global economy. For instance, 56.9 percent of Niger's 26 million inhabitants are younger than eighteen, yet the country represents only 0.016 percent of global GDP. That is 1/20th of what their population size would suggest if Niger followed the global average. In other words: despite ageing, most value still sits with the 'old countries'. So is it fair to describe Europe as the old man, or even as the world's care home, as if it is nothing but a problem and a constraint for Europe?

Does this have to do with our capacity for innovation and entrepreneurship? Here, the criticism is probably better placed. What few people realise, however, is how many of the biggest innovations originally came from Europe, only to truly break through via the United States. The list is long, and I will mention only a few here: the web, the mobile phone and SMS, Linux (and therefore indirectly Android OS), Bluetooth, wind and solar power, nuclear fusion, CERN, CT scans, CRISPR-Cas9 DNA treatments, mRNA vaccines, cultivated meat, and so on. So it is not that we got stuck in the 1970s when it comes to innovation; the most promising transitions in energy, food, climate or healthcare come from Europe. And yet we fail to scale those innovations economically, in the way the United States – and, more recently, China – do manage to.

One of the main causes is the lack of cohesion and a culture of boldness within Europe. Where American companies operate in a unified home market, with uniform regulation, tax structures and language, European innovators work in a fragmented landscape of 27 countries, with differing legislation, markets and languages. That makes rapid scaling harder, discourages investors and raises the barrier to cross-border growth. As a result, many innovations get stuck in national niches, after which they are outplayed by a handful of hyperscalers who, globally and according to the winner-takes-all principle, scoop up a particular market niche and push local offerings aside. Who still remembers the social networks in Belgium (Netlog) or the Netherlands (Hyves) from before Facebook? Who knows or uses local alternatives to Spotify, Netflix or Amazon these days?

In response, many European entrepreneurs have learned to be acquired by foreign players at an early stage, or to look for capital in the United States themselves, where scale and market access become possible. As a result, the European market is often the origin of world-changing technology, but rarely the place where that technology also matures economically. Our successful European entrepreneurs therefore become, de facto, American companies, and over time are even fully absorbed into the major global players through takeovers.

In addition, our financing and entrepreneurial culture also plays a decisive role. Europe has top universities and excellent fundamental research, but the translation from laboratory to market is weakly developed. What holds Europe back here is a natural reticence that is absent in the United States. American venture capitalists are willing to invest billions in ambitious moonshots, while European investors are far more cautious and operate with less money. What is more, European financiers also invest a disproportionately large amount in American stock markets, to the detriment of European listed companies.

Europe clings more strongly to its values, norms and ethical considerations. That leads to the familiar regulation and, as a result, often slower market introductions. That is valuable from a societal perspective, but it also means that others – usually American companies – can build commercial traction more quickly. Many local entrepreneurs are deeply frustrated by the apparent constraints these rules are said to impose on them, and they see this as the main explanation for Europe's lag behind the United States. Later in this book I explain why that is only partly a valid argument. What is more, we are now seeing at breakneck speed how, in the United States, the absence of this kind of socially protective regulation can potentially go off the rails. As a result, many entrepreneurs have become more nuanced in their criticism of Europe's rules. I will come back to this later as well.

Europe excels at imagining the future, but fails to build it itself at scale and strategically. Because of globalisation and the strong bond between Europe and the United States, that was not a real problem for a long time. If you wanted to grow a strong European idea, you would simply head to the United States to benefit from a more favourable climate: the doors were wide open to talent and entrepreneurs. Now that this situation is changing rapidly, we in Europe need to take the necessary measures to compensate for our weaknesses in successfully bringing things to market. The good news is that the scorched-earth policy currently unfolding in the United States is putting so much pressure on entrepreneurial and investor confidence that the United States' overly dominant position in that area is at risk of eroding. That creates a level playing field and opens up more opportunities to innovate and, at the same time, to build businesses.

Where the European shoe pinches most, however, is the role Europe has played on the political world stage over the past few decades. Compared with the geopolitical sabre-rattling of the United States, and the violence of Russia and some other 'democratic' countries, Europe has indeed not meant much. Our geopolitical importance was limited. Even the Ukraine crisis did not trigger strong and unambiguous responses in Europe. Time and again, we hitched our wagon to the Americans, who set the course as the world's police officer – with both hard and soft power. That slavishly follow-the-leader attitude is becoming harder and harder to sustain. As a result, we in Europe are now being confronted with qualities we barely needed, or did not need at all, for decades: clear, strong leadership and faster, more efficient decision-making structures, to name just two. As long as the United States set the economic and geopolitical course, Europe merely had to follow – united, or not.

I would actually rather not see Europe as the sick old man of the world, but as the intelligent and developed, yet spoiled teenager who keeps calling on the help of hard-working parents. Our teenager certainly has talent, but no longer knows how to roll up their sleeves. Until the parents cut the lifeline and the teenager suddenly has to stand on their own two feet again. Okay, I realise that comparison does not entirely hold up – how can Europe be a teenager when we are actually so much older than the United States – but still ... anyone with teenagers at home will understand what I mean.

Europe, Trump II and Davos

On the evening of 5 November 2024, I was in Amsterdam with one of my Dutch friends, an entrepreneur with a track record similar to mine: he had founded an internet company in the early days and has since remained involved in the digital scene in all sorts of ways, through many different companies. Unlike me, he was also politically active for a time and, with his degree in political science, absolutely qualified to reflect on both American and European politics. That evening I gave a keynote and afterwards we went out together, with one central topic of conversation: would Trump be re-elected that night, or would Harris still make it? Even though we could already sense what was coming, we still found it hard to imagine: Trump, president again?! His campaign had been one of the most toxic we had seen in recent elections, and his promises, statements, threats and claims were unworthy of a democratic leader.

Because the first exit poll results were expected around midnight, I decided to watch American television for a moment. Three hours later I crawled into bed with a leaden feeling: Trump had won again. The next morning that result was more or less confirmed. During the 4-hour drive back home, from Amsterdam to the Flemish Ardennes, I decided to write this book. The echoes of the conversation from the night before kept reverberating, pulling me back again and again to one question: why did people vote for Trump again? To my surprise, international reactions in the days after the election were largely positive. Stock markets rose sharply, cryptocurrencies went up, and entrepreneurs and CEOs suddenly had dollar signs in their eyes. Many non-Western countries too – such as India, Russia, China, Brazil and Saudi Arabia – were optimistic about the opportunities Trump's presidency would offer for their relations with the United States.

So was the fear my Dutch friend and I felt so unjustified? Or were we, in fact, voicing the pragmatic sentiment of Old Europe? A survey from January 2025, conducted by the European Council on Foreign Relations among nearly 30,000 respondents, showed that only 20 percent of Europeans still saw the United States as an ally. That stood in stark contrast to the positive sentiment in many other parts of the world, where Trump was seen as a peacemaker, good for the United States and for the global economy. The analysis of the results suggested that Europe risked marginalising itself even further in a world in which a new order was taking shape, based on great-power politics – something Europe apparently no longer had the weight to participate in as an equal player. A confirmation of that 'now that Trump is here we are all anti-Europe' feeling followed in Davos. The annual high mass for everyone with wealth, influence in business, or political power took place from 20 to 24 January 2025. An important topic of conversation was the results of the annual Global Risks Report, which maps out the biggest threats. For the first time, the World Economic Forum considered armed conflict the most urgent global risk in 2025, ahead of climate change and economic confrontation. Disinformation and the rise of a multipolar or fragmented world order were also on the list. Even more striking was the overall negative sentiment towards Europe. All the feelings and clichés of European decline described earlier came through more strongly, both in the corridors and in the official sessions. European optimism was so scarce that a few heavyweights felt compelled to use pep talks to tone down the pessimism. Laurence D. Fink, CEO of investment firm BlackRock, and Kristalina Georgieva of the International Monetary Fund, argued that there was too much pessimism about Europe and called for more confidence in the region's potential. Christine Lagarde, President of the European Central Bank, pointed to positive signals such as falling inflation and growth potential, but also warned of challenges in capital markets. It seemed necessary to give Europeans a bit of encouragement.

One thing was obvious: Europe was gradually becoming the world's loser. And under the inspired leadership of Trump II, the others would soon overtake us. Europe left the Davos circus with its shoulders slumped – and the worst was still to come.

28 February, the Zelensky incident

On Friday 28 February 2025, I was sitting at the table with my family. As is often the case at the end of a busy week – especially with our daughter, who is studying, just back from a week staying in her student digs – it was a hectic conversation that went off in every direction. Everyone had something to say about the past few days. But for me, that day there was only one event that mattered. I still remember our conversation going roughly like this:

Me: *'Remember this date forever. I think we witnessed something important today.'*

Family: *'What do you mean? What happened?'*

Me: *'Haven't you been following the news? Don't you know what just happened in the United States?'*

Family: *'Er, no, not really.'*

Me: *'The confrontation between Trump, Vance and Zelensky in the Oval Office! In the White House!'*

Family: *'Oh yeah, we saw that go by on TikTok. But what was so special about it?'*

Me: *'For me, a fault line has just opened up between the United States and Europe. I think we are suddenly living in a new world. This is one of those historic moments – put it in your diaries.'*

Family: **Sigh.**

I cannot reconstruct the rest of the conversation all that well, but I do remember the rolling eyes, and how the discussion quickly moved on to the order of the day (I think it was about which new series we were going to binge-watch). And there I was, steeped in the historic weight of what was unfolding, while apparently being the only one.

As it turned out, that last part was not true. The meeting, the goal of which was to sign an agreement on American access to Ukrainian rare earths, escalated into a heated exchange. Trump and Vice President JD Vance had clearly worked out a one-two, the kind we only know from top-level football. Within moments the tone shifted from positive and friendly to a toxic attack, with the Americans accusing Zelensky of ingratitude and disrespect. In one fell swoop, Zelensky and Ukraine were blamed for having caused the war themselves, and told they could no longer count on support from the United States. The way this happened was unprecedented in international diplomacy, certainly in front of the cameras. Afterwards there was plenty of speculation about whether the whole incident had been staged, so that Ukraine could be publicly abandoned and ties with Russia strengthened: a clear signal both to Trump's base and to Putin. The planned press conference and the signing of the agreement were cancelled, and Zelensky left the White House early, in a retreat that would not have looked out of place in *Game of Thrones*.

The comments in the hours and days that followed were telling, and I was clearly not the only one who marked the moment as historic. The general tenor in the media, political circles and among opinion-makers was one of astonishment, shock and concern about the future of the Western alliance and Ukraine's security. International media spoke of a 'scandal in front of the whole world' and stressed that it is unprecedented for an American president to publicly dress down an ally like that – certainly the leader of a country at war. French president Macron stated that it was clear who the aggressor was (Russia) and who the victim was (Ukraine), and that support for Ukraine remained unchanged. Italian prime minister Meloni called for an urgent summit between Europe, the United States and allies, because division would weaken the West. From Russia, meanwhile, the confrontation was greeted with obvious glee. Russian officials praised the 'restraint' shown by Trump and Vance towards 'bastard' Zelensky and called the situation 'historic'.

Historic it certainly was. For anyone who still doubted it, it was now clear: the United States was no longer the partner, let alone the leader, of the Western alliance that had held for almost a century. And yet this incident did not necessarily come as a surprise. Exactly two weeks before the Zelensky incident, American Vice President JD Vance gave a controversial speech at the 61st Munich Security Conference.

The core message was that Europe could no longer rely on the United States as protector or moral compass. The continent was given a dressing-down about its own shortcomings: migration policy that was too lax, restrictions on freedom of speech, and too little appreciation for the 'right' political parties (read: the radical right, such as AfD). According to Vance, Russia was not the great danger, but Europe itself – or rather: the decay of its own values. The message was clear: if Europe still wants to defend itself, it will largely have to do so alone – America has other concerns. And if Europe is worried about Russian tanks, then that is largely its own fault. That landed, although the impact still had not fully sunk in.

A few days later, Trump went even further. During a press moment at his beloved Mar-a-Lago estate, he suggested that Ukraine itself was responsible for starting the war. That happened after American and Russian peace talks in Saudi Arabia, to which Ukraine and Europe had not been invited – most likely because it was not really about peace at all, but about restoring trade relations between the United States and Russia. And yet even that did not fully sink in. So it took the slapstick politics of 28 February before no one could or wanted to deny it any longer: the world has changed, the United States is no longer what it was, Europe is even more alone, and a new world order is announcing itself. No: at the start of 2025, things did not look good for Europe.

The global shock

I have already referred to themes from my previous books: from digital transformation in the first works to the fundamental societal and business model transformations in the most recent ones. Each of those waves of change has its own terminology to describe the impact, severity and urgency of the disruptions.

In the early years, we spoke of digital **disruptions** (and disruptors) that changed the status quo of certain sectors and led to business model transformations, sometimes with consequences for an entire sector. By now we know that that impact often remained limited. Yes, Uber shook up the taxi business, and Netflix did the same for the film, TV and media industries. But outside those sectors, the influence of these tech challengers was small. That was true, by the way, for almost all digital disruptions, from education to banking, from retail to tourism. What is more, it often took far longer than expected to transform a sector. I estimate that, on average, it takes about twenty years from the emergence of a disruption to the intended winner-takes-all result.

Once my themes became more societal, I introduced other concepts. **The Metastorm** refers to a complex of perfect storms that occur simultaneously and reinforce one another. In the same period, work, mobility, housing, food, health, demography and other domains each undergo their own transformation, with mutual influence. The pandemic, for instance, accelerated working from home, which then changed the way employees organised themselves around housing, with a longer-term impact on mobility, because two cars per household are no longer necessary. However disruptive these societal and market shifts may be, their slow unfolding gives traditional players, in principle, enough time to respond adequately.

In *The Future Formula*, I introduce two concepts that come closer to our current reality. After the slow and limited impact of transformations and the metastorm, we are now faced with **systemic shocks**: events or developments that, in the short term, have an enormous impact on almost everything and everyone. When COVID-19 led to lockdowns and associated measures, the world was disrupted in one fell swoop, across all sectors and at every level. It was a textbook example of a systemic shock: fast, cross-cutting and global. The war in Ukraine is such a shock too: Russia's invasion immediately changed the way we look at military conflicts in Europe, our relations with Russia, our energy dependence and our geopolitical vulnerability. The next systemic shock that is now fully under way is, without a doubt, AI. The speed and scale of the possible change are unprecedented, and the consequences will be felt worldwide and across sectors.

In *The Future Formula* I describe this decade as the period of the **Great Imbalance**. By that I mean that many certainties are under pressure. That does not necessarily mean that our hard-won achievements will simply disappear or be replaced, but it does mean that we do not really know what will happen. We live in a time of imbalance and uncertainty – it could still go in any direction. The concept I introduce in this book is that of the **Global Shock**. I believe all the developments that came before are now culminating in a fundamental change in the world order. Disruptions are no longer slow and limited, but radical, all-encompassing and global. Trump's actions since his inauguration leave no one untouched and have negative consequences for friend and foe alike. As we look at the United States, we are moving from the uncertainty of the great imbalance towards a worldview that is becoming increasingly predictable: the emergence of a new world order, the first outlines of which are already clearly taking shape. The direction of the future is becoming visible – and it does not exactly make for cheerful reading.

The good news is that Europe seems to be waking up from a lethargy that has lasted almost a century. A growing awareness is emerging that we must – and can

– reduce our dependence, with the ambition of playing an autonomous and meaningful role in the new global game. We no longer have to fall in with the United States' strategic agenda, or that of emerging world powers. If we use the momentum well, we can legitimately claim a seat at tomorrow's table. But for that, we will need to develop a strong vision and sufficient clout. What that could mean, exactly, is the subject of this book.

3. What was that old world order again?

If we want to understand why Europe is now so often viewed with contempt by others, and with a sense of inferiority by Europeans themselves, it is useful to look at the evolution of the world order over the past 150 years. The difference in significance between Europe back then and its current position is huge. Time for a short history lesson.

The world order before WWII

At the end of the 19th century, Europe was at the height of its geopolitical influence. The great powers controlled almost the entire world through vast colonial empires. Great Britain dominated global trade with its economic strength and maritime supremacy. It did so not only militarily, but above all through the soft power of the economic and monetary influence it wielded over the rest of the world. France followed as the second colonial power, while Germany, unified since 1871 under the empire, industrialised rapidly and increasingly asserted its geopolitical ambitions. Russia, too, was a country to reckon with: despite lagging industrialisation, its sheer size made it an important player on the European stage. Austria-Hungary and the Ottoman Empire were still part of the puzzle, and Japan, too, was growing ever more ambitious in Asia, at the expense of China and other countries in the region.

In that era, the world order was a system of sovereign states competing with one another for influence and security, without a single dominant world power able to enforce the rules of the game. This multipolar structure was carried by European great powers that were both connected to one another through alliances and divided by deep-rooted mistrust. Diplomatic relations were fragile and strongly focused on bilateral deals (where have we heard that before?), more than on the robust multilateral structures and global agreements that only emerged after WWII. Relations between states were competitive and based on power, opportunism and common enemies, rather than on shared principles.

These relationships led to a complex system of alliances that was initially intended to preserve peace through a balance of power. Yet this system proved fragile and a source of great misfortune. Germany's rise around the turn of the century disrupted the existing equilibrium, while nationalism and the arms race in Europe further fuelled tensions. The situation culminated in 1914 in WWI, when the conflict between Austria-Hungary and Serbia escalated through those earlier, peace-oriented alliances and treaties, dragging everyone into a world war. That war brought an end to the power of the great European empires and fundamentally reshaped the world map. Afterwards, there were attempts at stabilisation, such as the creation of the League of Nations, the predecessor of the UN, but these proved insufficient. Germany felt deeply humiliated by the Treaty of Versailles, was economically exhausted by reparations for its war debt, and was politically unstable. The Great Depression after 1929 intensified tensions worldwide. In this context, authoritarian regimes seized power, with the most dramatic consequence being the rise of National Socialism in Germany.

At the same time, the United States grew into a decisive factor. Even before 1914, the United States had become the largest industrial power economically. Although the country traditionally kept its distance from European politics, American participation in WWI was an important step towards a more outward-facing geopolitical posture. After 1918, however, the United States largely withdrew from the world stage once again, which had consequences for the effectiveness of international institutions such as the League of Nations – which it had, in fact, helped to establish, but of which it ultimately did not become a member. We can say that the motto of this period was 'divide and rule' – and in that respect the parallels with the world order the United States under Trump II appears to be pursuing are striking. Economically, globalisation initially flourished under European leadership, with free trade and stable financial systems as its foundation. Of course, that came at the expense of colonised countries, which served as a cheap engine for Europe's economic success. But after WWI, and certainly after 1929, this, too, shifted: protectionism, currency crises and economic nationalisation undermined international trade and increased tensions.

The 1930s were marked by growing aggression, combined with a lack of effective collective security in Europe. The League of Nations had no means of stopping these worrying developments, while democratic states hoped to avoid further war by giving in to Hitler. The annexation of Austria and the invasion of Czechoslovakia showed the failure of diplomacy without clout (something Europe is accused of today in the context of the war in Ukraine). In 1939, the invasion of Poland put an end, once and for all, to the illusion of peace. WWII had begun, and with it the definitive end of the world order of that era.

The new bipolar world order that sculpted the modern face of Europe

After the catastrophe of WWII, and based on the lessons drawn from the period before it, an entirely new world order emerged. It became the foundation for eighty years of peace and progress – at least for us. At the same time, it marked the end of Europe's dominance as a world power, and the beginning of the inferiority complex that today prevents us from believing in a strong Europe within the future world order. Where Europe had once been the geopolitical centre of the world, after WWII the centre of gravity shifted irreversibly to the United States and the Soviet Union. The old European great powers emerged from the war exhausted and became dependent on support from the new superpowers in order to rebuild themselves. In this way, they ended up in the sphere of influence of one of the two new power blocs.

In this new bipolar world, rivalry between Washington and Moscow shaped international relations. The most important symbol of that division was the Iron Curtain, which quite literally split Europe in two: in the west, countries came under American influence; in the east, the Soviet Union installed communist regimes under Moscow's control. Where the interwar period had still been characterised by disorderly competition between many powers, after WWII the United States and the USSR sought to enforce stability through spheres of influence and ideological blocs.

Military institutions such as NATO and the Warsaw Pact, and multilateral institutions such as the UN and the IMF, set new rules of the game. They made far-reaching cooperation possible and at the same time served as instruments for managing conflict. Europe was no longer master of its own continent, but became a pawn in a larger geopolitical game of chess.

The consequences for Europe's role in the world were far-reaching. The colonial empires crumbled at speed, and with them disappeared an important foundation of Europe's global power. What remained was a Europe that was forced to reinvent itself and, in doing so, largely turned inward. Western European countries tried to create new relevance through economic cooperation such as the ECSC (European Coal and Steel Community) and the EEC (European Economic Community). In doing so, they laid the foundation for what would grow into the European Union. The nuclear threat changed the dynamics of power and warfare. The doctrine of MAD (Mutual Assured Destruction) paradoxically ensured that major military conflicts did not occur. Although Europe literally became both the stage and the frontline of the Cold War, it nevertheless remained one of the safest continents. That does not mean there were no military conflicts between the two superpowers, but they were usually fought via proxy wars on the edges of 'our world': Korea, Vietnam, Afghanistan. As I wrote earlier, that did not reduce the perceived threat in Europe. From the 1960s until the end of the 1980s, an all-destroying nuclear war hung over Europe as a tangible threat.

Despite that tension, the post-war world order was not based purely on confrontation. The creation of a series of partnerships shaped a new attempt at global cooperation. The United Nations (UN), the International Monetary Fund (IMF), the World Bank, the GATT/WTO, UNESCO, COMECON, the International Court of Justice (ICJ) and the World Health Organization (WHO) were, one by one, symbols of this era. Despite, or perhaps precisely because of, the loss of global impact, Western Europe focused mainly on its internal functioning. It grew into a bastion of democracy, social welfare and the market economy. Eastern Europe, by contrast, experienced a long period of dictatorship, economic stagnation and repression until the fall of the Iron Curtain.

Although the Cold War is usually presented as a duel between two superpowers and ideological enemies – the United States and the Soviet Union – China already played a role on the world stage before the fall of the Iron Curtain. At first it naturally settled into the Soviet-dominated Eastern Bloc, because of ideological affinity and dependence on Soviet technology. That alliance began to crumble in the 1960s, after which China turned against the Soviet Union and began to chart its own course. This produced a remarkable spectacle: communist China turning away from Moscow and seeking rapprochement with Washington. Under President Nixon, ties were strengthened and the West embraced the enemy of its enemy. China thus became a unique third force: ideologically independent, economically still largely closed, but geopolitically already busy reinventing itself. Only much later would it truly break through as a global player, but the seed was planted in this period of ideological rupture and pragmatic diplomacy. As we have grown used to from China, the country was probably already looking more than fifty years ahead then. We could learn something from that.

From a unipolar world order to geopolitical chaos

In 1991, the world order changed again, gradually pushing Europe even further into the corner – although it did not seem that way at first. With the collapse of the Soviet Union, the great counterpart to the Western ideological, cultural and economic bloc, the only other great power besides the United States disappeared. And with it went the bipolar structure that had shaped and kept the world order in balance for so long. What followed was a new unipolar world order, in which the United States – without any real counterweight – began to impose the rules of the game for globalisation, security and international order ever more forcefully. And it did so, not without arrogance, with full conviction.

In the West, the 1990s were marked by optimism about liberalisation, democratisation and the strengthening of multilateral institutions. NATO expanded into Eastern Europe, the European Union admitted new members and grew in influence, and the liberalisation of former Eastern Bloc countries was celebrated as a historic success. In this 'sphere of progress', the American thinker Francis Fukuyama launched his well-known thesis of 'the end of history': liberal democracy had, in his view, won the ideological struggle and would establish itself worldwide as the endpoint of human development. Although that idea was widely embraced at the time, the years that followed showed just how wrong he actually was.

For many former Soviet republics, the Soviet Union's sudden dissolution was not a liberation, but a profound systemic shock. What followed was not a smooth transition to prosperity and democracy, but a period of disruption and loss. Economies collapsed; inflation, poverty and unemployment rose at breakneck speed. Politically, the new states struggled to build stable institutions and the rule of law – often resulting in corruption, authoritarian rule or even civil war. Ethnic tensions that had been suppressed for years rose to the surface and led to violent conflicts in various regions. The promises of independence stood in stark contrast to the reality of unemployment, demographic decline, emigration, violence and the loss of familiar certainties.

In that vacuum – which Russia also fell into – the breeding ground emerged for the power bloc we know today. Russia, humiliated by its loss of influence, regrouped under Putin and began to reassert its position as a regional power. Through economic pressure, military presence and political interference, the country sought, step by step, to strengthen its grip on the region. It actively meddled in the internal affairs of, among others, Georgia, Moldova (Transnistria), Belarus, Kazakhstan, Armenia, Azerbaijan, Kyrgyzstan, Tajikistan, and of course – since the annexation of Crimea in 2014 and the invasion in 2022 – Ukraine.

The unipolar 'brave new world' proved short-lived. In the vacuum that emerged, new forces grew that were far less predictable than the ideological blocs of the Cold War. China, which at the time positioned itself as an invisible and harmless third force, began from the 2000s onwards to turn its economic power into geopolitical influence. From 'the factory of the world', it developed, step by step, into an economic, military and geopolitical great power. That allowed it to assert itself ever more strongly internationally – among other things through the Belt and Road Initiative, the large-scale logistics project with branches across the world, especially in developing regions. On top of that came rapid military modernisation and an increasingly assertive diplomacy in Asia and Africa. And although their impact was still limited, other emerging regions such as India, Brazil and Turkey also began to make themselves heard more loudly in global forums – not to mention players in the Middle East such as Saudi Arabia and the Emirates.

And so, a multipolar world emerged again. No more clear east – west or north – south contrasts, but a playing field in which each player followed its own mix of ideologies, cultures, interests and historical drivers. At this moment, Europe finds itself in an existential search for its place in the new world order. Because of the recent developments at the start of 2025, Europe is being cut loose by the United States. After years of – voluntary or not – submission to both the bipolar and unipolar dominance of the United States, Europe is now on its own. In this new playing field, Europe must reinvent itself. No longer as the arrogant and dominant world leader of a hundred years ago, but also no longer as the numbed and flabby follower of the past eighty years. Europe must become a player with its own story, its own vision and ambition, and a strong and credible position in the new world.

The colonisation of Europe

In this final section on the historical world order, I want to put forward a somewhat controversial theory about the relationship between the United States as a great power and Europe as the weaker little brother. There is, in fact, an explanation behind it. Anyone who looks with a critical eye at Europe's geopolitical position after WWII can hardly avoid a provocative but interesting conclusion: the Americans did not simply help Europe during and especially after the war – even then, their support was highly transactional. More than that: without Europe and WWII, the United States would probably never have grown into the world power it is today.

When WWII broke out, the average American preferred to look the other way. The trauma of WWI still ran deep, and the economic malaise of the 1930s had further undermined confidence. Isolationism was widespread in American society. In polls, more than 90 percent of the population said they were against intervening in the European conflict. The America First movement grew rapidly and managed to mobilise this sentiment politically. It showed ideological similarities with European fascism, and figures such as aviation pioneer Charles Lindbergh did not hide their admiration for strong leaders such as Hitler and Mussolini – or even their antisemitism. The message was clear: let Europe fend for itself. The parallels with today's America are striking.

Opposed to that was another current: a coalition of economists, cultural leaders and strategists who warned that American security was inseparable from Europe's fate. President Roosevelt steered a course between the two camps. While he publicly promised that no American soldiers would ever again die on European soil (it ultimately came to 185,000), behind the scenes he did, in fact, provide material support to Great Britain. That deadlock was broken on 7 December 1941, with Japan's attack on Pearl Harbor. The outrage was so great that public opinion flipped completely. The United States declared war on Japan, after which Germany and Italy promptly did the same to the United States. Where the average American had still been protesting against the war a day earlier, now lines of people formed at the gates of the recruitment offices.

America's self-image changed fundamentally. From neutral spectator, the country rapidly became the engine of the Allied war effort. That immediately also meant a radical shift in the role the United States would go on to play as a world power. Until then, the idea that America could – or should – develop into a world power had existed only in limited circles: a handful of strategists, thinkers and military planners saw the geopolitical opportunities, but their vision found little resonance with a population and political class that mainly wanted to focus on America itself. The large-scale mobilisation for WWII, however, gave the pro-great-power camp the chance to push its vision through and to seize the war as an opportunity to realise the latent potential for global dominance. What had previously been an elite thought experiment became, after 1941, a broadly shared self-confidence: America as the pivot of a new world order.

The transactional side was already visible then: we help Europe win the war, and afterwards we turn it into a kind of economic and geopolitical colony of the United States. I realise many readers will probably raise their eyebrows at this, but factually that is exactly what happened. Through the Marshall Plan, the equivalent of 150 billion euros in today's money was pumped into the reconstruction of 16 European countries. That money was not only meant to restore destroyed infrastructure, but also to encourage European countries to cooperate more closely and, gradually, to form a united Europe. A unified Europe, under American influence, was seen as an important weapon in the fight against communism. In the same period, NATO was founded, intended to organise collective security against the new enemy that had replaced Nazi Germany: the Soviet Union. The influence the United States gained through this was immense. A united Europe also meant a united market, one from which American companies in particular would be able to profit handsomely. Politically, almost all European countries aligned themselves with American ideology, and open sympathies for communism were immediately nipped in the bud. The Americans had several instruments at their disposal to make sure of this.

American intelligence services, which had barely existed before the war, grew explosively. At the height of the Cold War, there were estimated to be around 30,000 agents active. In many cases, European intelligence services functioned as a kind of extension of their American counterparts. Of course, these agents contributed to our security, but first and foremost they served American interests – even if that meant illegal and undemocratic actions being carried out on European soil. The permanent military presence was also built up significantly. At present there are still around 84,000 American soldiers stationed in Europe, but at the height of the Cold War there were almost half a million. European armies were rebuilt, but continued to operate in a fragmented way. NATO served as the connecting factor – under central American command, of course.

Although the United States is now criticising our military dependence, it has always taken an ambivalent stance on this itself. If you want to understand that, you also have to look at the economic dimension of defence. Of the hundreds of billions of euros that Europe invests each year in defence equipment (within the NATO framework), two thirds is spent on purchases from American suppliers. Since WWII, Europe has repeatedly tried to organise itself in a more militarily independent way, but those initiatives were each time slowed down as soon as there was a risk that Europe would strengthen itself outside NATO – and therefore reduce American influence, both militarily and financially.

For me, the most important influence the United States has exerted over the past eighty years has not been in the military or political domain, but in soft power: the Americanisation of our culture and economy. English became the lingua franca (to the great frustration of, for example, the French), American companies dominated our markets – whether or not through takeovers – and our capital flowed into American stock markets. Long before Netflix took over our viewing habits, it was already Hollywood films and American series that ruled our screens, and most major hits came from American music studios. By now, the tech sector, too, is almost entirely American. As *Star Trek* fans have known for a long time: 'resistance is futile'. In many areas, Europe was slowly but surely assimilated into the American worldview. Although many thinkers remained critical of that Americanisation, it did not stop it from developing. Why would it? We ourselves chose the comfortable path of least resistance – and the most luxury.

That our dependence on American products, technology and platforms is not without risk is being demonstrated by the change of course in the United States. Much of what we saw as harmless stimuli – influences that gradually nudged our behaviour in a certain direction – also turns out to have the potential to be deployed as a weapon. Think of American politicians openly criticising European values and meddling in our elections; cultural products that function as subtle propaganda; social media that is explicitly used to influence elections; or high-tech products threatened with being switched off if we do not behave 'appropriately' – such as Musk's Starlink or the kill switch on John Deere tractors (something the Russians discovered when they removed these from Ukraine). And since the Belgian telecom scandal of 2013, we have known what our 'partners' are capable of: for years, communications leaked via backdoors on routers of a Belgacom subsidiary to British and American intelligence services.

Europe did not just become a colony of the United States – in many respects you could say we were simply occupied. From Europe, we helped build the United States into the world power it still is today. If we fully realise that in Europe, we also understand how much influence we can have over our own future – especially now that the United States, just as in the 1930s, is once again turning away from strong transatlantic partnerships.

4. The world order is being redrawn, part 1: The familiar players

As we saw in the previous chapter, we have gone through a circular movement in geopolitics and world order. Barely a hundred years ago, we still lived in a multipolar world dominated by Europe. Through complex structures and strong self-interests of rapidly developing nation states, a field of tension emerged that ultimately led to two world wars. The subsequent bipolar order kept the world in balance, with a Western and an Eastern bloc. Western Europe then entered one of the longest periods of stability and security, but it did so at the cost of surrendering a significant part of its geopolitical significance, in favour of the United States. Eastern Europe, by contrast, fell into a long period of dictatorship, under Moscow's yoke.

Since the early 1990s, we have seen how the fall of the Soviet Union led to a unipolar hegemony of the United States, with only one centre of power left in the world: America. Over time, however, that evolved into the chaotic, multipolar situation we now find ourselves in. Where, up to Trump II, the United States still seemed to have the ambition, as the only world power, to ensure dominance, balance and stability, we now see how its own actions are actually reinforcing that new multipolar order. At the same time, it is retreating into a form of isolationism and nationalism that strongly recalls America in the 1930s. In the next two chapters, I analyse the forces underpinning these shifts. First, I discuss the players we already know, such as China, Russia and India, who are actively working to restore or expand their influence. After that, I focus on the new forces which, through the current Trump government, appear to be aiming for an accelerated redrawing of the world order.

Russia's resurgence as an old new enemy

If there is one player that wants to claim a prominent role again in the new multipolar world order, it is Russia. Where, shortly after the fall of the Soviet Union, there still seemed to be the beginnings of liberalisation, other internal forces ultimately proved stronger. The Russia of today is, without doubt, the direct heir to the Soviet Union. Many of those currently in power come straight out of the structures of the Eastern Bloc. Under Putin's leadership, the country has become steeped in a conservative worldview that runs counter to the liberal, rules-based model the United States put forward after WWII. Russia's vision of the new world order sits somewhere between the multipolar Europe of the 19th century and the bipolar world of the Cold War. In both models, a limited number of great powers define their spheres of influence, by exercising power or by striking deals and agreements. In that worldview, small states are not autonomous actors, but satellites that fall in line with the interests of their dominant patron.

Where Washington positioned itself after WWII as the protector of a global order based on freedom, law and market logic, Moscow is now projecting an image of pragmatic power politics and cultural conservatism. International structures and organisations that safeguard peace, security and global interests worldwide barely have a place in that worldview. Many of their members and representatives are seen by Russia as puppets of America, and therefore not as representative of the interests of new geopolitical players. Russia therefore fundamentally opposes the unipolar model of the 1990s and the American dominance it embodied. Putin does not see that period as a time of liberation, but as a historic humiliation in which Russia was marginalised. He does not regard NATO's expansion as a security instrument for former Soviet republics that asked for it themselves, but as a military encirclement by the United States and a direct threat to Russia's sphere of influence.

Putin's view of geopolitics is not purely ideological, but also a reinterpretation of Russian identity, with the restoration of 'lost greatness' at its centre. He sees present-day Russia not only as a modern nation state, but also as the legitimate continuation of two historic empires: the Russian Empire and the Soviet Union. From that double legacy, he builds an ideological foundation for his geopolitical ambitions. Putin presents himself as the restorer of a historic continuity that was interrupted by the chaos of the 1990s. Whether he truly believes that, or mainly uses it as an almost messianic legitimisation of worldly objectives, we will probably never know for sure.

Russia positions itself vis-à-vis the United States as an equal great power, although that claim rests mainly on military capacity. The war in Ukraine has shown that its conventional military clout is far smaller than the West long assumed, but Russia compensates for that with its nuclear deterrent. Economically, Russia is no match for the United States, Europe or China. With a GDP of 2,200 billion USD, it lags far behind Europe and China, and the United States takes the crown with 30,000 billion USD. It is therefore no surprise that a key part of Russia's strategy consists of making itself relatively stronger by weakening others from within – an approach it has used for years against both Europe and the United States.

Europe occupies a particular place in Russia's worldview. Moscow does not see us as an independent geopolitical player, but as an extension of the United States. As I argued earlier, that is – however unpleasant – not an inaccurate assessment. While Russia likes to portray Europe as 'weak and decadent', with geopolitical pretensions but without a military backbone or political unity, it simultaneously does everything it can to undermine a stronger Europe. Russia is adept at using its limited resources to disrupt other great powers. It masters the art of hybrid warfare like no other: sabotage, espionage, cyberattacks and disinformation serve to weaken European society from within. Another front of Russian influence lies in the political arena. Through proven financial support for populist parties, Moscow influences elections and fuels distrust of the EU. In that way it seeks to undermine Europe's political cohesion and structurally erode citizens' trust. There are strong indications that part of the negative sentiment among the population is indeed the result of direct and indirect Russian actions. Russia has understood well that the West does not have to lose a war – as long as it gradually weakens itself, little by little.

As confrontation with the West has intensified since the war in Ukraine, Russia has been seeking ever closer ties with China. What began as a pragmatic request for support has by now grown into a strategic partnership, based on shared distrust of American hegemony and a joint drive towards a multipolar world. At the same time, there is fear in Russia of becoming subordinate to the Chinese power bloc, and behind the scenes the balance of power within this 'friendship without limits' is being monitored closely. A recently leaked document from Russia's FSB intelligence service shows just how deep that distrust runs. As in the West, China is also active in Russia in the field of (corporate) espionage. At the same time, it appears that Russia itself is spying on the Chinese, by hacking WeChat and phone traffic.

Since Trump II, Putin seems to have found an unexpected ally in the American president. In a later chapter I analyse Trump's vision of the new world order, but there are clear parallels here, too, with the way Putin looks at the world. If the United States were to slide further towards autocracy and lose the trust of the rest of the world, Putin would have achieved at least one goal of his hybrid warfare: the weaker the United States as a great power, the greater Russia's relative strength, and the closer a new multipolar world order comes.

China, the true new great power

China does not want to remain on the sidelines. Where Russia primarily focuses on disruption, sabotage and military threats, China presents a strategy of gradual influence and structural presence to the outside world. China and Russia find common ground in their pursuit of a multipolar world order in which each aspires to an important role, but their approach differs fundamentally. While the end goal may be the same, China rarely seeks direct confrontation, unlike Russia. In their own words, it is about a peaceful, just and inclusive order, in which sovereignty, non-interference and multilateral cooperation are central. Those could have been the words of the United States, fifty years ago ... The UN is put forward here as a legitimate anchor point – not coincidentally an organisation that China is increasingly trying to get a grip on. Xi Jinping is focused on redrawing the rules of the game: trade norms, digital standards, geopolitical alliances – everything must gradually shift towards a model in which China's position is anchored. Not as the sole unipolar great power, but as one of the dominant parties at the table of the new multipolar order.

Beijing is also positioning itself as a representative of the Global South, a collective of countries in Asia, Africa and South America that felt marginalised within the Western order. China wants more influence within institutions such as the IMF and the World Bank, while at the same time building its own alternatives such as the Asian Infrastructure Investment Bank, the Shanghai Cooperation Organisation and BRICS+. That not only generates goodwill among those countries, but also access to raw materials, markets and political support – all crucial elements in the long-term strategy of global integration without American dominance. Oddly enough, China's approach of acquiring geopolitical influence through soft power among emerging countries strongly resembles that of the United States after WWII. The vacuum now being created by the United States' withdrawal from international humanitarian and development initiatives is therefore eagerly filled by China with its own projects. A striking example is Trump's recent decision to drastically cut funding for Radio Free Asia – a broadcaster that was specifically intended to provide independent reporting in authoritarian regimes. Up to early 2025, RFA broadcast on sixty frequencies in the region. Those broadcasts have since been stopped, and China has taken over the frequencies to spread its own propaganda.

The relationship between the United States and China is fundamentally competitive. Washington is actively trying to curb China's technological and economic rise and to limit its influence in Asia and beyond. Under Trump II, China becomes the United States' new great enemy. Despite rising tensions, however, China does not want to ignite a new Cold War. For Beijing, the core question is not who becomes the world leader, but what multipolar leadership tomorrow should look like. Europe, too, plays a key role in this vision. For China, the EU is both a crucial economic partner and a possible geopolitical counterweight to the United States, especially now that America under Trump II appears to be calling off cooperation with Europe. It is therefore not surprising that China has since launched diplomatic and economic charm offensives. In doing so, it not only signals that it is a stable and reliable partner as an alternative to the United States, but also that Europe may see itself as a new Western great power.

And yet China's economic opportunities and diplomatic charm cannot remove European concerns about the nature and consequences of the Chinese worldview. A first risk is that closer cooperation with China creates new strategic dependencies that threaten Europe's autonomy. Those dependencies are no accident, but part of a broader strategy of economic leverage and political influence by China – a strategy that strongly recalls what the United States has long done. If we go too far along with this, we risk simply swapping our dependence on the United States for dependence on China.

On top of that, there are the moral questions. From a European perspective, China represents an authoritarian regime that runs counter to our liberal democracy, in which individual freedoms are subordinate to the interests of the state and party control. The systematic repression of minorities, large-scale censorship, the rolling back of rights for certain groups, its threatening stance towards Taiwan, active espionage in the West, political influence through propaganda, and the absence of an independent judiciary – for Europe these are not side issues, but fundamental obstacles to trust. China's tacit support for Russia in the war with Ukraine is also a thorn in the side. For Europe, this is not a matter of indifference, but a direct challenge to its model of democracy, transparency and multilateral cooperation. The question is whether Europe is willing to take a pragmatic stance on this, especially now that the United States, too, seems to be taking the moral dimension of its leadership less seriously. What is more, the other potential players at the future multipolar table are hardly paragons of democracy or European values either.

One final interesting element is the relationship between China and Russia. As discussed earlier, there is deep historical distrust between the two countries. At the same time, they find common ground in their position vis-à-vis the West – and especially the United States – and in their pursuit of an alternative model of international order. Both want to push back American influence, but China does not want to jeopardise global stability, which underpins its own growth. Ironically, there is a growing suspicion that Russia will emerge so weakened from the conflict with Ukraine that, in the longer term, it will become subordinate to China. In that case, it would squander its own geopolitical future while simultaneously strengthening China's power base. The comparison with post-war Europe is hard to ignore: exhausted and weakened, Europe became, de facto, a vassal state of the United States, which in turn was able to build its world-power position. Could something similar now happen between China and Russia? In the Chinese view, the old world order is not only crumbling because of military aggression or electoral disruption, but also because of the patient work of a great power that gradually manages to anchor its own norms, networks and worldview into the foundations of a new system. The question is: will the United States accept this development? And what position will Europe take, now that for the first time in a long while it must set its own course?

India's ambitions

In the list of potential candidate great powers vying for a position in the new world order, India cannot be left out. The country is climbing steeply economically and has worked its way up to become the world's 4th largest economy, while presenting itself as the growth engine of the Global South. Because of the suspicion Trump harbours towards China, India has become an attractive alternative for manufacturing Western goods, which will further increase its importance in the global economy and therefore its growth. That rise is impressive, especially in combination with the expected growth figures for the coming years. Even so, for now India still remains at some distance from the economic heavyweights of the United States, China and Europe.

Diplomatically, India is also playing an increasingly active role. It navigates skilfully between the United States, Russia and China, without fully binding itself to any one camp – which gives it a unique geopolitical position. The recent tensions caused by the tariff war in mid-2025 seem to be pushing India more in China's direction, away from the United States as a strategic partner. How that develops further remains to be seen in the near future. In multilateral structures such as BRICS, the UN and the G20, India is making itself heard as a voice for developing countries and as a defender of a multipolar world order. That role is recognised internationally, but also viewed with a degree of caution: India's vulnerabilities limit its ability to take on that role consistently and credibly, because it still does not have enough power to project structural influence worldwide – as the traditional great powers do. India is therefore not China's or the United States' equal, but it is already a serious factor in the new balance of power of the 21st century. It will be interesting to see how Europe will engage with this emerging player.

And many more are waiting in the wings

Alongside the classic great powers and a challenger such as India, we see many other candidates that want to play a growing role on the multipolar world stage. Although they often show little sympathy for our Western values, norms and democratic principles, these countries do not share a uniform ideology or strategy. Usually, they have a few characteristics that make them internationally interesting: rapid growth, a strategic location, or access to essential raw materials. Countries such as Brazil and Indonesia stand out because of their major demographic and economic potential. Nigeria is a strong grower in Africa, with a young population and abundant raw materials, but it is hampered by internal instability. Countries such as Turkey and Mexico position themselves as bridge countries between great powers, while Saudi Arabia and the Gulf states use their oil wealth to pursue geopolitical ambitions.

In all these cases, we are talking about countries that are increasingly tipping the balance in international forums, trade blocs and diplomatic negotiations. They are seeking autonomy and agency within the new multipolar order, and no longer want to function as subordinate vassal states of the old great powers, but as independent actors with their own agendas. Despite their growth, their global impact is still limited, and yet it is increasingly these countries that have been taking the initiative in recent years to exert influence in regional conflicts. Their handy, opportunistic manoeuvring between the current great powers ensures that they keep open lines with both the United States and China, with both Russia and Europe. Their rise is real and irreversible, but how exactly they will form part of the new world order is still unclear.

Will a handful of great powers succeed in once again pulling smaller parties exclusively into their ideological, economic and military camp? Or are we still evolving towards the fragmented multipolar order from before the two world wars, in which everyone tries to claim a place and prioritises their own interests, but now on a global scale? And will that happen with respect for the international order, guaranteed through global rules and structures that are recognised and respected by all?

Or will the dynamics of the new world be determined by brutal abuse of power and convenient, businesslike alliances and deals? Presumably, reality will be an evolving mix of several of these possibilities, which makes it a fragile and explosive geopolitical blend. Much will depend on how China builds its position in the world, the extent to which the United States continues to distance itself from the international order of the past eighty years, and the role Europe will play in all this.

To make matters even more complex, in recent years new forces have emerged that also exert influence on the world as we know it. These forces are often detached from countries and nations, but their greatly increased influence does, in fact, help shape the positions those countries take. In the next chapter I discuss a number of these currents, how they have become visible through the presidency of Trump II, and how, through that presidency, they suddenly appear to have the most disruptive impact on the world order.

5. The world order is being redrawn, part 2: The new forces

How the United States is dismantling its own world order

As I wrote earlier, something remarkable is happening right now. Since Trump II, the United States, the architect of the current world order, has been acting as the biggest challenger to its own model. What stands out is that the White House does not simply see this world order as an outdated system that fails to take account of the current interests of Russia, China, India and other emerging countries – which is what those countries themselves argue. Trump and his entourage see the existing world order as a weapon being used against the United States. During the first meeting of his cabinet, Trump, with his well-known subtlety, blurted out that 'the EU was founded to screw America'. That today's Europe – the EU, its institutions, its defence policy and its weak position in the world – is in fact the result of American policy is something Trump conveniently seems to forget.

The United States was able, through a brilliant combination of economic, military and normative dominance, to structure and conduct the world order for decades. The foundation of that power lay first and foremost in the financial system it designed itself, with the dollar as its pivot and decisive positions in institutions such as the IMF and the World Bank. This not only allowed the United States to set global economic rules, but also to systematically use the financial system as a weapon against anyone who deviated from its vision. With this economic hegemony, Washington could pressure opponents worldwide to achieve its goals without mobilising a single soldier, tank or aircraft. The dollar, trade, credit and capital markets were crucial pieces in a geostrategic chess game that served American interests, far more important than the military power the United States possesses.

If this economic and financial pressure was not sufficient, the United States still had its military machine, which functioned as a safety net for allies and a deterrent to rivals. With the largest and most modern army, and its dominant position within NATO, America could exert pressure and intervene far beyond its own borders. Yet it was not only brute economic and military force that helped build American hegemony. Through diplomacy, development aid, care and cultural soft power, the United States built an image of moral leadership, and slowly and steadily spread the liberal Western worldview. Democracy, human rights and free-market principles were promoted and funded worldwide, although a critical look at the actions of the West – and of the United States in particular – shows that this was often done in a highly selective and hypocritical way. Even so, many countries were drawn into the United States' political, military and economic sphere of influence, keeping them away from Europe, Russia and, of course, the rising power: China. It was precisely this mix of hard and soft power that enabled the United States to function as the pivot of the world order: economically coercive, militarily assertive when needed, yet culturally seductive and politically guiding. And it is precisely that mix that is being dismantled under Trump II. On all these fronts, the United States seems to be detaching itself from its historic partners and from its dominant position on the world stage.

Trump's second presidency breaks with the foundations of American hegemony as it has been built since 1945. What began as rhetoric around 'America First' is evolving, in his second term, into a deliberate dismantling of America's soft power infrastructure. Institutions that for years functioned as pillars of American foreign policy are being hollowed out or abolished. Officially, this is done under the guise of eliminating inefficiencies or correcting alleged discrimination, while it is clear that these operations are, first and foremost, aimed at dismantling institutions that do not align ideologically with Trump's worldview. Where previous administrations still viewed diplomacy and development cooperation as strategic instruments,

Trump reduces them to useless baggage. At the same time, he is pulling the United States out of crucial multilateral cooperation: from climate agreements to human rights treaties, one international commitment after another is being terminated or ignored. Where America under previous presidents still steered between pragmatism and symbolic leadership, Trump is letting go of that position. The negative attitude towards historic allies is no longer hidden behind diplomatic euphemisms; it has now become official policy. The leaked Signal messages from Trump's team, in which European partners are dismissed as 'freeloaders' and 'pathetic', are illustrative of the brutal contempt with which the United States now looks at its partners – and at Europe.

On top of that, the United States is sawing off the military leg of its own international power apparatus. Threats to leave NATO or withdraw soldiers from Europe, and the undermining of Article 5 (where an attack on one member state counts as an attack on all member states, activating collective defence), erode confidence in American defence as a global guarantee. While each of Trump's statements can be seen as a negotiating tactic from the 'art of the deal' toolbox, they still constitute a threat with structural consequences for the members of these old alliances, who are being forced to reinvent and strengthen themselves. The repeated turning off of military support for Ukraine also shows that Trump is willing to go beyond threats and bluffing. So does America have no interest anymore in what happens beyond its borders? It does – but the focus is now entirely on building power in the Indo-Pacific, where China is explicitly designated as the biggest systemic rival. The message is clear: the United States is willing to leave Europe to its fate, in order to shift its resources and attention to Asia. This is a fundamental change of course.

And that brings us to the most disruptive action of the Trump administration: undermining its own dominant position on the global economic and financial stage – the most powerful instrument the United States had for geopolitical intervention. On 2 April 2025, during so-called 'Liberation Day', Trump announced a tariff war with almost every country in the world, in a staggering display of economic incompetence. The barrage of tariffs – some of them unprecedentedly high – shook global trade to its core. How poorly prepared this was became clear, among other things, from the fact that the Heard and McDonald Islands were also hit, where, bizarrely enough, only penguins and seals appear to live. The market uncertainty created by this is unprecedented. And the fact that tariffs are frozen, reintroduced, or seemingly randomly raised or lowered only amplifies that uncertainty. Remarkably, at the time of writing, one of the few countries that escapes these tariffs appears to be ... Russia.

The actions of the current Trump administration, briefly discussed above, weaken America's international position, its alliances, and the individual positions of its partners. They leave behind an unprecedented leadership vacuum in domains in which the United States has set the tone since WWII. This forces the abandoned partners to reposition themselves in each of those domains, in order to strengthen their own position in the new world order. At the same time, it gives America's rivals the chance to expand their influence. Given Europe's earlier described near-vassal status vis-à-vis the United States, the consequences are enormous on every front. The need to reinvent ourselves is vast, but fortunately that awareness has now truly set in. Which brings us to the million-dollar question: why is Trump doing this, what is the grand master plan, and what world order is the United States pursuing?

The new Trumpian tripolar world

Donald Trump's worldview represents a fundamental break with how we think about international order. Where American administrations for eighty years clung to a model of global leadership based on (more or less) universal values, Trump seems to be introducing a radical alternative: a world divided into three spheres of influence, led by the United States, Russia and China – three great powers that keep one another in balance. This tripolar vision is not merely rhetoric: it is translated into policy choices based on power politics and territorial thinking. In this vision, the international system – built on shared interests and multilateral agreements and cooperation – is no longer seen as a platform for collective progress. Instead, the global market becomes an arena for rough negotiations in which each power secures its own space.

This is known as the Realism doctrine, in which the role of power (and the abuse of power) and self-interest in state behaviour is central to international relations. The doctrine starts from the assumption that nation states are once again the most important actors in a chaotic world order. Realism argues that, in times of chaos, states are primarily motivated to safeguard their own security and survival, which leads to a focus on military strength and strategic alliances. Ideological and moral considerations are subordinate to pragmatic decisions. In this doctrine, it is perfectly logical for the strongest parties to use their power to force others to give them what they want. Trump's remarks about Greenland, Canada or Panama are illustrations of that behaviour. The parallels with the 19th-century dynamics of multipolar nation states in Europe are strong – and the consequences of that period are well known.

Trump does not see Russia and China as dangerous deviations from a liberal world order that need correcting, as previous American administrations did. Instead, he regards them as legitimate great powers with an obvious claim to their regional sphere of influence. For him, it is not inherently problematic for Russia to dominate Ukraine or for China to exert power in the South China Sea, because these are logical expressions of great-power politics. Even so, there is a fundamental difference in how Trump views Russia versus China. In traditional American foreign policy, China was seen as a rising systemic rival, but with room for cooperation. Russia, by contrast, was mainly viewed as a dangerous, revisionist power that needed to be prevented from further expansion. Under Trump, that perspective shifts fundamentally: China becomes the primary existential threat to American hegemony and therefore has to be pushed back economically, technologically and militarily. This perception of China as the main enemy is rooted in Trump's conviction that economic competitiveness is a matter of national security. As early as 2017, he identified China as a 'rival power' that 'is trying to change the status quo in the world, to the detriment of the United States'. Russia, by contrast, is reduced to a manageable regional player (much to Putin's irritation, by the way). By strengthening relations between the United States and Russia, Trump believes he can drive a geopolitical wedge between China and Russia.

This recognition of 'natural' spheres of influence is, for Trump, a strategic move to limit international conflicts: if each of the three poles controls its own territory, the risk of clashes is smaller. But because today's world is a complex puzzle of intertwined interests and dependencies, this vision is simplistic and even dangerous. Boundaries of influence are rarely clearly defined. Here too, we can once again learn from the 19th-century situation and how it ultimately led to two world wars. In Trump's framework, states are essentially competitors, and international politics is a succession of transactions that you can win or lose. It is no coincidence that Trump often frames his geopolitical worldview in real-estate terms: who owns what, who picks up the costs, and who can sell at a profit. That reduces geopolitics to something best understood through transactions, rather than through institutional checks and balances and broader societal interests. In Trump's logic, geopolitics is boiled down to negotiable assets – from Greenland and Canada to Ukraine's raw materials and the Panama Canal. However hard that may be to square with the way we see the world today, it is essentially how the world was carved up between power blocs until the 19th century.

Trump's vision leaves no room for Europe as a strong and independent geopolitical actor. Instead, Europe is reduced to a junior partner that must adapt to

American strategic priorities, or risk being left behind. In the worst case, Russia can simply absorb (part of) Europe into its sphere of influence. In addition, in the tripolar vision, regional powers such as Turkey, South Korea, Indonesia or Brazil are forced to align themselves with one of the three dominant blocs, whereas today they are often still sitting on the fence and can manoeuvre strategically between multiple parties. In Africa, South-East Asia and Latin America, this creates a new risk of geopolitical competition, in which development, infrastructure, military support and the digital connectivity of local states become instruments in the struggle for loyalty to one of the power blocs. It is therefore not difficult to foresee how conflicts could once again arise between neighbouring countries that orient themselves differently towards a great power, and in doing so become the battleground for proxy wars of the kind we saw so often during the Cold War.

If this tripolar order becomes reality, the space for autonomous regional development by independent states will shrink, just as the playing field will shrink for countries that do not want to turn to the United States, China or Russia. Trump's worldview is a return to a system of great powers that keep one another in check through mutual pressure, threats and respect for hard borders. This approach fails to recognise the complex, interdependent reality of the 21st century. The question, then, is whether this plan has any chance of success. Do China, Russia, Europe and other countries even want to play along in Trump's story? Or are current American actions mainly a wake-up call that pushes other states to chart a different course, to design a strong new world order in which the United States is no longer the model's architect but perhaps simply one of many parties at the table? The coming months and years will show which direction things go in and which model we ultimately end up in – but it is important to believe that we ourselves hold some of the keys.

There is another striking aspect at play in current American policy: a new ideological link between the United States, Russia and even China. Both Trump and Putin see Europe as a 'bastion of decadence' and view the values Europe stands for as a threat. This shared antipathy towards European liberal values, and our long tradition of democratic government, forms an unexpected basis for an American-Russian rapprochement. For Europe, this means it is being marginalised in Trump's new world order not only geopolitically, but also ideologically.

Is the United States an autocracy?

The problem with writing a book about current affairs is that you never know what the world will look like in the months after you submit the manuscript. I am answering the question of whether the United States is an autocracy based on what we know now, even though that means reality may already have changed completely by the time you read this book. Perhaps, in the midterm elections in 2026, the Democrats will once again hold a majority in Congress and Trump's power will be limited. Perhaps the situation will have deteriorated sharply and the United States will have slid further into an autocratic regime.

When we look at the political evolution of the United States, it is hard not to sound the alarm. What is happening in the United States strongly resembles what we saw in Germany in the 1930s and, more recently, in countries such as Hungary, Poland and Turkey. You could call it an 'electoral autocracy': a form of regime that looks democratic, with elections, parliaments and media, but is authoritarian in essence. Elections still exist, but they lose their meaning when institutions are hollowed out and political opponents are neutralised. The appointment of ideologically loyal judges, the purging of Trump critics in federal agencies, bypassing Congress through executive orders, attacks on the media and law firms, censoring books in libraries, rewriting history in American museums, and ignoring judicial rulings – all of these are signals that something is fundamentally wrong with the democratic quality of the United States.

This drift towards less democracy is also reflected in the results of the Bright Line Watch survey, published in early 2025. Based on polling hundreds of political scientists, it maps the state of American democracy. The decline is extreme: the democracy score falls from 67 to 55 in barely three months, confirming that Trump's statements are now also translating into day-to-day reality in the United States. One striking note in the report is the unprecedented speed of that decline: where countries such as Hungary and Turkey take years to roll back democratic achievements in subtle ways, Trump and his entourage seem to want to achieve this in a matter of months.

But what drives Trump to pursue such a course? Countless books have already been written and films made about the man and his view of the world. Is he power-hungry, with nostalgia for lost American supremacy? Is it all one big negotiation, in search of the right deal? Is it about personal loyalty to his ego? Is he really that stupid, or much smarter than he lets on, manipulating the truth as part of his game? Does he now truly see himself as a messianic leader, who is only still alive – and therefore rules the United States – because he was chosen by God? Is everything he does politically driven by self-interest? The answer to these questions will probably always remain a great enigma.

The question I am trying to answer in this book is this: is Trump's current draconian policy really Trump's policy, or rather that of a consortium of forces that want to carry out their agenda through him? And, more importantly: if these forces truly set the United States' agenda, are they an exclusively American phenomenon, or does their influence reach further – into the rest of the world? In the preparatory conversations for this book, I was often asked why I pay so much attention to what is currently happening in the United States. That question implies that everything will more or less normalise once Trump leaves the stage, and that it will not get quite that bad. What I want to show with the next chapters is that Trump and his administration, in my view, have become a vehicle for power, steered by other forces. Those forces remain active after Trump is gone, and they influence the rest of the world – including Europe. If we want to think constructively about a new world order and Europe's role within it, it is necessary to understand this dynamic.

The Trump Gang

There is something odd about the way Trump has seized power within the Republican Party, but also about how others are using the momentum to pursue their own objectives through Trump. Trump's first term in office was characterised by the actions and approach of a president who perhaps never expected to win. What he did was populist, loud, brutal, provocative, and focused on the themes he could use to please his initial MAGA base (Make America Great Again). Those themes tapped into a deeper current of alienation, frustration and distrust that had been simmering for years under the surface of American society, and which Trump exploited in a sly way.

What is interesting is that Trump himself probably has little ideology. His goal was to become president, and his approach was to mobilise part of the population with a populist and conservative agenda, using talking points for which it was clear his inflammatory style was ideal for delivering the message. To win his first election, it was not enough to have only the MAGA base on board, which is why he struck unexpected alliances. The most striking was with right-wing Christians (especially white evangelicals). Although there was initially a great deal of resistance to the uncouth and morally questionable Trump, the movement strategically chose to support him, mainly because of his hostility towards left-progressive ideas. Trump's promise to appoint a conservative majority to the Supreme Court fulfilled an old dream of these conservative Christians and was rewarded with a historic score: no fewer than 81 percent of conservative Christians voted for Trump in 2016. This opened the door to right-wing religious organisations that will prove to be of great importance in his current policies.

The impact of his first term was rather limited. Trump was still inexperienced as president and, when it came to his most radical ideas and actions, he was kept in line by an army of advisers and career politicians in the right positions. But after his defeat to Biden and in the run-up to his re-election, something remarkable happened. Behind the scenes, a range of other movements and interest groups were gearing up to push through their own agenda via a new potential Trump presidency – with Trump as a battering ram. This time, well-organised groups took a seat at the table to help Trump secure re-election. The way I see it, this amounts to another power grab, in which the agenda and the tighter ideological line no longer come from Trump himself, but are dictated by interest groups that have gathered under the MAGA umbrella. Trump's vision is no longer his alone: it has been expanded and professionalised by other stakeholders. Trump has become the face of groups that see their chance to – often after years of operating behind the scenes – come out explicitly with their worldview. This insight is crucial, because it makes clear that Trump's departure as president will not necessarily lead to different policies – perhaps even the opposite. Another reason this matters is that these forces are global and are not limited to the United States alone. If we want to think about the future world order, and about the choices Europe has to make in order to chart its own course within it, then it is important to properly understand what those forces are and what kind of worldview they are pursuing.

So who are the various stakeholders behind current Trump policy? It turns out to be a fascinating mix of hardline MAGA supporters, traditional Republicans from the Grand Old Party (the GOP, as they affectionately call their party), radical right-wing religious organisations, American oligarchs and techno-libertarians. Below, I briefly describe who they are, how they are linked to one another, and who their most important representatives are – often at the very highest level of the US government.

The MAGA movement

Although the original slogan was first launched by Ronald Reagan in 1980 as 'Let's Make America Great Again', it was recycled by Trump, who used it to ignite the MAGA movement. 'Make America Great Again' became the collective cry of nostalgia, restoration and resistance. It expressed a deeply rooted feeling that the America of yesteryear was slowly disappearing. Whatever you may think of Trump's abilities, he has managed masterfully to spot this undercurrent of loss and cultural uncertainty and to mobilise it skilfully for his own ends. With his uncouth style and unconventional performance, he gave a voice to people who had long felt unheard. The danger of the MAGA movement is that, under the guise of ordinary people's legitimate concerns about purchasing power or illegal immigration, an ideology is hiding with far broader implications. The slogan 'Make America Great Again' sounds like a patriotic sentiment, but the implicit message is that America used to be better – read: whiter, more male, more Christian and more homogeneous. That nostalgic worldview and the underlying cultural insecurity are turned by the MAGA movement into political mobilisation. It is a movement that feeds on fear, but presents itself as a movement of restoration. That gives it a veneer of legitimacy that makes it dangerously effective.

MAGA is not an ideology in the strict sense, but a framework through which people interpret their world. It offers not so much policy solutions as a story: of loss, of being betrayed by the elite, of the need for struggle. And that, above all, is what makes it hard to counter with arguments or facts. MAGA is not oriented towards debate, but towards loyalty. Criticism of Trump, in the eyes of many supporters, is not a substantive judgement, but an attack on their identity. That emotional bond is precisely what makes the movement so tough and durable, and what sets it apart from traditional electoral politics. And as long as those underlying feelings of loss, alienation and cultural insecurity persist, the MAGA feeling will keep flaring up in old or new forms, both within the United States and beyond.

Anyone who imagines a typical MAGA supporter as an angry, poorly educated white labourer from the Deep South is only seeing part of the story. The movement is indeed dominated by white, Christian men of middle to older age. These men are often retired and have plenty of time for politics, are noisily present in the streetscape, or troll everyone and everything on social media. But the stereotypical image of the economically disadvantaged rural resident does not entirely hold up: a substantial part of Trump's base has a higher-education degree, lives in or near major cities, and many are well above the low wages we picture when we think of the caricatured MAGA fan with his red cap and pick-up truck. In the 2024 election, Trump also managed to attract more female voters than in 2020, especially among conservative mothers who worry about 'woke' education, gender teaching and crime. In 2024, Trump could also count on more support among ethnic minorities and young male voters, thanks in part to economic promises, his hard line on crime, his macho behaviour, and a carefully thought-out campaign that played on their frustrations with the Democratic Party.

What really binds supporters is the feeling that they are being economically and culturally outpaced by forces beyond their control. They share a worldview that revolves around three axes: cultural preservation, economic nationalism and distrust of institutions. That ideological cocktail is not new, but under MAGA it is formulated and propagated with unprecedented sharpness. The fear of cultural replacement is linked to resistance against immigration, gender diversity and the feminisation of society. Add Trump's economic protectionism to that – with hard rhetoric against international trade and globalisation – and you get a movement that presents itself as the guardian of a threatened American ideal. Distrust of the media, science and even its own party leadership completes the picture.

A large part of MAGA's success is due to the influence exerted within its own media universe, which gratefully draws on Trump-friendly outlets such as Fox News, but just as much on the countless MAGA influencers who build and maintain their MAGA echo chambers through podcasts, YouTube channels and social media. Thanks to these alternative media channels, many supporters live in a parallel information reality in which their worldview is constantly affirmed. In that world, Trump is not a controversial leader, but a martyr being attacked by the system. Migrants are an existential threat, elections are stolen, climate policy is a globalist ploy, and scientists and journalists are agents of the left. These alternative facts create a reality in which political opponents are not opponents, but enemies, making democratic debate all but impossible.

It is important to see how other interest groups, in the meantime, are making use of the MAGA movement – 'the face of the people' – to carry out their own agenda. The real money flows behind MAGA run through so-called Super PACs (organisations that can raise and spend unlimited amounts of money to support political candidates or campaigns) and donors who often have little affection for the movement's folksy character, but who use MAGA's energy for their own ends.

If we draw the link with similar currents in Europe, we see that the underlying social discontent is just as present. This often explains the rise of populist politicians and parties that explicitly model themselves on Trump and his MAGA movement.

Unlike the near-omnipotence MAGA has acquired on the right in the United States, European populist movements operate in a far more diverse political landscape. Existing far-right organisations do benefit from the Trump vibe, but they have to do so alongside a range of other parties, both to the left and right of the political centre. Whereas (as I discuss in the section that follows) Trump has taken over the Republican Party in the United States and reshaped it into a bastion of conservative populism, that is far less successful in Europe. In most cases, alongside the extreme populist currents in the European party landscape, there are still stable right-conservative forces that do not take the radical route, yet still try to claim citizens' concerns about purchasing power, illegal migration and other sensitive issues. This spreads part of the social discontent across multiple parties and acts as a buffer. Although populist parties in some countries can attract up to a third of the vote and can indeed come to power through coalitions, it remains difficult to form a central bloc like the MAGA-dominated Republican Party in the United States.

The traditional Republicans

Within the Republican Party, there remains a substantial group of traditional Republican voters who struggle to identify with the style and worldview of the MAGA movement. They are the heirs to a conservatism embodied by figures such as Ronald Reagan, George H.W. Bush and John McCain. Their convictions are anchored in a classical liberal framework: small government, free-market capitalism, strong defence, and a certain degree of social order – but packaged in moderate, institution-minded language. Where MAGA hammers on enemy thinking and culture wars, these Republicans speak of 'religious freedom', 'citizenship' and 'constitutional values'. Their loyalty to the party led them to vote for Trump in 2016 and 2020 nonetheless, but often reluctantly. Crucial moments, such as the storming of the Capitol, marked fault lines: where MAGA saw it as protest, traditional Republicans saw it as an attack on the rule of law and democracy. The difference between the two groups is not only substantive, but also stylistic. For traditional Republicans, style matters: they value leaders who are rational and unifying – the 'Reaganesque' president who radiates optimism and treats opponents with respect. The 'clownish' Trump, with his insulting tweets, tirades and chaotic approach, is the opposite of what these traditional Republicans stand for.

Even so, it would be wrong to think the Republican Party consists only of these two groups with opposing visions. In reality, the party is made up of multiple factions that vary in ideological emphasis, tone, style and worldview. Where, in the past, classical conservatives set the party line, they have now been pushed to the margins. The centre of gravity now lies with the conservative-populist wing, with MAGA as the dominant point of reference, but other, more radical factions have also gained influence. The party's ideological recalibration is also actively fuelled by external forces, such as The Heritage Foundation, the organisation behind the famous Project 2025, which I will return to later. Party policy no longer comes from the classical centre, but from the new radical periphery that has taken the reins.

Through his MAGA movement, Trump has de facto taken over the party and then opened the door to other, more radical factions that together are shaping America's extreme agenda. This did not happen through formal restructuring, but in the typical Trump way: through the abuse of power, pressure and deals. Anyone within the party who still wants to build a career now knows that opposing Trump amounts to electoral suicide. The most visible critical voices were purged long ago, and to this day internal resistance has been minimal – out of fear of reprisals from Trump. What began as a protest movement has now become the conservative centre of power, at the expense of the old Republican order. The question is whether the latter will still stir if the United States slides even further towards autocracy.

The radical right-wing religious movement

In the previous pages, we saw how the MAGA movement is largely based on a white, male and Christian nostalgic image of society from the 1950s. What few people realise is how deeply this ideology is now rooted in today's United States, and which powerful players are now trying to seize the momentum to push their convictions further.

When, as a young teenager, I became a fan of the American musician and composer Frank Zappa, I could not have imagined that 45 years later I would be reaching back to that period. I discovered Zappa in the early 1980s. Through my brother, who was three years older and in turn had older friends, the first albums by this eccentric genius made their way into our home. Both the music and the lyrics were unconventional and, in terms of content, shocking. It is therefore no surprise that Zappa became the target of attacks by a new right-wing religious lobby: the Moral Majority. I still vividly remember how the eccentric rock musician, sharply dressed in a suit, appeared before the US Congress in 1985 and delivered a fiery argument against the proposals of the PMRC, the Parents Music Resource Center.

Those proposals effectively amounted to the censorship of music and related cultural expression. This was the first time I was confronted with attempts by right-wing religious movements in the United States to use their influence against the liberalisation of society. I was seventeen then and had no eye for the underlying motives, let alone for the initiatives of this conservative current. What they were doing seemed anecdotal to me at the time, and not at all influential in the development of the United States, Europe or the rest of the world. I fear many people shared that analysis, which meant that the activities of these well-organised movements largely remained under the radar in the decades that followed.

What began as a cultural crusade against music, abortion and pornography slowly but surely grew, from the wings, into one of the most powerful political forces in the United States. In the 1970s, figures such as Jerry Falwell (television evangelist and founder of the Moral Majority) and Paul Weyrich (political strategist and founder of The Heritage Foundation, which I will return to later) mobilised a broad coalition of evangelicals and conservative Catholics. That the two sides of the Christian spectrum – Protestants and Catholics – found common ground in this was, in itself, unique. They initially positioned themselves as moral watchdogs, but soon discovered the value of strategic political operations, lobbying and judicial appointments. The Moral Majority was only one of many organisations that emerged in that period, all pursuing a similar conservative agenda. These organisations were not merely pressure groups: they increasingly became breeding grounds of political influence, which they deployed in subtle ways, election after election. Although Trump's power grab was still to come, the Republican Party gradually shifted along with them: whispered moral themes became party positions. The religious right learned the rules of power – and how to bend the game to its advantage. Over the past fifty years, their influence has been unmistakable, but never did it become as explicit as it has since Trump first came to power. As I wrote earlier, Trump needed right-wing religious voters and was willing to deliver on a number of their agenda points if he were elected.

And so it came to pass. Under Trump's first administration, three conservative Supreme Court justices were appointed – a milestone for these movements, and enormously important in the many legal battles the current Trump administration is embroiled in. With these appointments, and the takeover of the US Supreme Court, the dream that began to take shape back in the 1980s was realised. This long march through the institutions shows that the religious-conservative project is not a spontaneous impulse, but a carefully considered plan that has been under way since the 1970s. What did that plan look like?

After WWII, a wave of liberalisation took hold, and Western society took the shape we now know: secularisation; the separation of church and state in the form of a liberal democracy; emancipation and liberation; freedom and equality in terms of gender, culture, religion and sexuality; access to education and development for everyone; the building of a welfare state; and an unprecedented level of medical and scientific progress. You could argue that it is impossible to be against this evolution of the past eighty years, and that everyone goes along with it. But reality shows that this is not the case. There are people for whom these developments are horrific: an outgrowth of progressive decadence, an attack on a social order that for hundreds, even thousands of years has been based on conservative mechanisms and convictions. In itself, as someone who holds democracy in high regard, I have little objection to the fact that people hold these views and try to defend their conservative interests. Through elections, they can try to find a parliamentary majority to translate their principles into policy and laws. That is precisely the strength of democracy: if you manage to mobilise enough people, you can influence policy. If you find a majority of like-minded people, you can change the system, even if that means liberal progress is rolled back towards a more conservative worldview.

If we look at the figures in the United States, however, we see that only 25 to 30 percent of Americans support an far-reaching religious-conservative policy agenda. That is therefore far removed from a legitimate democratic majority. And yet that is precisely what these organisations have been striving for all this time, and what they have now achieved with Trump's re-election. More than that, they have made it the central theme of his policies. To achieve this, they have harnessed the mobilising dynamic of the MAGA movement described above to use MAGA discontent – which mainly revolves around core themes such as illegal immigration, the economy, purchasing power, anti-establishment sentiment and a nostalgic sense of loss – as a vehicle for introducing a much deeper right-wing Christian agenda.

The right-wing Christian impact on today's United States

The core ideology of these movements revolves around a patriarchal, Christian vision of society and morality. The traditional nuclear family serves as the moral anchor: the father as breadwinner, the mother as caregiver, children in obedience. Sexual diversity and gender equality are rejected as signs of moral decline. This family ideology is more than nostalgia: it is a blueprint for the social restructuring that we are now also increasingly seeing reflected in the executive measures of Trump II. Religion, economics and politics are brought together in a worldview in which the authority of God and man is central. In this vision, a secular state is not neutral, but a hostile force that undermines the natural order. The economic vision of this movement is closely intertwined with its cultural values. The 1950s are idealised as a period of family stability, religious commitment and economic prosperity based on one income. This leads to legislative proposals or executive orders in which tax benefits are granted to large families, childlessness is discouraged, and reindustrialisation is pursued along the lines of the 1950s model. In this retro-vision, economic policy acquires a moral dimension: the goal is not efficiency, but virtue. The economic agenda is therefore not neoliberal, but morally conservative: jobs should support families, not enrich shareholders. Here we see a first major field of tension emerging within the MAGA camp, because the interests of the right-wing religious groups on this point run directly counter to those of the American oligarchs, who have also rallied behind Trump.

Within the broader Christian-conservative field, there are even more radical currents, such as the supporters of Christian Reconstructionism. This movement argues for the reintroduction of Biblical laws into state structures. Their vision, in which homosexuality and apostasy are punishable offences, is extreme, but it finds indirect resonance among policymakers in Trump's orbit. You could almost call it a Christian variant of sharia. The ultimate goal of various right-wing Christian groups is the realisation of a so-called post-liberal society. They argue that liberal democracy fails because it is morally neutral, and they strive for a society in which all institutions are once again organised on the basis of 'Judeo-Christian' values. Universities, the media and civil servants are seen in this model as hostile bastions of progressive thinking, to be purged or re-educated. Political leaders such as Vice President JD Vance explicitly speak about subordinating liberal freedoms to higher moral laws. This trend marks a break with the conservatism of traditional Republicans, which defends individualism and freedom. Post-liberals want order, hierarchy and moral clarity.

If we map Trump's policies and actions since his inauguration, we see that – alongside personal acts of revenge against anyone who has ever crossed him – the echoes of the right-wing Christian agenda are clearly present. If you have ever wondered why Trump has suddenly adopted such radical, religiously infused positions, when in the past you would have needed a magnifying glass to find his moral compass, the answer is clear: it is not Trump's own agenda, it is the agenda of the right-wing Christian organisations, behind Trump, behind MAGA. A few examples can illustrate this, without going into detail. The most striking is, of course, the purge of everything seen as woke or progressive. This is not only happening within federal government agencies, education or the military: the corporate world, too, is under heavy pressure to stop all DEI initiatives (Diversity, Equity, Inclusion). Even European companies and governments have received forceful calls from US embassies to immediately end every DEI programme, in order to remain in America's good graces. The political argument behind this demand is that such programmes lead to discrimination against white, traditional values and people, and to progressive indoctrination. In reality, this is undoubtedly the top priority of the right-wing Christian agenda: rolling back progressive developments that they regard as decadent.

In the same way, the overt attack on educational and knowledge institutions in the United States can also be understood. By quasi dismantling the Department of Education, it becomes harder for many Americans to access education, which in the longer term may lead to a larger group of unskilled people. The attack on top universities fits within the belief that these institutions are bastions of progressive and woke thinking, and therefore irrelevant or even threatening to the post-liberal world being pursued. In that world, a highly educated society, with high-quality dissemination of knowledge across all groups, is not a priority. Truth-seeking science has no place in it either; on the contrary, it runs counter to the Christian dogmas invoked by many figures in the right-wing religious world.

From this conservative perspective, the economic measures are also easier to understand. Through a tariff war, Trump is trying to bring back classic industrial activities, as they were dominant in the 1950s, when the hard-working, white man was the breadwinner of a large family. The economic risks that come with this matter less to the right-wing religious base: they look for a 'return on moral investment', not corporate profits. In the same vein, there is a whole series of policy measures aimed at restoring the traditional family as the cornerstone of American society. The Trump administration is pursuing a coherent, ideologically motivated family agenda in which the traditional, heterosexual family is affirmed and protected as the only legitimate form. This is reflected, among other things, in scrapping recognition of non-binary identities. In that way, the traditional male-female model is once again affirmed as the only valid basis for forming a family. While reproductive rights are being curtailed – for example by removing coverage for the morning-after pill – access to fertility treatments such as IVF is, by contrast, being encouraged. These reforms are intended to reinforce the traditional family ideal, in which only male-female pairings are seen as legitimate. Family policy thus becomes a pivot in the broader restructuring of American society along Christian-conservative lines.

The sweeping rollback of global support programmes can be framed in several ways. First of all, many health programmes focus on HIV treatment, sexuality, contraception, abortion, reproduction, and so on – all so-called expressions of perversion and Western decadence. It is clear that this runs directly counter to the conservative view of sexuality, so it is only logical, from that perspective, that all support for it must stop – including, by the way, within the United States itself. The fact that many of these projects take place in countries with non-Christian societies certainly plays a role in ending the aid, given how conflictual this is with the Trump administration's Christian priorities.

The most explicit manifestation of the influence of right-wing religious factions is the introduction of religious elements into the American state apparatus. What began as something of a meme after the failed attempt on Trump's life – where it seemed almost impossible that God himself had not intervened to save him – has by now become a structural part of American policy. In the current White House, there is no longer any question of the separation of church and state as enshrined in the US Constitution. It openly presents itself as a Christian bastion, and Trump has repeatedly played down the separation of church and state. The creation of the Task Force to Eradicate Anti-Christian Bias calls on federal officials to report alleged discrimination against Christians, reversing the classic human-rights logic in which the protection of minorities is central. And, as the icing on the cake, on 21 May 2025 a special mass was held in which Brooks Potteiger, the pastor of Secretary of Defense Pete Hegseth, led the prayers. What characterised this service was that Hegseth opened with a prayer emphasising the importance of national submission to the leadership of Jesus Christ. Potteiger's sermon went a step further still: he declared that President Donald Trump had been 'sovereignly appointed' by God to lead the country, and prayed for Trump's protection as the nation's moral beacon. The service drew sharp criticism from secular organisations, who called it a flagrant violation of the First Amendment and a troubling example of religious propaganda now penetrating the heart of the machinery of government.

As stated earlier, Trump himself has little or no ideological bent. For many observers, it therefore seems as if his countless – often undemocratic – executive orders are based on little or nothing. The opposite is true, however. In the first months of Trump II's administration, a roadmap that had been years in the making has been implemented in a rigorous way. To understand that, we need to look at The Heritage Foundation, at Project 2025, and at the strategic positions in the White House. To realise all these plans, a team was needed that would support and carry out even the most radical policy decisions. At first glance, it seems logical to think the team members were selected because of their loyalty to Trump. I do think loyalty was indeed an important selection criterion, but not necessarily exclusively to the president. If we look at the current Trump administration through the lens of religious orientation, what stands out in particular is its deep anchoring in right-wing Christian currents. These religious affiliations clearly influence the policy priorities and rhetoric of everyone involved. They form a common thread in the current governing culture of the White House. I list a brief selection in *The religious colour of Team Trump*.

The religious colour of Team Trump

- **JD Vance**, Vice President, highly visible internationally and, as we have already seen, never averse to provocation when it comes to the far right and democracy (see also later in the paragraph on techno-feudalism). Converted to Catholicism in 2019 and has since been very active in the Catholic Church.
- **Marco Rubio**, Secretary of State, is affiliated with traditionalist Catholicism, an ideology that strongly emphasises hierarchical order and the revaluation of traditional social structures. This movement has its origins in resistance to the reforms implemented after the Second Vatican Council (1962 – 1965). Traditionalist Catholics want to return to, or hold on to, older forms of liturgy (in Latin), theology and church life as they existed before the modernisation of the Church in the 20th century. Rubio's faith is reflected in a foreign policy that stresses the preservation of 'Judeo-Christian values' as a foundation for international cooperation.
- **Pete Hegseth**, Secretary of Defense, has an evangelical Protestant background. This denomination within Protestantism strongly emphasises personal conversion, mission, and a literal belief in the Bible as the highest authority. Hegseth is known for advocating classical Christian education and resisting secularisation.
- **Kristi Noem**, Secretary of Homeland Security, comes from the Foursquare Church and regularly expresses herself in Christian-nationalist terms. This means she strives for a society in which the 'nation under God' is governed on the basis of a literal and conservative interpretation of the Christian faith. She sees her political role as part of 'God's plan', which

translates into security policy with a strong ideological charge, including her hardline positions against LGBTQ+ rights.

- **Linda McMahon**, Secretary of Education, and **Pam Bondi**, Attorney General, are both also linked to traditionalist Catholicism, like Rubio. They advocate a family-oriented, religiously inspired policy that safeguards religious freedom primarily for conservative Christians. In their joint policy, there is a clear priority on institutionally strengthening religious-moral norms in American society.
- **Russell Vought**, Director of the OMB (Office of Management and Budget). He is a central figure in the Christian-nationalist movement and the chief architect of Project 2025. His policy vision links budgetary discipline to moral purity: scrapping progressive programmes is presented as a moral necessity.

The Heritage Foundation and Project 2025: The plan was already in place

I have already referred several times to The Heritage Foundation and Project 2025, with Russell Vought acting as a bridge figure between this organisation and the current Trump administration. In the pages that follow, I briefly describe the importance of this conservative initiative and its impact on Trump's current agenda. The Heritage Foundation was founded in 1973 in response to frustration in conservative circles about President Nixon embracing the 'liberal consensus' (even though he himself can hardly be described as progressive). The founders wanted to go further than the, in their view, overly meek and sluggish think tanks that had little impact on political debate. With short, accessible policy papers, they directly shape the voting behaviour of conservative members of Congress. The first real breakthrough came under President Reagan.

More than forty years ago, the Foundation wrote a first handbook for conservative America. The Reagan administration embraced the 1,100-page *Mandate for Leadership* as a blueprint for a conservative revolution in the White House. Within one year, well over 60 percent of Heritage's proposals had been translated into conservative policy. You could see this as the beta version of what The Heritage Foundation has recently developed in order to have deep and definitive impact on current American policy: Project 2025. In the decades after Reagan, The Heritage Foundation grew into the ideological backbone of conservative America. In the process, the think tank increasingly shifted towards activism. Its exceptionally large multi-million budget allows it not only to write policy documents, but also to exert direct pressure on lawmakers. A key distinction from other conservative think tanks became increasingly clear: Heritage does not only intervene in political, economic or fiscal debates, but also takes a stance more and more often in the culture war around religion, abortion and family. In this way, the Foundation has grown from a technocratic policy institute into an ideological compass, a political campaign organisation and, by now, the underground architect of the current Trump administration.

The Foundation's leadership sees Trump's first term as a missed opportunity, because of a slow start and – as described earlier – an unorganised, chaotic approach. In 2021, they launched Project 2025. The goal is that, if Trump is re-elected, they will be properly prepared this time – with more than just a plan. The approach is ambitious and methodical: 22 million dollars is invested in a coalition of more than a hundred conservative organisations working together on an extremely conservative policy package. Fundamental to this strategy is the compilation of a list of 10,000 potential candidates to fill positions and thus actually implement the policy through active staffing and the restructuring of the American bureaucracy. A crucial instrument within Project 2025 is the 180-Days Playbook, a roadmap intended to steer Trump's actions from the moment of his inauguration.

At the heart of Project 2025 lies the idea that full control over the federal apparatus should be placed in the president's hands. That implies a radical reform of the civil service and largely dismantling the administrative state. The Schedule F reform (a measure Trump introduced in 2020, under which federal civil servants lose their permanent appointment and protection against dismissal) aims to replace thousands of neutral civil servants with ideological allies. The federal agencies that are to be tackled first are neatly listed for abolition or restructuring: the Department of Education, Justice, the FBI, Homeland Security, Commerce, and independent agencies such as the Federal Communications Commission (FCC) and the Federal Trade Commission (FTC). With this document in hand, Musk's DOGE actions are cast in a different light: this is clearly not an efficiency exercise, but an ideological purge following a pre-planned script. Whether Musk himself was aware of that, or genuinely thought he could reform the government the way he has done with his tech companies, is unclear.

The social agenda of Project 2025 is at least as outspoken and radical. Anti-abortion measures, such as a ban on the abortion pill, are combined with renaming the Department of Health to the 'Department of Life'. LGBTQ+ rights are systematically rolled back, including the withdrawal of legal protections against discrimination. The Christian moral compass serves as the guiding principle, which runs directly counter to the First Amendment of the US Constitution. Legislation discouraging Sunday work and new rules that define gender strictly in biological terms are also on Project 2025's roadmap. The Mexico City Policy is being reinstated, meaning organisations lose all American support if they provide direct or indirect assistance related to reproductive healthcare. On immigration, Project 2025 returns to earlier Trump-era policies: plans for mass deportations are ready.

Finally, Project 2025 reaches far beyond America's borders. Foreign policy combines isolationist reflexes with sabre-rattling. The United States must become militarily stronger, and sovereignty must outweigh multilateral agreements. The defence budget and investment in nuclear weapons are set to rise, while confrontation with China intensifies. That also makes it immediately clear where the Trumpian tripolar world order comes from. Trump's economic agenda, meanwhile, reads like a chapter from the Project 2025 playbook: tax cuts, radical deregulation, fossil energy, and even the tariff war and industrialisation plans are explicitly included in this blueprint.

According to the most recent data at the time of writing, the Trump administration has so far already implemented around 47 percent of the guidelines from Project 2025. This is shown by the official 'Project 2025 tracker', which monitors the extent to which the policy recommendations in the playbook have been translated into concrete measures. For some other proposals, initial steps have already been taken, but no full policy has yet been introduced; other points are still waiting to be implemented. This makes it abundantly clear that Trump's policies do not really come from him, but are the rigorous execution of a well-developed conservative plan that has been in preparation for almost fifty years. The architect of that plan, The Heritage Foundation, has long since ceased to be a classic think tank, and has become a shadow cabinet that is trying to embed a conservative revolution, step by step, policy paper by policy paper.

What does all this have to do with the new world order and with Europe?

The reason I deal with this theme in such detail is because it is one of the determining forces behind US foreign policy and the pitting of partners against one another in the current world order. Almost all measures and actions become easier to understand if we frame them within the right-wing Christian agenda of organisations that have been working behind the scenes to roll back the Western liberal order. The explicitly negative attitude towards 'progressive and decadent Europe' shown by Trump and his associates is not only about our failure to meet, say, our defence commitments, but about a genuine aversion to the values and norms that form the basis of modern Europe.

In that aversion, they look for partners worldwide, and they readily find them among other autocratic regimes or populist leaders who are already poised for an autocratic revolution of their own, whether openly or not. Trump does not hide his preference for autocratic leaders. He shares with them his brutal way of getting things done and, although he himself probably cares little about it, the people who truly shape his policy share the same aversion to decadent Western values. Although China is officially the United States' new arch-enemy, there is sympathy for Xi Jinping's autocratic style, for China's resistance to too much liberalisation in its own society, and equally for China's condemnation of Western decadence. The Trumpian tripolar order can also be explained through this ideological affinity: a culture war waged by three world powers against anything they deem too progressive within their own countries, and, of course, within Europe and the rest of the world.

Europe occupies a fragile position in this force field. The complexity of its internal structure and the multitude of clashing interests in an electorally fragmented landscape make it relatively easy for external actors to find openings for influence. In practice, this means Europe is being played from multiple directions in an attempt to weaken our Union from within. Ironically, geopolitical and nationalist opponents find common ground in this shared objective. The rise of anti-EU and far-right populist currents within Europe is enabled in part by these external forces. Far-right parties such as the RN in France, the AfD in Germany, Fidesz in Hungary, Vlaams Belang in Flanders, the PVV in the Netherlands and the Lega in Italy consistently position themselves as defenders of national sovereignty against 'patronising' European institutions. With their narratives about migration, climate and identity, they attract a large group of dissatisfied voters who no longer feel heard by traditional politics. These parties form a European mosaic that operates as a fifth column within the EU: they undermine consensus, block joint policy, and in doing so offer an opening to hollow out European unity from the inside. Although strongly nationalist in nature, the irony is that these movements receive financial and ideological support from forces outside Europe that have an interest in a divided continent.

If we look at how the influencing of these local parties works, we see strong parallels with how Trump managed to capture Americans' discontent around a number of topics that mattered to them, and then open the door to a far more conservative agenda. We now see the same thing happening in Europe: populists gather a large following around themes such as migration, the economy and dignity, while in the meantime pursuing a much more conservative agenda. Would American and European voters who have voted radically – for example because they want less migration – be aware of the far-reaching right-wing Christian agenda of the forces that support and help build up their parties? Probably not really. Research in Hungary from 2021, conducted by Amnesty International and the Háttér Society, shows that 59 percent of Hungarians support same-sex marriage, and 90 percent believe the government does not need to interfere in this. Yet that same year, the conservative parliament passed a controversial anti-LGBTQ law, with 157 votes in favour and 1 against.

Behind this European fragmentation lies a network that reaches deep into the United States, Russia and even China. While Russia focuses on disinformation and direct financial support for, for example, populist parties such as the AfD or French far-right movements, the American connection is subtler, but at least as influential. Through evangelical networks, conferences such as the World Congress of Families, and proxies such as Steve Bannon or Tucker Carlson, a culturally conservative ideology is systematically exported. Younger voters, meanwhile, are affected by influencers such as Andrew Tate, who promote an outright toxic view of relationships between men and women. Since Trump's inauguration, this influence has gone into overdrive. Figures such as Elon Musk, JD Vance and, of course, Trump himself, no longer mince their words: they openly support far-right parties and berate Europe when it comes to our democratic and liberal structures. These 'culture wars' are no longer directed only at issues such as abortion and LGBTQ rights, but also at the core values on which the EU is built: pluralism, liberalism, the separation of church and state, the protection of citizens and consumers, and human rights.

The growing influence of American right-wing religious organisations on Europe does not mean that there are no comparable European initiatives. Within Europe too, a coordinated network of right-wing Christian organisations is gaining strength. Organisations such as Ordo Iuris in Poland, Mathias Corvinus Collegium (MCC) in Hungary, and CitizenGO in Spain use legal tools, lobbying and grassroots campaigns to roll back progressive gains. They operate in international networks such as Agenda Europe, which hold annual meetings and jointly set strategies. Their agenda aligns with that of American conservative think tanks and evangelical funds that support them with financial resources and ideological backing.

Europe, too, has its oligarchs who, besides their fortunes, share something else: their drive for a religiously inspired conservative Europe. The best known is undoubtedly Vincent Bolloré, the French billionaire who rose from inheriting a small paper mill to becoming one of the country's biggest industrialists. He gained his societal influence by steadily buying into a range of media companies, from Canal+ to CNews, Europe 1 and *Paris Match*. By analogy with American Fox News, his news outlets give the far right a platform to systematically tell their story, helping far-right figures and parties to normalise their ideas. More recently, the French billionaire Pierre-Edouard Stérin has also come onto the radar. He made his fortune through gift vouchers, until at a certain point in his life he went looking for meaning and found it in a mission 'to earn even more billions in order to serve Christ and France'. Stérin worked for years on a secret plan, called Périclès, through which he has, among other things, financially supported numerous far-right figures in France. Through various projects, he aims to exert political influence to help shape his religious-right vision of France. One of the biggest is Politicae, through which he wants to 'prep' candidate politicians so that they are ready for the municipal elections in 2026. The aim is to train 4,000 candidates, in the hope of getting 3,000 elected. The parallels with America's Project 2025 are striking: not only is there an ideological plan and playbook, but thousands of people are also being lined up to 'step in' as soon as election results allow it. As I write this, several investigations are under way in France into Stérin, including in connection with illegal political financing.

The consequences of this ideological influence are visible in a wide range of policy choices. Countries such as Hungary have developed into laboratories for a new kind of illiberal democracy, in which the classical separation of powers is hollowed out and media freedom is under pressure. These countries block or delay European decisions on sanctions against Russia, climate policy or a common asylum policy, and in doing so actively work against European unity. At the same time, we see far-right parties gaining greater weight within European structures and the European Parliament through their electoral successes. As a result, the political spectrum shifts to the right, which has a structurally slowing effect on the implementation of the European agenda on climate, migration and human rights.

What once began in the United States as a conservative moral protest movement is now one of the most important geopolitical factors. Through the judiciary, policy influence, financial support, international networks and the media, the American and European Christian right has emerged as an ideological world power. Its influence stretches from Washington to Warsaw, from churches to courtrooms, from family policy to foreign aid. This movement wants to remake the world in its own image: patriarchal, religiously inspired and hostile to liberal freedoms. Recognising that the rightward shift within Europe is not only the result of normal electoral evolution and respect for voters' views, but is also strongly influenced by these external conservative forces, is fundamental to understanding both the new world order and the position Europe can and wants to take within it. The Trumpian tripolar world order presents itself as the perfect playing field to build this conservative world. But for that to happen, decadent and liberal Europe must first be further dismantled – and how better to do that than from within?

In the next part of this book, I discuss Europe's response to the explicit upheavals in the United States and the challenges we are now facing. The speed at which the United States is changing is creating not only a shock, but also momentum – even a collective European awareness. If we play it well, this could turn out to be our salvation, allowing Europe to claim a place at the table of the new world order.

The rest of this book asks whether that is even possible, and what we in Europe can do to make that ambition a reality, but first I will discuss two more groups of stakeholders behind the Trump administration who also shape the face of its policies.

Tech bros: the new oligarchs in a world with fewer rules and more power

It was a strange sight at Trump's inauguration. Looking somewhat sheepish and unsure of themselves, the richest and most powerful people in the world stood behind the newly sworn-in president: Elon Musk (Tesla and SpaceX), Jeff Bezos (Amazon), Mark Zuckerberg (Meta/Facebook), Tim Cook (Apple) and Sundar Pichai (Google) were given a place of honour, ahead of ministers and other prominent political figures. The fact that each of them had donated at least one million dollars to support the event financially will no doubt have helped them secure that spot. If you look closely, it is not entirely clear whether they are standing there from a position of power, with influence over the president, or rather as a symbol of surrender. The progressive forces of Silicon Valley, the all-powerful tech bros, finally bent to the will of the conservative president. That they did so out of economic self-preservation is obvious: you simply do not rub Trump up the wrong way. On the other hand, many tech CEOs will also have scented opportunities in a president willing to cut taxes, scrap regulations and put Europe under pressure over the many constraints on tech companies. On that cold 20 January 2025, many of them will have been counting their future profits. Whether that was still the case a few months later is very much open to question. Elon Musk is, of course, a special case. In the months in which he was allowed to be Trump's First Buddy, it became clear just how much unchecked power the richest person in the world could wield. The fact that this bromance ran aground in May 2025 in a dramatic and hilarious fashion made it clear that Trump tolerates no co-president at his side – certainly not one who came with such a price tag.

Once Musk, too, had been neutralised, it became clear that the tech bros had become more of an instrument for Trump and his autocratic policy than Trump was a president under the influence of this lobby. Even so, we can say that a natural symbiosis has emerged, with the Trump regime and the tech bros looking for ways to support and strengthen one another. The comparison with the oligarchs who were able to become extremely wealthy after the fall of the Soviet Union thanks to the new regime – on condition of unconditional loyalty and serving as instruments of that regime – is striking. Yet there are differences, and they make this American variant of tech oligarchs even more dangerous.

What once began as a generation of idealistic engineers, dreamers and entrepreneurs in Silicon Valley has by now grown into a new economic aristocracy with a direct political agenda. Unlike earlier industrialists, who exerted their influence mainly through lobbying and party donations, these new oligarchs are not afraid to place themselves actively on the political battlefield. Elon Musk, Jeff Bezos, Peter Thiel and others use their media, platforms and personal wealth to exert direct influence on policy, public opinion and even foreign relations. This new oligarchy differs fundamentally from the industrial elite of the 20th century. Their power is not only economic, but also structural and communicative. They own the digital infrastructure on which the entire world runs, and that makes them unprecedentedly powerful. If, under pressure from the new regime, they open up their digital platforms to the interests of Trump and his circle, the global impact will be unprecedented.

These digital platforms already control markets, information flows and public debate. Until now, the driving force behind the manipulation of user behaviour was mainly economic and profit-driven. If – or rather, when – these platforms are deployed for (geo)political purposes, the impact could be enormous: they can manipulate the public sphere in real time, mute dissenting voices and shape political preferences. This is not science fiction, but everyday reality: algorithms that steer conversations, moderation that prioritises certain opinions, accounts that 'suddenly' disappear. Whoever has access to the internet's distribution logic has the power to decide what is visible and therefore what exists. The concentration of that power in the hands of a small group of billionaires, under the authority of an autocratic president, undermines democratic principles – not only in the United States, but worldwide. It is no coincidence that Google's original 'Don't be evil' has long since been replaced in its values by the much vaguer 'Do the right thing'. But who decides what 'the right thing' is?

An interesting observation is that this rightward shift in the tech scene goes beyond mere submission to Trump. Where tech companies once fought heroic battles with dictatorships over issues such as censorship or human rights, most companies now seem to have cast those moral objections aside. There is growing cooperation between the American tech elite and authoritarian regimes worldwide. The days when Google, Facebook or Twitter resisted interference by dictatorial regimes are long behind us.

One possible explanation is that they have gradually developed an aversion to 'bureaucratic' regulation and public oversight, which they increasingly see as a constraint on their freedom to operate. In recent years, these companies and their leaders have come to feel culturally and strategically more aligned with autocrats than with liberal democracies. Their resistance to European regulation – such as the Digital Services Act and the Digital Markets Act – is an illustration of this. What follows is a systematic campaign to undermine, delay or 'water down' European regulation. Since Trump II, this has happened with explicit support from American politics, with Trump openly threatening trade measures against countries that 'obstruct their tech companies'. Tech billionaires are not acting here as neutral entrepreneurs, but as geopolitical actors forging alliances to protect their interests – even if that means working with populist and anti-European forces.

Their impact is no longer confined to the economic or digital domain; more and more tech entrepreneurs are pursuing ideological dominance. What began as innovation and disruption – often driven by an idealistic urge to improve the world – has evolved into the building and exercising of cultural, political and even military power. The major tech companies have long since stopped focusing on e-scooters or dating apps, and are now working on AI-driven autonomous killer drones or AI-powered facial recognition, designed to strengthen their own nation states or to be sold to the highest bidder.

Ambitions go further still: techno-feudalism as a future form of government

A significant number of tech oligarchs subscribe to ideologies that are both bizarre and influential, and that far exceed the commercial interests of their own companies. There are various forms and variants, which, for convenience, I group under the term techno-utopianism. This is an ideological framework that brings together beliefs and ideas grounded in the assumption that technology is capable of fundamentally changing society, improving it – and even saving it, but, if we are not careful, also destroying it. Among its adherents are some of the richest and most successful tech entrepreneurs, who in some cases fashion a messianic mission for themselves. Although it is hard to imagine a greater contrast with the conservative right-wing religious currents described earlier, both ideologies converge in their end goal: a post-liberal world that escapes the current constraints of the international order.

In preparation for this section, some time ago I listened to a hilarious podcast in which two American women offered a devastating analysis of masculinity in the tech world, and of the techno-overlords now at the helm of some of the world's most important companies. Despite their personal bias, they hit the nail on the head, as far as I am concerned. The essence of their argument was that people like Musk and Bezos are the rich version of the typical pale, spotty programmer. You know the clichés: they wear Iron Maiden or AC/DC T-shirts, they shower only once a week, eat mainly pizza, and avoid daylight so completely that, without make-up, they could play a vampire in *True Blood* without any effort. Aside from their water-cooled computer with four large monitors (invariably set to dark mode), their universe consists only of Tolkien, the original *Star Wars*, and playing *Dungeons & Dragons* in a basement, beer in hand. They are out of touch, hopeless at relationships, have a bizarre concept of empathy, believe in UFOs, think *The X-Files* is real, and regard the other sex as an unknown species they only know from the internet. In the two women's analysis, our tech CEOs are simply these kinds of nerds, with one small difference: if you put the five richest tech entrepreneurs together for an evening of *D&D*, they are worth as much as the GDP of Sweden and Belgium combined. Okay, the podcast was a bit exaggerated and not particularly respectful towards the many programmers who really are not nerds – but think back to the photos of Musk before his hair transplant and Bezos before he discovered the gym, and you can see where they got it from.

There is a lot of truth in this caricature of tech leaders. It is true that much of their ideology was shaped by a youthful fascination with science fiction, heroic storylines and futuristic utopias. Elon Musk, Peter Thiel and other icons grew up with books by Asimov and Tolkien, in which technology, heroism and overcoming failing societies take centre stage. Those literary influences are not merely youthful nostalgia, but form the foundation of their vision of the future. Peter Thiel's company Palantir, which sells controversial data services to governments, is named after a magical artefact from Middle-Earth; the names and activities of Musk's companies Neuralink, Starlink and SpaceX could have come straight out of a 1980s sci-fi film. I myself have been allowed to come up with quite a few company names, but they never sprang from my favourite teenage fantasies. Otherwise, I would have had a Galactica BVBA or an Adama NV (that one is for those in the know). Not so.

More important than their companies' names is the founders' deeper motivation: for them, these are not just companies, they are manifestations of a worldview in which private power must correct the failure of public institutions. It becomes even more unsettling when this translates into a form of technological messianism, in which tech leaders no longer see themselves as entrepreneurs, but as saviours. They are not building products, but infrastructures for a new civilisation – with themselves, of course, at the helm. Media and cultural scholar Joseph Vogl notes that they use their monopoly positions not only to dominate markets, but also to take over state functions. Musk's Starlink already plays a more important role in many places than many traditional telecom providers – to the point where Musk can personally decide the course of military conflicts simply by switching his satellites on or off (as he did when Ukraine was planning an attack on Crimea). In January 2025, a proposal was launched to use AI for nuclear security in the United States, in a collaboration between OpenAI and the US Department of Energy. These are examples of a new reality, in which democratically legitimised institutions increasingly cede power to private actors with a quasi-religious vision of the future.

The mix of these overlapping currents is often grouped under the ideological umbrella of TESCREAL (even that sounds as if it has walked straight out of *Terminator 2*). According to this ideological constellation, humanity must technologically enhance itself into a cyborg with brain interfaces and extended life (transhumanism), expand its consciousness and civilisation indefinitely (extropianism), prepare for a near-term singularity in which AI becomes superior to human intelligence (singularitarianism), spread life to other planets as a moral duty (cosmism), base all decisions exclusively on rational models and data (rationalism), provide help where it measurably has the greatest impact (effective altruism), and, in doing so, weigh the wellbeing of future billions of souls more heavily than that of people today (longtermism). In the 2025 film *Mountainhead*, these ideologies are mocked in a barrage of hilarious and cynical conversations that, for those in the know, tick off the whole list of -isms. Unfortunately, it also becomes painfully clear how a bunch of post-adolescent, multi-billionaire tech friends (modelled on Musk, Altman, Zuckerberg and co) start to see themselves as 'masters of the universe', and are willing to let civilisation go to the dogs because it fits their TESCREAL worldview. Granted, it is once again a parody of reality, but anyone who digs deeper into the motivations of many figures in the tech world will notice that ideals like these increasingly do, in fact, form their underlying tone.

These ideologies share an almost religious faith in technology as a saviour, and in the idea that human life can and must be radically improved – even transcended. Artificial intelligence is seen as the key to overall progress: it could cure diseases, prevent conflicts, solve poverty and, ultimately, free our consciousness from the human body. AI could also destroy the world, but apparently that is a risk we are willing to take. What these ideologies share is their tendency towards scaling up: this is not about the here and now, but about the future of billions of unborn people, or even consciousness as a cosmic phenomenon. Longtermism is a pivot philosophy in this. It argues that our moral duty lies above all with future generations. If we believe that trillions of people could live in the distant future, then we must do everything now to secure that future – even if that means making painful or unpopular choices today. In 2022, *What We Owe the Future* by the young Oxford philosopher William MacAskill appeared, and he has since become the figurehead of longtermism. He described it as a moral wager: it is rational to make sacrifices now if the potential benefits are immense. Elon Musk, who publicly praised MacAskill, sums up that idea with his obsession with 'expanding the light of consciousness through the universe'. Critics rightly point to the dangers of such a shifted morality. If the end is sacred – the survival of the species, the colonisation of space, control over superintelligent AI – then the means can quickly seem justified, even if they undermine democratic norms.

We see this, for example, in the rise of the e/acc movement in Silicon Valley. e/acc is yet another term that sounds as if it has wandered out of a sci-fi universe. It stands for effective accelerationism, a current that argues that technological progress must be accelerated as much as possible – regardless of the risks. AI, biotechnology, space travel: everything must be faster, bigger, more radical. Only then can humanity be 'saved'. Regulation, for this group, is an obstacle; caution is a weakness. They see acceleration as a moral duty, with slowing down equating to betrayal of the future.

That ideology of acceleration is not neutral. It increasingly translates into concrete policy choices – often without democratic debate. In 2024, President Trump put Elon Musk in charge of the Department of Government Efficiency (DOGE), where, through brutal cuts and technocratic data analysis, he reformed government institutions without parliamentary oversight. Engineers replaced civil servants; algorithms determined who was dismissed. This is technocracy in its purest form: policy as an optimisation problem, not as social deliberation. Musk's power within DOGE symbolised the shift from public to private authority and showed how far technocratic thinking can reach.

The anti-democratic dimension becomes even clearer in the embrace of ideas from the so-called Dark Enlightenment. Figures such as Curtis Yarvin and Nick Land argue for a world in which democracy is replaced by a hierarchical technology elite. Yarvin compares countries to companies: governance should be top-down, with CEOs above voters. Peter Thiel, investor, ideologue and the man behind Palantir, once said that 'freedom and democracy are incompatible'. For these thinkers, equality is an obstacle and deliberation a waste of time. Their ideal is a rational elite that uses technology to decide humanity's fate, unimpeded by participation, checks and balances, or public accountability. This translates, among other things, into the concept of the network state: a new, digital form of statehood in which communities organise around shared values, technology and capital, rather than physical territory or democratic structures. The idea, originally introduced by former Coinbase CTO Balaji Srinivasan, holds that individuals detach themselves from existing nation states by founding virtual nations via online platforms, based on shared ideological convictions. Once these virtual nations are strong enough, they can materialise in the physical world – here on Earth, or, for example, as a new colony on Mars.

In theory, this promises a hyper-modern form of self-government, but in practice network states risk becoming elite shadow states, accessible only to those who are rich, mobile and technologically literate enough. They undermine the concept of public space and equal citizenship, and form a technocratic alternative state model that seeks to evade international rules, national legislation, tax systems and social protection. In essence, the network state is a feudal system in digital form. Where medieval lords based their power on land, military force and personal loyalty (often wrapped in divine legitimacy), we see a similar structure returning in the network state – but now driven by infrastructure, data and access. The founder acts as a digital sovereign: he sets the rules, owns the 'land' (meaning: server space, platforms, protocols), and grants access and protection in exchange for obedience and value creation. Just as serfs were bound to their lord's land, members of a network state depend on internal economies, reputation systems and token structures in order to function within the network.

The legitimacy of this power structure does not rest on elections or representation, but on ownership, technology and exclusive access. Socially, too, network states reflect feudal thinking. Citizenship is not an inalienable right, but a status that can be earned, bought or lost. There is no shared legal order, but a contractual dependence on the lord's rules – or rather on those of the founder, the investors, or the underlying DAO (Decentralized Autonomous Organisation, from the world of crypto and blockchain). Just as in the feudal era, there is no public domain: everything is private, everything is conditional. Instead of a democratic community, a hierarchically organised tech enclave emerges, where freedom is equivalent to participation under conditions, governed without elections, and with total control over behaviour, data and infrastructure – the ideal playing field for those who value efficiency above democracy. For proponents of the concept, network states form the ultimate basis for capitalism: no regulation and bureaucracy as an obstacle, no social rights as an inefficient relic of the past. Everything becomes a market service: education, healthcare and security are all delivered by private providers within the closed ecosystem of the network state.

The ideologies of TESCREAL, e/acc and the Dark Enlightenment are intertwined and reinforce one another. They legitimise the concentration of power in the hands of tech leaders by presenting that power as necessary for the survival and flourishing of the species. They combine futuristic salvation narratives with neoliberal management thinking, and treat democratic institutions, human rights and social equality as obstacles to their mission. The societal implications are enormous. Not only is policy power shifting from elected bodies to billionaires, the public sphere – media, infrastructure, even wartime information – is increasingly coming under the control of their private platforms.

It is clear why a large part of the tech world has fallen in behind Trump. His worldview – dismantling the old order – resonates far more with their objectives than that of previous presidents, who were more favourably disposed towards democracy and sought to rein in technology companies through rules and lawsuits. It therefore stands to reason that an even more values- and regulation-based Europe is seen as the enemy above all. So it is understandable that they are hitching their wagon to the Trump locomotive, which wants to dismantle all of this for conservative ideological and geopolitical reasons.

What is striking is how the ideas and execution of these tech ideologies ultimately align closely with the conservative agenda of right-wing religious organisations. Although religious-conservative movements and techno-liberal ideologues, at first glance, draw from entirely different sources – one from faith, the other from technology – their agendas show remarkable similarities that, in practice, increasingly converge. Both are pushing towards a post-democratic order in which traditional public institutions are seen as slowing, corrupt, or morally bankrupt obstacles. In their place, they want to install a new elite: either pious and God-fearing, or smart and tech-driven. Their shared support for Donald Trump functions as leverage in that process: not because he embodies their ultimate vision, but because he is the ideal catalyst for undermining the liberal status quo that stands in both their way.

And then there is also the far from negligible role of Peter Thiel: an influential German-American entrepreneur, investor and thinker. He is known as a co-founder of PayPal (together with Elon Musk) and Palantir (a data company that works for governments). Strikingly, he combines explicitly Christian-conservative convictions with Silicon Valley's techno-optimistic vision. Thiel is the pivotal figure in the remarkable fusion of these two worldviews. As an outspoken Christian, he directly links his faith to his technological and political ambitions: he sees progress in science and technology as rooted in Christianity, with the ultimate goal of building 'the kingdom of God on earth'. This vision positions Thiel as a bridge-builder between Silicon Valley and the religious right, with Vice President JD Vance – deeply Catholic and economically shaped by Thiel – as his political extension. The relationship between Thiel and Vance goes further than most people realise. Vance was able to start his career in the financial world after Thiel hired him for one of his investment firms. Thiel introduced Vance to the wonderland of Silicon Valley and also supported him financially in his successful Senate campaign. Finally, Thiel introduced him to Trump as a vice-presidential candidate. The significance of this cannot be overstated. At 78, Trump was the oldest person ever to become president, which makes it possible that JD Vance, as vice president, could one day succeed him before the end of his term. In that case, the candidate of one of the most important figures in this line-up suddenly becomes the most powerful man in the world.

Figures such as Garry Tan (CEO of Y Combinator – one of the most important tech incubators in Silicon Valley) and Trae Stephens (founder of the high-tech defence company Anduril, and also once a Thiel protégé) illustrate this trend too: both are active in the Epic Church, where tech investors come together around a shared belief in spiritual and technological salvation. In this network, the boundary between religion and technology blurs, between transcendence and transhumanism. The ideological overlap lies in a shared desire for order, direction and a higher purpose – whether via Jesus or via AI. Thiel's project is a deliberate attempt to reconfigure power and meaning within the American elite. The link between these two seemingly opposing movements thus becomes far more understandable – and far more logical.

How long will this unusual marriage last?

With that, I come to the end of my analysis of the forces behind Trump, which are far more complex than they seem at first glance. Exposing this network explains the seemingly inexplicable policies of Trump and his administration: their domestic ambitions, their vision of geopolitical reshuffling, and their stance towards Europe. There is, indeed, a masterplan, and it has been years in the making. The unexpected coalition of all these forces gives Trump II unprecedented power to dismantle the liberal order. And that is also the only thing that truly binds them. The question is when the first cracks will appear, because this complex marriage of convenience contains so many contradictory principles and convictions that it is not a question of if, but when, it falls apart. In time, the fundamental tensions between these power blocs will prove irreconcilable. The TESCREAL elite – futuristic, secular and AI-driven – stands in direct opposition to the religious right, which regards transhumanism as heresy and AI as blasphemy. Traditional oligarchs, meanwhile, fear the disruptive impact of both Trump's trade wars and the long-term technological ambitions of, for example, network states on existing markets. MAGA supporters see all of these actors as elites who betray their interests: they distrust tech, despise globalist billionaires, and regard 'Old GOP' figures as traitors. Repeated public clashes – and even attacks – between Musk and Steve Bannon are, in that respect, illustrative of this explosive co-existence.

For the choices Europe must make in tomorrow's world, it is essential to know and understand these forces. They already answer one crucial question: does this evolution stop once Trump disappears from the scene? The answer is no. The underlying forces that today make use of Trump II, MAGA and similar European populist movements and figures do not simply disappear. They are inherently part of our world, in which one part of people strives for progress and freedom, and another for order and preservation. That this tension leads, through democratic means, to electoral swings is healthy. That it happens through radical and brutal means, as we are seeing today in the United States, is problematic. If we want to build a strong Europe, we must understand these forces in order to be able to manage them. Not to be against technology or religion, but to avoid technology and religion turning against Europe.

Part 2
Balancing towards a brand-new Europe

6. Europe takes a step back

And then things got serious ...

I was clearly not the only one who saw the Zelensky moment in the White House as a turning point in history. That incident, together with a piling-up of unprecedented statements by Trump and his closest associates about Europe, Russia, Ukraine, Greenland, Canada, Gaza, or the Panama Canal confronts us with the United States' new position towards Europe – and, by extension, towards all its historic partners. Faster than we thought possible, our reaction shifts from denial and initial disbelief to a collective realisation: the United States no longer sees Europe as a self-evident partner. On the contrary, if it is up to Trump, we will be left to our fate – even if that means aggression from Russia. In just a few weeks, Europe realises that the world order has fundamentally changed. Ursula von der Leyen put it this way in an interview with the German newspaper *Die Zeit*: 'The West as we knew it no longer exists.'

The first reactions from European capitals initially range from diplomatic shock to quiet resignation. How are we supposed to deal with the seemingly arbitrary diplomatic antics of Trump and his White House? Ignore them, in the hope that it will blow over and that he will change his mind again tomorrow? But the barrage of brutal statements quickly makes it clear that this is not caprice, but a radical shift in international relations: the transatlantic cooperation that held for eighty years is under threat. The question arises of how Europe should respond. Can old strategic doctrines be rewritten, and are new alliances possible? Many are divided on how independent Europe really can and should be, especially in the context of military autonomy and the relationship with NATO. In the business world, the attitude is initially still cautious and mercantile-pragmatic: as long as economic stability is guaranteed and there are profits to be made, why should doing business with authoritarian regimes be a problem?

Then an unprecedented transformation unfolds: the atmosphere and rhetoric shift from confusion, disbelief and concern to the realisation that action is needed. An analysis by the Atlantic Council, a US think tank, points to a growing belief in closer European cooperation, in response to the already existing geopolitical uncertainty that is being brought to a head by the United States' recent stance towards Europe. External pressure acts as a catalyst, along with the realisation that Europe must reinvent itself or risk becoming completely irrelevant. Can Europe present itself as the only Western power bloc in which institutions still function robustly and cooperation is still valued in its own right?

In political circles, there is suddenly a surge of pro-European positions. Keir Starmer, Prime Minister of the United Kingdom, openly argues for strengthening defence and NATO, with a core group of countries willing to go beyond the minimum. He sees this coalition not only as a military vehicle, but also as a political statement of European resolve. Frans Timmermans, former European Commissioner and now leader of the Dutch socialists, emphasises the need for political and defensive cohesion and calls for planning from the darkest scenario: a Trump who abandons Europe entirely, and a Putin who exploits division. In France, Macron seizes his chance: politically cast out by the French, he seems to find his footing again as a leader when he rises like a phoenix from his political ashes, as one of the strong European figures arguing for a sovereign European project. In Poland and the Baltic states, the conviction grows that only a strong, integrated Europe can withstand the Russian threat. Donald Tusk, former President of the European Council and current Prime Minister of Poland, takes on a leading role here, although his forced cooperation with an ultra-conservative president leaves him in an awkward split.

Belgium announces additional multi-billion investments in defence, while also pushing for diplomatic renewal within the EU. In Denmark and the Netherlands, leaders speak in unprecedented terms about a 'geopolitically mature Europe'. Politically, everyone seems to realise that, in the current situation, any form of division is a risk, and that better cooperation must strengthen Europe's position. That also leads to unexpected candidates for closer cooperation within Europe emerging: countries such as Switzerland, Norway and even tiny Liechtenstein are exploring how they can tighten ties. Europe's political dynamic is visibly changing: from reactive to proactive, from cautious to determined. What for a long time seemed impossible – and in practice was also actively obstructed – is now taking on new contours: is it conceivable that Europe will no longer outsource its role as a geopolitical player to the United States, but will actively shape it itself, now that the US no longer regards us as equals? Is such a vision even credible in a fragmented, over-regulated and inert Europe, or is it nothing more than political rhetoric?

Recent history shows that slow, bureaucratic Europe functions best in times of crisis. Our joint approach to the pandemic, both in terms of vaccination and the recovery fund, was more efficient and effective than, for example, China's zero-COVID policy. During the eurozone crisis (2009 – 2012), too, the EU profoundly reformed its financial architecture, with new systems to limit future risks and the introduction of stricter European banking supervision. After the Russian invasion of Ukraine (2022), swift and unified sanctions followed, along with joint energy purchases and weapons deliveries, while work also began on a large-scale energy transition. In each of these moments of crisis, Europe proved capable of decisive action, solidarity and structural renewal, each time despite the complex decision-making process and the often stark ideological and political differences between member states.

Could it be that this crisis, once again, will translate into effective action? The facts already seem to point that way, in the form of several concrete policy measures that were put in place in just a few weeks. Programmes such as Readiness 2030 show that Europe is prepared to shift gear. Germany, for years the referee of budgetary discipline in Europe, takes an unprecedented step by loosening the debt brake and freeing up 500 billion for investments in defence, infrastructure and transition projects. To do so, it amended the constitution in a matter of weeks. For the first time in decades, a European dynamic is emerging that should enable us to become stronger on the world stage. This dynamic is proving to be more than political hot air: it is underpinned financially and politically, too. Quite apart from our capacity to actually deliver on this, the signal to the rest of the world is clear: Europe is ready to take its future into its own hands, and is using the break with the United States as momentum. What is needed now is a collective story that can motivate and mobilise politically, economically and socially. A vision of the future that moves people, motivates them and brings them together, grounded in the realisation that Europe must reshape itself in a world that has fundamentally changed. The question is no longer whether we must be autonomous, but how we can achieve that in a credible way.

Trust arrives on foot and leaves on horseback

Whatever happens in the months and years ahead, European and global trust in the United States as a stable, democratic superpower has been damaged for a long time. More than the incidents and unprecedented diplomatic statements in the first weeks after Trump's inauguration, it is above all the political decisions and actions in the months that followed that have undermined that trust. The dismantling of democratic institutions, the normalisation of ideological purges, and the rise of autocratic rhetoric fundamentally erode America's moral leadership. The speed and intensity with which Trump, by executive order, bombards the US (and the rest of the world) with agenda items from Project 2025 makes Europe do more than raise an eyebrow. Where powerholders in countries such as Hungary, Russia and Turkey took years to bend the rule of law to their will, it is happening in the US in a matter of months. The fact that we can, so to speak, follow in real time how the US is taking on autocratic traits – and what impact that has on minorities or groups branded as ideologically decadent – is, for many, a wake-up call and a reminder of the past.

Do we want to experience this again in Europe? Although Europe, too, is seeing a shift to the right, the American experiment with democracy goes too far for most people. However conservative or populist some parties and individuals may be, the initial enthusiasm for the Trump and Musk bulldozers has cooled for most Europeans. The US is losing its status as a moral beacon, especially now that Trump appears to have more sympathy for other 'strong leaders' than for his traditional democratic allies. The rapid dismantling of these foundations under Trump is confronting for Europe, but also mobilising: the American experiment goes too far. A survey by the Belgian weekly magazine *Knack* in March 2025, among just over 1,000 Belgians, shows that trust in Trump is as low as trust in Putin – a telling result.

One of the most visible elements undermining European trust is the US stance on defence. Sowing doubt about America's loyalty to NATO, threatening to withdraw US troops from Europe, and even announcing that future weapons systems will only be supplied to 'European partners' in stripped-down versions – because it is no longer clear whether they can be trusted in the long run – are, one by one, signals that erode this fundamental pillar of decades of transatlantic cooperation.

Economically, the US is disrupting the global order with provoked trade wars and renewed protectionism, putting pressure on trust in America as a standard-setting force in world trade. Less visible in Europe, because we do not experience the consequences directly, is the ideological pressure on American culture and science. Law firms, journalists, the press and media companies are attacked and crippled through lawsuits with damages claims running into hundreds of millions. Most settle out of fear of repercussions. Universities and research institutions lose subsidies and support for research and activities that no longer align ideologically with the conservative agenda. Projects on reproductive healthcare, vaccination, mRNA treatments, research into infectious diseases such as avian flu, cleantech and sustainability are being scaled back or dismantled entirely, as is a large part of US healthcare provision. Prestigious universities are financially forced to comply with White House demands, amounting to direct interference in their academic functioning and independence. Even banning books, such as *The Diary of Anne Frank*, has by now become common practice in certain states. But perhaps the most dramatic development in the long term is the American stance on climate. Withdrawing from international agreements, structurally sabotaging earlier climate legislation, and ending funding for ambitious programmes – both inside and outside the US – marks the end of America as a climate leader.

Now that we can no longer trust our historic partner, we will have to organise many things ourselves. What may seem like an impossible task is, at the same time, a huge opportunity. The gap the US is leaving in the international order will be filled by new players. Europe can take on its own role within that space, taking into account our historic weaknesses, but also by leveraging our strengths – and the system of values and norms that sets us apart from the rest of the world.

7. The momentum for a strong Europe

Readiness 2030: More than defence

On 4 March 2025, barely one day after Trump halts military support for Ukraine, Ursula von der Leyen launches the Rearm Europe initiative: a concrete plan for a new European security architecture. It is an ambitious five-point plan that mobilises 800 billion euros for Europe's rearmament, in response to the potential consequences should US military support genuinely fall away. The plan combines fiscal flexibility, new financial instruments, a reorientation of EU budgets, and the involvement of both the European Investment Bank and private capital in accelerating the build-up of Europe's defensive capacity. The focus is not only on traditional weapons systems, but also on technological and infrastructural capabilities, such as AI, cybersecurity, and the protection and expansion of critical infrastructure.

Under pressure from both Italy and Spain, the plan is quickly renamed Readiness 2030. Their arguments are persuasive: there is not only a threat from Russia on Europe's eastern flank, but also a range of other challenges that endanger security – from climate change and shortages in food supply to uncontrolled migration movements, to which southern Europe is more sensitive. The name change also reflects a broader ambition: not just military readiness, but an integrated approach to security. In doing so, Europe positions itself as a strategically mature player on the world stage, now that the American shield is wobbling.

What fundamentally sets Readiness 2030 apart from earlier European initiatives is its level of ambition. Unlike the original Rearm Europe, the scope of this programme goes beyond merely building additional military capacity. The aim is to give Europe the resilience and readiness it needs across a range of domains that are expected to put the stability of our society under pressure in the future: energy, health, food and digital infrastructure. It assumes that modern threats are far more than tanks crossing borders or missiles that sow death and destruction from a distance. As we experienced in 2020, a pandemic can be just as disruptive as a cyberattack; turning off a gas tap in Moscow can be as effective as soldiers in trenches; and a targeted sabotage of a country's electricity grid can do more damage than an entire army. Readiness 2030 aims to prepare Europe for those kinds of challenges, but also for crises without a direct enemy, in which our European model is nevertheless at risk. Think of natural and climate disasters, but also disruption caused by new pandemics – a scenario that is far from inconceivable given global warming.

What makes Readiness 2030 so important in our story is the embedding of European cooperation as the norm. If there is one point of (often justified) criticism of how Europe functions, it is that there is so little unity between member states, which leaves Europe effectively hamstrung when it comes to major decisions, except in times of crisis. By embedding cooperation with other countries and partners in the DNA of Readiness 2030, it becomes an important instrument for achieving closer cooperation in crucial areas, and therefore for building a coherent and powerful Europe. In the past, such initiatives often ran aground on national silos and fragmented competences, whereas Readiness 2030, from the outset, is geared towards deeper integration. Yes, I know: 'the proof of the pudding is in the eating', but the programme still has the potential to be a fundamental lever for future European cooperation and clout. The launch of mechanisms such as HERA, EFSCM and SAFE shows a clear trend: in times of crisis, the EU dares – and is able – to centralise resources and act in a coordinated way.

HERA, the Health Emergency Preparedness and Response Authority, was set up after COVID-19 to deal with future health crises. EFSCM, the European Food Security Mechanism, was established in response to the war in Ukraine to address key vulnerabilities in food supply. The SAFE loan instrument is part of Readiness 2030 and helps member states jointly procure defence equipment, with an emphasis on ammunition and strategic weapons systems, while encouraging them to buy European. Readiness 2030 is therefore also an institutional experiment: what if we see solidarity not only as a moral virtue, but as a strategic necessity – as part of a European identity? If crises are cross-border, then the response must be, too. For the first time, that realisation is truly taking shape – not in fine declarations, but in budgets and plans. Not because we want it so badly (it was comfortable under the American umbrella), but because we have to.

Another key pillar is the focus on technological sovereignty. The war in Ukraine, the chip shortage during the pandemic and dependence on American cloud infrastructure show just how digitally vulnerable Europe is. Here, too, Readiness 2030 aims to drive change. Investments in AI, quantum technology, chips and satellite communications are no longer seen as innovations belonging to the start-up and tech sectors, but as a strategic necessity for Europe. The European Chips Act, the AI Act and programmes such as IRIS2 (a home-grown satellite network) reflect a new mindset: Europe wants control over the critical systems on which our economy and security depend. To make this succeed, more is needed than money alone. For thirty years we have accepted that scaling up – often of innovations conceived in Europe – happens in Silicon Valley and, now, also in China. The ambition to make Europe technologically independent will become one of our biggest challenges, but also one of vital importance, both economically and geopolitically.

The amount being discussed within Readiness 2030 is 800 billion euros. How realistic is it that this can drive real change? To put that in context, we can compare it with the budget the US invested in rebuilding Europe after WWII. Through the famous Marshall Plan, just over 13 billion dollars was pumped into Europe between 1948 and 1952. Converted to today's value, that is just under 120 billion euros. That means Readiness 2030 has almost seven times as many resources as the Marshall Plan did back then. And that is without taking into account the structural increases that are planned in the coming years for NATO contributions.

Even so, even the most ambitious plan will fail without public support. Readiness 2030 lays the technical foundations for a resilient Europe, but for now it still lacks the compelling story that brings citizens, local politicians and businesses along. The challenge is creating – and selling – a vision of the future that looks beyond the next crisis: what kind of Europe do we want to be in 2050? What is the narrative that connects, inspires and gives direction? What will make Europeans willing to move from a populist story full of meaningless one-liners to a complex but realistic plan that genuinely makes Europe better? What is the positive identity that makes Europeans feel European, despite all our cultural differences? Despite the reservations about current US policy, there are also lessons we can learn from them. They, too, as a society, made the shift – since Pearl Harbor – towards the ambition of becoming a global power. Can we do the same? But perhaps most importantly: can we learn from them how to feel part of a single nation, despite the melting pot of cultures, backgrounds, religions and beliefs? What has made America great over the past 150 years is exactly what we will also need in Europe: a positive and inclusive identity, oriented towards a European future, not a mythical and exclusive past.

Europe as a new superpower; our economic position

I can't drive a car any more. At least, not an ordinary one: one with a manual gearbox, no sensors, no cameras, no beepers, and no automatic handbrake stopping me from rolling backwards on any incline. I came to that conclusion a little while ago, when I was on a city break in Bilbao. We'd taken the train as far as the French border and hired a small car there to get to our destination and to do a few trips in the surrounding area. I parked the car in an underground car park, where the Basque engineers had done something rather special when calculating the gradient of the exit ramp. In practical terms: it was so steep that, once I reached the top – right before the barrier and the post where you scan your ticket – I simply couldn't get the car moving forwards again. Every attempt to find the (once so intuitive) balance between the handbrake, clutch and accelerator ended in a moment of sheer panic, each time the car 'dropped' metres back down the slope again. You can imagine the people waiting behind me retreating to a safe distance. After eleven years of high-tech electric driving, I'd completely unlearned what used to be second nature. Thankfully, we were with another couple who still knew how the old world works, and they got the car past the barrier without much trouble. I didn't drive again for the rest of that holiday.

Somehow it feels as if we in Europe have ended up in a similar situation. We're standing on a slope and we've forgotten how to move forwards. For eighty years we could rely on American support, defence and technology. Now that we want to get past the barrier ourselves, we no longer know how to do it – or whether we even still can. How naïve is it, really, to think that Europe can claim the role of a new superpower? Is that delusional and lacking in realism, or have we simply unlearned what used to be second nature, like driving a manual gearbox? In early March 2025, Donald Tusk spoke these memorable words at the end of a meeting with European leaders: 'Just listen to how it sounds: 500 million Europeans begging 300 million Americans to defend them against 140 million Russians. If you can count, count on yourself. Not in isolation, but with full awareness of your potential. These days, what Europe lacks is not economic power or people, but the belief that we are a world power.' In the meantime, that has become the attitude – and the belief – of many people: now that we have to, we can, but it won't be easy. Let's first analyse just how strong or weak Europe actually is, compared with the other major powers.

If we look at economic potential, Europe remains, without a doubt, a major player. The European Union's GDP, at 19,400 billion euros, is just above China's (17,100 billion), but well below that of the US (28,490 billion). If we want a more accurate picture, we need to convert these figures to purchasing power parity. That means we also account for price differences between the same goods and services in different countries, so you can infer how much you can actually buy in each country with the same amount of money. With one billion you can produce more weapons in Russia than in Europe, because costs there are substantially lower.

This gives a more realistic comparison: China is number 1 with 32,000 billion euros, the EU follows closely with 29,180 billion, the US is third with 25,000 billion, and Russia lags far behind with around 5,000 billion. That puts us at almost the same level as China, which has more than three times as many inhabitants. The EU's 450 million inhabitants are also among the richest consumers in the world and – unlike the average American – live far less beyond their means. The average EU citizen has three times as much savings, invests less in the stock market (which makes us less vulnerable to fluctuations), and is more likely to own their own home. In short: economically, we're not doing badly at all – and we combine that prosperity with an unparalleled level of wellbeing and care.

It gets even more interesting if we zoom out a little. Imagine that a new Western Economic Alliance were to emerge, in which the EU, the UK, Switzerland and other European countries that are not yet part of the EU – supplemented by Canada and Japan – begin to cooperate closely on economic matters. This economic union would become the largest economic bloc in the world, both in nominal GDP (28,560 billion euros) and in purchasing power parity (33,500 billion euros). If we calculate the total population, we end up at 757 million inhabitants. And it just so happens that these are precisely the countries that, in these turbulent Trump times, are the first to tighten their ties with one another as an initial response to the economic uncertainties arising from the tariff war.

Europe as a new great power; our military position

When it comes to defence, we are less well positioned than the US, but even here Europe is stronger than we often think. To make that clear, I use figures, budgets and numbers that roughly reflect the balance between the different actors. Depending on the source and the period these figures relate to, the real, more recent numbers may differ, but in principle that does not undermine the logic set out below.

Just as in the economic comparison, Europe is in second place in the ranking: the US spends approximately 900 billion euros a year on defence, Europe just under 400 billion, China 215 billion and Russia 140 billion. Europe has, including Ukraine, more than 2 million active soldiers, compared with 1.3 million for both the US and Russia (though that latter number may now be lower due to the high number of war casualties). If we look at available hardware (tanks, aircraft, ships, and so on), then in almost every category we have to concede ground to the other power blocs.

One of the key debates at the time of writing concerns NATO and the contributions that the various NATO members should or should not be paying. It is an understatement to say that this has been a point of frustration for Trump for years. In his view, Europe and other members contribute far too little, meaning that the Americans are the organisation's biggest sponsor. The nuance that gets lost here is that, in principle – apart from a few billion for the organisation's day-to-day running – there is no direct transfer of money to NATO. When we talk about the NATO budget, we mean the sum of the individual defence expenditures of all NATO members combined. That comes to just under 1,400 billion euros, of which the Americans pay about 900 billion and Europe just under 400 billion. To be crystal clear once again: that is the amount the Americans and the other countries spend on their own defence, which is therefore counted as their NATO contribution. So there is no such thing as a NATO bank account where all the money sits, and with which NATO can wage war.

Trump claims that the US takes responsibility for Europe's defence within NATO, and that this is 'very, very unfair'. If we look at the facts, however, we see a completely different picture. Of the US defence budget of 900 billion euros (and therefore of the US NATO contribution), at most 70 billion goes towards the defence of Europe. The remaining 830 billion goes towards American interests in the US and in regions such as Asia and the Middle East. In concrete terms, this means that, out of NATO's total budget of 1,400 billion euros, only around 470 billion goes towards the defence of Europe, of which 400 billion is paid by Europe itself.

In other words, Europe pays 85 percent of its own defence; it is therefore factually incorrect to state that the Americans pay the lion's share of our defence. And when you realise that two thirds of our European purchases of defence equipment are made from American suppliers, Trump's claim becomes even more bitter.

All these figures show that Europe's problem is not necessarily the absolute level of investment in defence, but the fragmented and inefficient way in which defence is organised. As a result, our performance is lower than what we should be able to achieve with our collective potential in people and resources. As we have already seen in the paragraph on the colonisation of Europe by the US, the American strategy has always been aimed at placing investment and the development of individual armies with the European countries themselves, while keeping the command-and-control structure within NATO, where the US military holds the reins. In this way, NATO ends up with a kind of 'army on demand': a tightly organised American base layer, supplemented by additional troops and equipment sourced from fragmented European suppliers. Remove the American command and no effective European army remains. Remove, too, the strategic instruments supplied by the US, such as satellite data and intelligence, and large-scale military operations can no longer be carried out at all. Now that confidence in American leadership within NATO is declining, it is not necessarily necessary to invest much more in matériel and soldiers, but in coordination across the board: from central command to standardised weapons systems. This is potentially a greater challenge than simply ordering more weapons, because it requires a central European mandate that runs directly counter to the model of, on the one hand, national fragmentation of armies and, on the other, central NATO (American) control.

Europe as a new great power; our industrial position

Some time ago I spoke with a young woman, CEO of a successful and innovative technology company. She was grappling with an existential question about her children's future: whether, by staying in Belgium and, by extension, Europe, she was depriving her young children of opportunities. Would she not be better off moving to the US with her young family, because that is where the future lies, while in Europe nothing is really possible any more? Every day, my work takes me into boardrooms, executive offices, or halls where my audience typically consists of representatives from the business world. For years I have been hearing the same thing: Europe no longer matters industrially and all the exciting things are happening in the US or in China. Time and again, European CEOs lobby for support, because wage or energy costs here are so high that they can no longer compete with companies from outside Europe. If you base yourself solely on this dynamic, it does indeed seem as if Europe is industrially dead. But if you look further, you see that, in certain areas, Europe still belongs to the world's leading group, especially in a number of strategic sectors. In the semiconductor industry, the Dutch company ASML, thanks to its advanced lithography machines, is essential to the manufacture of microchips. They have grown into the global leader and are involved in the production of almost every chip in the world.

Despite pressure from the Chinese and the malaise in the sector, European car manufacturers still have trump cards in hand, especially now that they too are accelerating their electric transition. A company like Renault shows that it is possible to withstand the Chinese onslaught, with a strategic focus on EVs, attractive models such as the new R5, and competitive pricing. BMW, too, seems to have found the right direction and is delivering markedly better results than direct competitors Mercedes and Audi. Although Chinese consumer brands are putting heavy pressure on the market, they also remain highly dependent on suppliers of components, which account for 80 percent of a car's production costs. Without exception, the most important players here are German (Bosch, Continental), Canadian (Magna International) or Japanese (Denso). In sustainable energy, companies such as Ørsted, Siemens Gamesa and Vestas are pioneers, while BASF and Umicore are leading the way in the development of local circular processing, new materials and chemical innovations. In biotech and pharma, BioNTech, CureVac, Roche, AstraZeneca, GSK, Sanofi and many others confirm Europe's culture of innovation.

Due to the demolition politics that the Trump administration is currently pursuing in each of these domains, our relative position is being strengthened as well. Investments that previously went to the US are now heading towards Europe, and we can also expect a brain gain from talent that can no longer find a home in the US or is no longer welcome there because of their foreign nationality. This industrial backbone is further reinforced by a dense network of leading knowledge institutions, universities of applied sciences, universities and research centres, which translate fundamental research into economic value. A notable recent shift can be seen in the attitude of the captains of industry and CEOs I mentioned earlier. Whereas, up to 2025, it was nothing but complaining that European companies and people would move to the US because of high costs and an unattractive, heavily regulated Europe, we now increasingly hear voices from the heart of industry endorsing Europe's technological potential and naming it as a strategic lever for a strong Europe. Peter Wennink, former CEO of ASML, emphasises that Europe has all the necessary building blocks: companies, knowledge, infrastructure and creativity. According to him, the European ecosystem is perfectly capable of developing and deploying key technologies such as AI, quantum computing and new forms of energy. Wennink argues that Europe must invest fully in technological sovereignty so as not to become even more dependent on American or Chinese technology. Thomas Leysen, one of Belgium's leading entrepreneurs with experience across many sectors, speaks in terms of resilience and adaptability, and sees the possibility of a robust industrial base in Europe, adapted to the new geopolitical and, at the same time, ecological reality.

Europe as a new great power; the policy

Europe does indeed have the potential to become one of the geopolitical great powers, but it is doing so from a strategic disadvantage that has been built up over recent decades. That makes it difficult, but not impossible. An exceptional illustration of such a turnaround comes, remarkably, from the US itself. In the 1930s, the US was in the Great Depression, with mass unemployment, economic stagnation and social unrest. As we saw earlier, the dominant political discourse was one of protectionism and America First, without any ambition to dominate the world. Under President Roosevelt's leadership, however, the foundations were laid for their later status as a world power. In response to the deep crisis, in which confidence in the free market and democracy had collapsed, Roosevelt launched the New Deal: a series of government programmes aimed at economic recovery, structural reforms and social security. The construction of infrastructure, such as dams, roads and railways, led to mass employment and a modernised economy. At the same time, Roosevelt shifted more powers to the central federal level and succeeded in restoring confidence in democracy and government.

In this way, the New Deal laid the industrial and logistical base necessary to build the American war economy. But its real impact was that the US was the only country in the West ready, after the Second World War, to help shape the world order and to emerge from it as a great power. More than an economic programme, the New Deal was a strategic recalibration of ambition and belief in its own capabilities. The parallels with the current situation are striking, both socially and politically, with Readiness 2030 as a contemporary version of the New Deal. If we want to achieve the same effect, then the short-term objective is to absorb the US's separation and build strong alternatives within Europe. In the longer term, this could lead to us being able, with good reason, to claim a seat at the table of the new world order, based on the intrinsic strength that Europe will then project. Just as in the US in the 1930s, certain foundations are missing on which this new Europe must be able to rest, and we must therefore build them as quickly as possible. Economically and culturally, Europe struggles with stubborn internal fragmentation: instead of one coherent internal market, a patchwork remains of ideological differences, national pride, legislation, tax structures and policy frameworks. This division hinders the development of strategic capacity, whether in defence, AI, battery technology or cloud infrastructure. It is no coincidence that the Readiness 2030 project identifies the promotion of cooperation between member states as one of its spearheads.

The most important foundation of a strong Europe of the future is strategic autonomy, whereby Europe is able to take its own decisions and also implement them independently. As a result of our status under the wing of the US, contemporary Europe has above all been built as a market project and a union of values. The focus has been on building a free market through economic integration and free movement within the EU, with moral principles such as democracy and human rights as the legacy of the European Enlightenment. De Vos argues that we must evolve towards a Europe as a state project and a union of power: a political entity with its own strategic interests and decision-making capacity, with greater competences, so that it can position itself assertively on the world stage.

Such a transition confronts us with major challenges, because it implies that a thorough reshuffling of competences is required. In core areas such as defence, foreign policy, the economy or climate, national competences would, at the very least, have to be partially transferred to a central European level. Because people realise how difficult this is today, there is increasing talk of different coalitions of the willing. In this way, not all countries have to go along every time with structural forms of cooperation that are hard to sell to their constituencies, or where politicians are in power with an anti-European sentiment. In the final chapter of this book, I will go into this in more depth. The most important coalition now emerging concerns fundamental cooperation on defence, where countries – in this case even from outside the EU, such as the United Kingdom – can join voluntarily and thereby give an important mandate to that structure. It is still unclear where, alongside what, or under what these coalitions will sit, also in relation to NATO, but that vagueness is probably a deliberate part of cautious European diplomacy. In time, strong new structures can replace existing ones, exist in parallel with them, or optimise them from within, in the interest of a more centralised Europe.

The European Union must be able to function as a political entity with federal characteristics, comparable to the US. This shift of competences towards a central point seems an almost impossible task, because it runs counter to the lack of engagement among many citizens and the growing distrust when it comes to Europe. In part, this is justifiably based on the Union's distant, bureaucratic character and its not always positive track record. A significant part of this sentiment, however, has been deliberately created by populist politicians and anti-European parties, linked to conservative movements that have for years sought to weaken liberal Europe. Now that we have recognised the patterns and tactics behind this, it will be an important priority to counter this active disinformation and mobilise the population around a realistic, critical and compelling project. This de facto shift – from values to power, from market to state – cannot succeed if we do not embed it in a democratically legitimate structure. That requires social and political support, and momentum.

That momentum is here now, with Europe's calculated response to the chaos Trump is creating. The problem with momentum is that it means nothing if it is not seized, if it is not followed by action. Readiness 2030 may be for Europe what the New Deal was for the US in the 1930s, and it already points the way to some extent. Even so, Europe will still have to make fundamental choices if it is to become strong again in a credible way. In this book, I set out my vision of what can help Europe to choose an innovative strategic, economic, technological, philosophical and moral direction. Despite the great uncertainty and geopolitical chaos, I think the stars are aligned for Europe. But for that, we need a compelling story that can spur all of Europe into action, even if that requires sacrifices, ideological differences to be set aside, and unexpected alliances to be necessary.

Can we even compete at all?

Let's assume that, up to this point, you've been following my argument. Perhaps I've been able to make you relatively enthusiastic about the possibility of transforming Europe into a new great power. I have shown that we are not doing nearly as badly as we often think. And yet one pressing question remains: can Europe actually compete with the rest of the world? For years it has been clear how dependent we have become on others for almost everything we need and use every day. In the technology sector, the situation is dire. Roughly every online platform we use, our email, our social media, the streaming services we watch, the smartphones we use, our computers, and so on: almost nothing is European any more. The hardware comes from China, the applications are in the hands of American giants. It is estimated that 80 percent of all European data sits in some American cloud, and the entire corporate world runs on Microsoft's technology. After thirty years of internet development, we have managed to keep almost nothing of any technological importance in Europe (with a few strong exceptions such as SAP). While the US and China are pumping billions into research and development, we are left behind with an investment level that is only a fraction of their budgets. In areas such as AI, consumer electronics or cloud infrastructure, we have become structurally irrelevant.

Anyone who looks further sees a long list of dependencies that place Europe in a vulnerable position. For rare earth metals, Europe is almost entirely dependent on imports, mainly from China. In terms of energy, too, Europe has historically been reliant on external suppliers: oil, gas, coal and even the uranium for our nuclear power plants largely come from outside the continent, which, in times of geopolitical tension, repeatedly leads to panic and costly emergency measures. Even in agriculture, once a source of European pride, we are too small-scale and fragmented compared to the industrial scale of American and Brazilian production. Agricultural seeds are patented and controlled by a handful of multinationals, and our already highly fragmented farmland is being bought up by yet other multinationals. Our energy costs are so high that energy-intensive industries can barely be profitable, and our demographic development means that we no longer have young workers to deploy in our economy. Add to that the structural lack of our own (mass) production of consumer goods and the lag in the electrification of mobility, and the picture is clear: in many respects, the EU has become an import union, dependent on others for its food, its energy, its security and its technology.

Yet this does not have to be an insurmountable problem if Europe is to realise its new ambitions.

Transition thinking as the basis for European leadership

The key to a strong Europe lies in a different way of thinking, not in copying or competing with the models of the old world. If we want to hold our own economically and industrially against China, Russia, the US and their classic approach, the fight is lost before it even begins. The solution lies elsewhere, and is driven by meta-developments over which we have little influence, but which could be the key to a strategic approach that can once again make Europe an economic great power. The fundamental insight is that the world is at a turning point anyway, with a series of transitions already under way that are necessary for the survival of people and planet. Some of these transitions arise from the climate and biodiversity crisis, others are the result of geopolitical and demographic developments, and yet others are the next logical evolution in technology or scientific progress. What is interesting for Europe is that this is a case of the advantage of a late start, and that it can work in our favour.

The sectors that will be fundamentally transformed into something new over the next 25 years are the very sectors and methods in which the US or China have perfected themselves and are now dominant. China is aware of this and pragmatically commits to a mix of both preservation and innovation. The US, by contrast, seems, with its current policy, to be clinging even more tightly to the old models, which everyone now acknowledges are finite. The transitions unfolding are disruptive for the current industries that have developed around those major domains: energy, food and agriculture, mobility, housing, care and health, to name just a few. Each of these sectors has a stable landscape of players, in which, through a tangle of monopolies, consolidations, state interventions and hyper process optimisation, the spoils have long since been divided. Given the scale and efficiency of the leading companies, it is almost impossible to continue competing here. Under normal market conditions, that makes them unbeatable, but at the same time sluggish and vulnerable in times of change.

From our experience with digital transformation, we can draw lessons that are crucial for the future of these sectors. A basic rule is that incumbents, the traditional market leaders, have become so large and sluggish that they cannot cope with disruptions that disturb their status quo. At first they will deny those disruptions, then minimise them, and then try to absorb them within an organisational structure that is not designed for that. With a few exceptions, all the fundamental transformations of the past twenty years have been driven by digital challengers, not by the established players. Often, these disruptions mean the end of sectors (think of video rental shops) or of individual companies that cannot adapt. In most cases, digital transformation has led to new players entering the market with alternative solutions and new value streams, which have very quickly become dominant. The incumbents do survive, but they have to give up market share and adapt to a world that is unfamiliar to them.

Europe's industrial weakness is very real if we look at it through the classic lens, but becomes an opportunity if we reason from transition thinking. If Europe is to be economically competitive, we must fully commit to developing and commercialising transition sectors. We should not compete over natural gas or oil, but invest in a profitable market for sustainable energy. We cannot beat the agricultural giants, but we can become a leader in new ways of creating food. We are barely competitive when it comes to Chinese electric cars that are dumped on our market, but we can devise and roll out innovative and socially relevant mobility solutions.

Of course we are not alone in this vision; quite the contrary. China is already investing heavily in it, and until the arrival of Trump II, the Americans were leading the way in many innovations, preparing for their own transitions. The big difference with the old industrial approach is that the market for transition industries is still in its early stages and is often actively held back, sometimes even sabotaged, in order to protect entrenched interests. The spoils have not yet been divided, and this time Europe does indeed have the chance to develop the smart solutions that already exist at an accelerated pace and make them the future global standard. The budgets that form part of Readiness 2030 can be used to accelerate our positions in transition sectors and, through our contemporary version of the Marshall Plan or the New Deal, strive to realise a very clear vision.

Focusing only on these transition industries will not be enough. In other areas too, we will have to reclaim our strategic sovereignty: digital platforms and media, artificial intelligence, digital services, communications technology, and so on. We currently source most of these solutions from outside Europe as well, but there is no good reason why we should not be able to bring them back into our economy and into our European ideological framework. In part 3 of this book, I go into detail about what I call the recipes for a strong Europe. In it, I analyse the various strategic industries that we, as Europe, must build ourselves. Many of these ideas focus on transition sectors; others are about how we can rebuild our digital strengths with a focus on Europe.

Energy as an example of transition thinking

The energy transition is the most important force of a new world and of a sovereign Europe. Our energy dependence has determined our geopolitical course for decades. Since the oil crisis of the 1970s, we have been aware of the power that oil-producing countries hold over the rest of the world, which is why, ever since, we have often set aside our European moral principles in order to secure our energy supply. Yet we know this is a finite story, because climate change will ultimately force everyone to make the energy transition. If Europe decides to commit to this, we enter a market in which we no longer have to compete with the old models and suppliers of energy. In strategic transition thinking around energy, one concept is essential: traditional energy can be seen as a commodity, renewable energy can be seen as a technology. The impact of this distinction is immense.

Traditional energy sources such as gas, oil and coal are raw materials that are extracted and traded as commodities via global energy markets. Every shock leads to price volatility: wars, geopolitical risks, artificially keeping production low, stock-piling reserves or disruption to supply chains all have a direct impact on the price and therefore on the global economy and on Europe. The knowledge that these fuels are finite means that, in principle, the price can only rise as demand and supply of affordably extractable fuels fall out of balance. In the traditional energy sector, there is almost no innovation possible that can push down the price of energy in the long term. Moreover, Europe can hardly fall back on local sources of oil or gas, which entrenches our dependence in the long term. None of these arguments even take into account the negative effects on climate and public health, and the expected rise in costs due to climate measures to adapt to possible consequences in the long run.

Once we realise that renewable energy sources such as solar and wind are, in fact, technologies, they also follow the logic of the technology world. The more we invest in development and innovation, the cheaper, more reliable and more efficient installations become. The cost of the energy they generate falls. Once the installations are operational, they have hardly any fuel and maintenance costs, which leads to price stability and energy independence. Innovations continuously improve performance and costs, which, over time, will make energy ever cheaper. These innovations do not have to be limited to optimising what already exists, but can also lead to completely new forms of sustainable energy generation. Healthy, competitive market dynamics, in which new solutions put existing ones under pressure, will further accelerate the entire wheel of innovation and lead to ever more, and cheaper, energy. Because of the local and decentralised character of the new installations, the place of production is closer to the place of consumption, which significantly reduces dependence on geopolitical backroom dealing and abuse. In addition, this increases the involvement of local communities in energy policy: in the future, the energy they use will also have been generated by themselves, which both creates greater energy awareness and can generate additional economic activity. While traditional energy as a product remains bound to the logic of scarcity and conflict, renewable energy as a technology offers a path towards sustainable growth and sovereignty for Europe.

Although solar energy is now, on average, already up to 50 percent cheaper than energy generated from gas, we are still far from a full shift to renewable energy. One of the causes is the unpredictability of generation: you can run a gas-fired power plant steadily, but with solar and wind we are dependent on external factors, which means there are regularly periods of too little or too much energy generation. Energy storage could offer a solution, but we are still a long way from having sufficient capacity to buffer all energy needs stably through storage. In addition, there are industries with energy needs so large that current renewable sources are insufficient; stable solutions will have to be found for those as well.

If, within Readiness 2030, we set out a project aimed at cracking these codes, and we position it in the market as the next high-tech race, then it is very likely that we will solve this problem too within the foreseeable future. For this, Europe has already earmarked almost 115 billion euros in subsidies to address the energy storage challenge. If we were to treat that money as a commercial investment fund for innovative energy technology companies, and match it with the same amount from private investors, then an enormous lever could be created to make Europe a leader in energy and independent of the rest of the world. Although China benefits from enormous resources and economies of scale in this area, Europe is betting on technological expertise and research, while the US risks falling far behind by ending American support for these kinds of initiatives.

Europe can never win the fight over oil and gas as an energy source, so we should not take it on. The transition sector of sustainable energy is still in its infancy and is built on entirely different foundations: talent, innovation, technology and money. In that arena, Europe can reclaim its position, never to let it go again. And that takes me back in time.

A backwards-running meter

Just under twenty years ago, my wife and I decided to do something a bit crazy. Alongside super-insulating glass, above-standard insulation and a heat pump with underfloor heating, we invested in solar panels. As long as we didn't have electric cars, those forty panels generated virtually all the energy we needed, and our backwards-running meter worked like a de facto battery: what we used when there was no sun was neatly 'run back' when the sun was at its peak.

Our monthly total energy costs were effectively 0 euros, and throughout that time we had a fixed monthly repayment to the bank of 177 euros. In doing so, we replaced the costs of a product, a commodity, with an investment in technology. The repayment is now behind us, and the solar panels still work perfectly. Oh yes, they are German panels, from the time when the Chinese had not yet written world dominance in solar energy into their strategy as a top priority.

Defence as an example of transition thinking

Now that we have already devoted considerable attention to Europe's weaknesses in defence, it is useful to look at how transition thinking can offer a perspective here as well. The classic image of military superiority is still based on the size of armies, the number of tanks, fighter jets or aircraft carriers, and the size of the defence budget. In those areas, Europe simply cannot compete with military giants such as the US or China. Yet we should not underestimate Europe's military strength. Europe does, in fact, have a broad and high-quality arsenal of conventional weapons systems that can rival their American counterparts. Although the F-35 is promoted as superior, European air forces, with aircraft such as the Eurofighter Typhoon (UK, Germany, Italy, Spain), the French Rafale and the Swedish Gripen, have fully capable fighter jets. At sea, the FREMM frigates from France and Italy are advanced platforms for air defence and anti-submarine warfare, while the airspace is secured by Aster missiles and the Swedish RBS 70 NG, a laser-guided air defence system. On land, Germany's Leopard 2A7 is regarded as one of the most modern tanks worldwide, supported by Sweden's Archer artillery system. Several European countries have the SCALP/Storm Shadow cruise missile – comparable to the American Tomahawk – while MBDA, as a pan-European missile producer, develops a whole range of missiles deployed within NATO. Finally, radar systems, such as the Swedish Saab Giraffe series, provide advanced detection capabilities that are essential in modern warfare.

Europe's greatest weakness, then, is not the absence of high-quality technology, but the fragmentation of its defence apparatus. Where the US can rely on a centralised procurement policy and around 30 standardised weapons systems, Europe operates with dozens of fragmented national defence budgets and 172 weapons systems that are often not compatible. Each member state makes purchases according to national strategic, economic or industrial logic, which means European economies of scale and interoperability are lost. As we discussed earlier, it is this fragmentation that leads to higher costs, slower modernisation and lower operational readiness. In that context, it is therefore good news that the newly elected German Chancellor Friedrich Merz is presenting himself as an advocate for standardising weapons systems, with the aim of having just one type of fighter jet or tank across Europe in the future.

It makes sense, from Readiness 2030, to focus on streamlining and optimising this conventional capacity, but it would be a major mistake to stop there. Just as in the energy sector, the battlefield is also changing fundamentally. The war in Ukraine makes it clear that modern conflicts are no longer decided by brute force alone, but also by smart, flexible and technological strategies: cyber warfare, hybrid conflicts, AI-driven surveillance and, above all, drones. Flying drones, sailing drones, underwater drones, driving drones, crawling drones – all forms of manned or unmanned autonomous systems.

Ukraine's subordinate position has led to transformative innovation that is drastically changing the face of war: Ukraine has managed, in an unprecedented way, to convert consumer drones, which cost only a few hundred euros each, into powerful weapons capable of disabling tanks and other infrastructure. The deployment of thousands of cheap drones creates an asymmetric advantage on the battlefield that undermines classical doctrines. An estimated 75 percent of all casualties and damage on the Russian side are the result of deploying these dirt-cheap drones. In this new reality, Europe must rebuild its defence not only around better organising old structures, but also on the basis of a transformative technological mindset. Cyber warfare, hybrid wars, geopolitical soft and hard power – all of it belongs in the mix of the defence transition for a strong Europe. The good news is that this does not require extra steel or expensive high-tech components, but above all brains and the will to innovate.

Defence transition: a drone wall

Germany launched the proposal to build a 'drone wall' along NATO's eastern flank, including Ukraine. That wall would not consist of concrete or barbed wire, but of a network of autonomous, AI-driven air systems and drones, intended to detect Russian attacks in good time and neutralise them immediately.

This idea turns classic defence logic on its head: not thousands of soldiers or multi-billion budgets for tanks, fighter jets and missile systems, but an adaptive defence line that is smart and scalable, all for a fraction of the traditional cost. The most advanced consumer drones, with AI and autonomous functions, cost somewhere around 3,000 euros, while Ukraine is managing to build its drones for less than 1,000 euros each. For the budget of ten F-35 fighter jets, you could deploy 300,000, or more than one million drones respectively, in this alternative defence line.

The drone wall is an example of how Europe can develop as an innovator in the defence transition, rather than as an imitator and competitor of a traditional defence industry. Once you start digging into the subject, you notice that innovation thinking around defence is gaining significant traction in Europe: underwater drones being developed in Ostend, funding for German AI-driven air protection systems, many other high-tech defence start-ups, Swedish killer drones with names that refer to their mythology – it is almost as if the war in Ukraine has set an entirely new high-tech ecosystem in motion, one that eagerly attracts funding and talent.

Alongside guarding our land borders with tanks and soldiers, in the future we will also have to defend digital borders. In chapter 12, I discuss in detail the various initiatives Europe is taking to build technological sovereignty. Yet we will never function with full technological autonomy. Meanwhile, almost all our devices are becoming smart and internet-connected, from cars to lawnmowers and from dishwashers to doorbells. With the expectation that AI robots will find a place in our companies and homes in the coming years, this trend of smart devices will only increase. We may be able and willing to build some of these products in Europe ourselves, but a substantial share will continue to come from the US and especially

China. We must not be blind to the risks of this evolution. In the 2023 film *Leave the World Behind*, there is a hilarious scene in which hundreds of white Teslas drive autonomously to the same location and crash into one another there, completely blocking the motorways. This is a – admittedly fictional – example of how civilian infrastructure can be used as a weapon in a connected world.

Recently, a report was published describing how backdoors have been found in internet-connected Chinese inverters for solar panels which, in theory, make it possible to take over the devices and exert control over them if desired. If this is done maliciously, it could cause an energy blackout, as was the case in Spain on 28 April 2025. Experts I know assure me that there is no indication whatsoever that this incident was caused deliberately, but in theory it is perfectly possible. Ask yourself what the most efficient form of warfare will be in the future: physically attacking Europe with missiles, aircraft and tanks, or rather shutting down the entire continent through a few targeted hacks on solar panels? I fear the answer speaks for itself. A major part of our defence transition will therefore have to consist of the technological capabilities to counter this: proactively detecting any backdoors and kill switches in devices we use at scale and ensuring that, in the event of malicious incidents, we can quarantine the threats so that they do not bring down our critical infrastructure. For this we do not need weapons manufacturers, but smart people who excel in both defensive and offensive hacks and in cyber security.

The list of possible transition sectors is extensive and offers Europe opportunities to compete with the rest of the world in a new, future-proof way. In addition to energy and defence, there are agriculture and food, housing, mobility, medicine and care, circular and local strengthening of access to raw materials, climate technology and, of course, everything to do with digital reinforcement. These sectors form the core of a strategic, future-oriented European model. They show that we do not have to be a world power according to the old recipe, but can help shape a new order through technological and social innovation. In part 3 of this book, I go into more detail about a number of these sectors.

Europe, a democratic beacon in the new order

In the world order that is now taking shape, Europe is not *the* centre of the world, but neither is it any longer the submissive vassal of the US. If we play it well, we will become one world power among others, with the chance to occupy a unique place – a place rooted in economic strength, innovation in defence and industries, and in our European values, history and structures. At present we have 450 million of the richest and best-educated citizens in the world, and with the right alliances that could rise to 750 million people. Europe's scientific and technological tradition is very much alive: from fundamental research to breakthroughs in biotech, climate technology, superconductors and medicine. Innovation no longer has to leave for Silicon Valley – the minds are here, and the investment climate is beginning to shift. That gives Europe a solid economic base not only to follow the major transitions of this century, but also to lead them actively. Not by endlessly extending yesterday's industrial revolutions, but by building the transition industries of tomorrow. Europe does not need to be ashamed of its position. On the contrary, there is much to be proud of, much with which to build a strong Europe. Europe has everything it needs, and today's geopolitical pressure is the lever to activate it.

We must stop looking to the US as the leading beacon, as the world's moral compass. Since Trump II, those days are over. Nor should we keep looking to China as the great example of industrial leadership. We can take up a middle position in which we primarily want to be the centre of the world for ourselves, doing things our way, with our values and standards, with our capabilities, focused on smart innovation and transition. What can set Europe apart is influence and power through positive, intrinsic strength, not through the brute force or demographic dominance that others rely on, nor by continuing an industrial model that is losing relevance.

Today's Europe stands for a worldview in which freedom, human rights and democracy are fundamental building blocks. If the new world order no longer takes these principles for granted, we must continue to embody them – not as moral crusaders, but as a legitimate power with a strong conviction of its own. That can make us unique: a significant economic, technological and military power kept in check by principles rooted in the legacy of the Enlightenment, in five centuries of striving for progress, scientific thinking, individual emancipation and pluralism. At the same time, we must recognise that, for many others on this planet, that same legacy calls to mind the darker sides that this period also brought: ruthless industrialisation, colonisation, slavery, pollution and climate change. But the ability to acknowledge this moral ambiguity and draw lessons from it can make us a credible player for others who aspire to geopolitical responsibility and nuance.

From a regained strength, we can seek balanced partnerships, even with power blocs that have a different view of the world. Unlike the US before Trump II, we do not need the arrogance of wanting to play the world's moral police officer, using military intervention, under the banner of democracy or human rights, to enforce our own geopolitical or economic interests. Europe does not need to become a copy of other great powers, but can, through smart investments in transformative defence and other transformative sectors, build credible power and deterrence. Only then can we act autonomously, without dependence on external patrons. Not to dominate the other power blocs, but to build enough weight of our own so that we can negotiate on equal terms with the US, China, Russia or India. The condition, however, is that we ourselves dare to act coherently, assertively and even aggressively. That means continuing to defend our values, even when the rest of the world advances different ideological principles.

We defend Europe's moral boundaries, not to wag our finger at others and export our system of values and norms like old-fashioned missionaries, but to safeguard our borders, literally and figuratively, against forces from outside that want to change Europe's DNA of democracy, freedom and progress. As I showed in part 1, those forces are present and they will not disappear once Trump is no longer there. A crucial element in Europe's current turnaround is recognising the patterns in how they operate and actively defending ourselves against them.

A stronger Europe through new alliances and partnerships

The Trump administration is pushing its historic allies into the arms of other partners. Instead of playing the old collaborations off against each other, Trump is indirectly creating new fronts and alliances, without the US. One commentator described it as 'from America First to America Alone'. Europe is taking a leading position here, continuing to pursue a course of openness, in contrast to American protectionism. What we are seeing emerge is not one new mega-alliance, but a series of mutual ties between different parties, brought together in larger coalitions of the willing or not. Through these alliances, the former allies do not necessarily want to break completely with the US, but they do want to reduce their dependence by diversifying their economic, technological and military ties.

One striking development is the rapprochement between the United Kingdom and the EU. The crisis Trump has created is accelerating the UK's post-Brexit ambitions. The summit that took place in London on 19 May 2025 marks a turning point: defence, trade, migration and geopolitical coordination are being redefined in a context of shared interests and shared threats with the EU. The UK is playing an increasingly active role within NATO, is offering itself as a pivot in European defence initiatives, and Prime Minister Starmer is one of the European front-runners trying to stabilise the relationship with Trump and the US. That role acts as a lever to kick-start broader economic and cultural cooperation, with the UK once again positioning itself as a reliable European partner, even outside the formal EU framework. There is a clear shift from the reluctance during the Brexit period towards a more pragmatic sense of connection with the rest of the continent.

About a month later, Europe reached another milestone. On 23 June 2025, Canada and the European Union signed a security pact – the Security and Defence Partnership. The agreement is not limited to defence and cybersecurity; it also extends into areas that have become inseparable from security in the modern world: the energy transition, digital regulation, and strategies around critical raw materials. Canada's potential participation in Europe's SAFE fund (the Readiness 2030 component designed to stimulate €150 billion in joint investment), along with its announcement that it intends to purchase more military equipment from European suppliers, underscores a shared determination to reduce structural dependencies on the United States. Where cooperation between Canada and Europe was previously primarily economic, it is now framed in terms of a common vision of strategic autonomy and democratic values. In response to rising US protectionism, relations between Canada and the European Union have climbed to a historic high. It is telling, for example, that for the first time in Canadian history a newly elected prime minister did *not* choose the United States as the destination for his first official foreign visit. Mark Carney's trip – just three days after his swearing-in – took him to Paris to further translate this renewed closeness into concrete cooperation.

A similar dynamic can be seen in the strengthening of relations between the EU and Japan. Shortly after Trump's election victory, the EU and Japan announced their own Security and Defence Partnership on 1 November 2024 – the first of its kind that the EU has entered into with an Indo-Pacific country. The cooperation includes maritime security, cyber defence, space, and support for Ukraine. As in the relationship with Canada and the UK, we see a deliberate strategic spreading of risks and a strengthening of joint capacity. The fact that Japan, too, is actively linking its defence industry with European partners illustrates how far this cooperation reaches. In parallel, work is under way to deepen cooperation on the economic and technological front. Through joint initiatives around hydrogen, electric vehicles, rare earth metals, AI, 5G/6G, quantum technology and cyber security, they want to increase their economic autonomy. Europe and Japan are not opting for isolation, but for a new form of connectedness: resilient, innovative, values-driven and future-oriented.

On the Latin American continent, the European Union has meanwhile also taken important steps. In December 2024, after 25 years of negotiations, the historic EU – Mercosur agreement was concluded, with which the EU established its largest free trade area ever. With a market of nearly 720 million people and a strong focus on agriculture, industry, human rights and sustainability, this agreement is seen as a symbolic response to the US's retreat from multilateral structures. The modernisation of the EU-Mexico agreement, announced a few days before Trump's inauguration, also shows that Europe is not waiting, but anticipating. In Africa, Europe has expressed its commitment even more strongly. The launch of the first Clean Trade and Investment Partnership (CTIP) with South Africa in March 2025 shows how the EU looks beyond purely economic interests. Through an investment package of nearly 5 billion euros, Europe is focusing on co-investment in transparent trade, sustainable economic growth, clean technology, skills and social development. This is not a neo-colonial project, but an initiative to build new ecosystems through investment programmes – linked to local labour markets and with respect for sovereignty and cultural differences. The aim is, in time, to roll out CTIP to other African countries as well. With a young, growing population and the same time zones, Africa is not only Europe's neighbour, but also a future economic beating heart that we must take into account.

Finally, India is also important in Europe's geopolitical reorientation. The talks between Von der Leyen and Modi in March 2025 have accelerated the negotiating process on an EU-India free trade agreement. Both parties are aiming to finalise it by the end of 2025, with the pressure Trump is exerting on the global order as an explicit driver. This is just a selection of the ongoing initiatives and talks with countries with which Europe is actively working to strengthen mutual relations. In Asia, a series of agreements have been concluded that are both economic and strategic in nature: digital trade agreements with South Korea and Singapore, restarted free trade negotiations with Malaysia and Indonesia, and a new security dialogue with the Philippines. With New Zealand, a 'green' free trade agreement was concluded on 23 June 2025, and with Thailand framework agreements and innovation programmes are also being rolled out at an accelerated pace. In Latin America, alongside the major Mercosur deal, there are also initiatives with Brazil and Chile – with a focus on raw materials, sustainability and strategic investments.

This broad wave of diplomatic activity underlines that the EU is not reacting passively to Trump's America, but is confidently building its own network of alliances. What is also striking is the speed with which the EU is concluding new agreements. This suggests that at least some of these diplomatic moves were already in development before Trump II's inauguration, probably even dating back to his first term.

The new alliances show that there is support for Europe as a world power alongside the US, Russia and China. Countries that do not want to align themselves with these players see Europe's course as a possible alternative model for positive development and progress. Yet we must not be naïve either. The US, China and Russia have not disappeared from the world stage; quite the opposite. China's role, in particular, is significant, with large-scale initiatives through which it has gained or bought so much influence in the Global South that Europe has almost no chance of bringing countries into its alliances there. However we look at it, in the new multipolar world order, different spheres of influence will emerge, competing geopolitically with one another, while many of the global structures that currently provide order will erode or disappear. Hopefully, in that world Europe will succeed in taking on the role the US is now relinquishing, so that countries looking for economic and social development can align themselves with a positive, constructive, pluralistic and democratic model.

While Europe plays its part from a newly regained position of economic and technological strength – combined with its values and norms – we will also need to build pragmatic relationships with the other power blocs. As I have said before, building a strong and sovereign Europe is not the same thing as blowing up our ties with the United States. The challenge will be to keep cooperating constructively – where possible and where necessary – through the turbulent ride the US seems poised to take both at home and abroad. The same applies to our relationship with China: a stronger Europe does not imply a rejection of China, but rather a permanent effort to recalibrate – again and again – a healthy balance between the interests of both major powers. Even our relationship with Russia will, at some point, have to stabilise and normalise. It is, and will remain, a neighbouring country with which we will have to coexist in the long run. What may change in each of these relationships is that the Europe of tomorrow can help shape them from a position of its own strength: with less dependency, and with the capacity – military or economic – to strike back if it must. We are not there yet, but if Europe continues to believe in this course and invest in it, it should become possible. I call this the achievement of *hybrid peace*. Europe must learn to operate in an environment that is neither purely peaceful nor explicitly hostile – an environment in which developing strategic autonomy and sovereignty is essential, and in which economic, cultural, military, and moral positions are actively defended using all the means at our disposal.

8. Is there enough support?

We are on a slippery slope of support

In recent years, I have done a lot of strategic work for cities and municipalities. They too see the world changing, and some genuinely have the ambition to be pleasant places to live and work by 2050. Alongside countless policy and practical challenges, the constant brake on real acceleration of innovation is the lack of support. No matter how many beautiful plans we have, how much money we throw at them, how strongly politicians argue for them: if there is no broad support among citizens and businesses, no major transformations will happen. And that, in these times of social discontent and polarisation, is precisely a major problem. Bases of support are the glaciers of our society: every day we see them melting away, and with it announcing a future disaster.

I truly believe there is political momentum to allow Europe to emerge stronger from the current crisis. The only question is whether European citizens believe in that too. If we want to bring this European project to a successful conclusion, we need the democratic support of all Europeans. The transformations and investments in transition sectors will lead to change and sacrifices, and we will have to seek consensus around positions everyone can live with. That means we will have to make concessions and many sacred cows will be slaughtered. In recent years, we have seen necessary measures meet resistance from citizens: removing paving, the tethered bottle cap, the concrete stop, low emission zones in the city, maximum speeds on the motorway ... they all lead to irritation and frustration. The issue is not so much that people do not support the underlying causes, such as road safety or the climate; the issue is that we do not understand how these 'pesty measures' contribute to a solution. The burden we experience is greater than the understanding we have of why the action is being taken. We live in a time in which trust in 'the system' is at a low point, and yet we are going to need that support to make the European turnaround. How do we tackle that?

There are several possible dynamics that can help here. The most obvious is creating a clear enemy image. A war works wonders in this respect: it unites a people, in all its diversity, and makes them endure unprecedented hardships without too much complaining, together against the enemy. Look at the situation in Ukraine, where the war has been going on for years now, and although Russia is strongly focused on demotivating citizens, the determination seems only to be increasing. Fortunately, Europe is not in a state of war, and hopefully it never will be. Something more peaceful, but just as efficient, is an economic and cultural enemy image. When Trump started acting out and proclaimed that Canada should really become a state of the US, that Justin Trudeau was downgraded to governor (the title for the head of an American state), and that Greenland was almost confiscated, outrage in those countries was widespread. From a kind of nationalist sense of unity, even people who are not nationalist by nature rallied behind their country's common flag. The consequences ranged from an economic boycott of American products to reducing the number of trips Canadians typically make to the US. Not to mention the complete European collapse in Tesla sales because Icarus Musk had flown a little too close to Trump's sun.

Major global shocks such as natural disasters and pandemics are comparable to wars. Although human selfishness usually rears its head immediately, for example in the form of looting or people jumping the queue for vaccination, in these moments we generally still see enormous mobilisation and solidarity: citizens join forces to help, or, without much complaint, accept restrictions that in fact disregard their democratic rights. Typically, this positive behaviour is usually of relatively short duration. The consequences of a disaster simply must not drag on for too long, because then the willingness to show solidarity drops rapidly.

There is another kind of shock effect that acts as an engine for mobilisation: the outrage of large groups of people when a moral boundary is crossed. That moment when something is not only wrong, but is also deemed unacceptable. When the US government openly began targeting universities such as Harvard, a broad range of students, academics and even critics closed ranks. Until then, they had often been loudly shouting at one another from opposite sides in the occupations of campuses that resulted from conflicting worldviews. But the danger that Trump's actions amounted to a frontal attack on academic freedom united opponents against a common enemy and around a common purpose. We saw a similar phenomenon when American ICE agents rounded up migrants in violent raids: even people who had previously argued for stricter migration rules were shocked by the images and voiced their disgust. Such moments create a temporary unifying effect, generating support for resistance or for action.

All the dynamics above are essentially negative motivators, aimed at short-term mobilisation, against something. The question is how you motivate people in the long term for something, for positive action. Our brains have evolved in such a way that we pay far more attention to negativity, which makes it easier to resist something that can threaten us now, while motivating people for something that could bring us an advantage in the longer term is much harder. And that brings us to the core question: what not only sets Europe in motion, but also keeps us moving in the long term? Negative motivators, however powerful, lack the ability to transform a society sustainably. They are the impulse that is creating the necessary momentum in Europe today, but not the force needed to achieve lasting change over the long term. What we need is a positive vision of Europe's future: an image that is credible and desirable. As I have described at length in earlier books, people are only willing to make sacrifices if they understand what those sacrifices lead to – and, more importantly, if they want to be part of it. So we need a clear story, an ambitious vision, that can inspire and motivate people for the long-term, collective 'why' of change.

To build support for this unprecedented European project, we need not only Readiness 2030, with the hundreds of billions that come with it, but also the imagination to dream up a story that citizens, businesses and politicians are willing to sign up to. Unlike a typical European communications campaign that runs for a few months, with a website, a few dull events and hideous blue-and-yellow brochures, this story will have to be profound and credible, and repeated for years. In doing so, we would do better not to model ourselves on the classic, uninspired European political communication, but rather on the ideological near-propaganda that the Chinese, the Emirates and others are so good at – provided, of course, that we do not start manipulating, lying or misleading.

The times democracy triumphed

I have a strange quirk. For years, I have followed international elections with above-average attention. While many people spend their Sunday evening enjoying their BBQ, Netflix, or trying to recover from a visit to the in-laws, I follow exit polls and political analysis. What strikes me is that, since Trump's inauguration, an interesting and hopeful pattern has been emerging when we look at the most recent elections. Despite the global shift towards populist ideologies, despite the souring mood and increased polarisation and, with that, the success of autocratic leaders, there are at the same time clear signals of resistance. Not from politicians, academics or opinion-makers, but from the population, which is making itself heard in the voting booth. The radical course Donald Trump has set in the US – with disinformation, institutional undermining and isolationism as its trademarks – seems, in many other democracies, above all to be a deterrent example. While some leaders copy him, there are more and more voters who see the dangers of that route and choose a different path. Yes, some of those voters are still generally against (illegal) immigration, still believe the system does not work, that the establishment rules from behind the scenes, that politicians are corrupt, and that our human rights are being curtailed (because what else can you call it if we are not allowed to drive 160 kilometres per hour on the motorway and we are no longer allowed to burn rubbish in our garden). And yet: the example of the US, where Trump threatens to plunge the country into an autocracy, really does go too far.

From January 2025 up to and including June 2025, there have been clear signals that citizens around the world are protesting against Trump in a remarkable way: by casting their vote. Various elections and recent polls show that the democratic idea is more durable than had been feared. Traditional parties that for years have seemed to be on the ropes are recovering and winning elections, or becoming more popular in the polls. Not because everything is suddenly going better, citizens have become less right-wing, or people have started believing in politics again, but because people realise what is at stake: what Trump is doing in the US must not happen here. A brief overview of recent, striking political outcomes.

- **Canada**. If you have been threatened with annexation by Trump for months, it is not surprising that Pierre Poilievre lost the election as Justin Trudeau's would-be successor. Poilievre positioned himself too emphatically as the 'Canadian Trump'. Voters preferred Mark Carney, a former banker and steady leader with a pro-European outlook. Under other circumstances, he would have stood little chance, but now he beat the populist candidate who until recently had been seen as the presumptive winner.
- **United Kingdom**. Keir Starmer's government was under a bad star anyway, but because of Europe's efforts to manage Trump's chaos, he has been able to restore his leadership both in the UK and in Europe through diplomacy and calm. The popularity of his rival Nigel Farage is still very high, but he is struggling as a result of his open admiration for both Trump and Putin.
- **The Netherlands**. In the polls, Wilders, despite earlier gains, is finding himself in a difficult position because of his ambiguity on Russia and his admiration for Trump, giving moderate pro-European forces such as Frans Timmermans greater appeal. Whether these polling results will translate into election outcomes remains to be seen, of course.
- **Germany**. Friedrich Merz won because he positioned himself as a centre-right alternative to the far-right AfD. That party was unable to benefit from associations with Trump, not even from the explicit support of Musk and Vance.

- **Ecuador.** In recent years, left-wing populists (yes, that is a thing) have been making significant gains. The moderate incumbent candidate Daniel Noboa, the son of a millionaire and a representative of the 'establishment', was challenged by Luisa González. She was the candidate of the left-populist 'Citizen Revolution', a movement that combines populist rhetoric with authoritarian tendencies. Her campaign, in which she flirted with anti-democratic proposals, made many Ecuadorians fear a return to the era in which the left-populist president Rafael Correa bent the constitution to his will, centralised power with the president, ruled by decree and took over the Constitutional Court, hollowing out the separation of powers. The expectation was that Luisa González would win, but to everyone's surprise the moderately conservative incumbent Daniel Noboa won by a wide margin of 11 percentage points. Luisa González screamed blue murder and accused the winner of having stolen the election. The echoes of Trump are clear.

Even in countries where there are currently no elections, such as Hungary and Serbia, we have seen public mobilisation against authoritarian leaders who model themselves on Trump's style. The demonstrations in Rome and Belgrade, and the unexpected popularity of Péter Magyar, Orbán's pro-European challenger in Hungary, show that citizens do not remain passive when fundamental values come under pressure. For me, one of the most meaningful, unexpected election outcomes is that of the new Pope Leo XIV. The papal election of 2025 turned into a geopolitical spectacle that fans of the TV series *Succession* would probably consider top entertainment. Quite unexpectedly, the conclave became the stage for a geopolitical struggle that until then had played out mainly in parliaments and polling stations. The election of Leo XIV – known in civilian life as Robert Prevost, an American cardinal with Peruvian experience and a reputation as a bridge-builder within the global Church – was, in substance, far more than an internal Vatican matter.

Right-wing religious forces in the US, backed by the Trump administration, saw the papacy as a strategic bastion from which to expand their cultural and ideological influence worldwide. They threw their weight behind the candidacy of Cardinal Timothy Dolan, Archbishop of New York and an outspoken opponent of Pope Francis' progressive course on migration, climate and social justice. Dolan, popular among American conservatives, was known for his hardline positions against abortion, same-sex marriage and 'woke ideology'. He was therefore actively supported by MAGA movement leading lights such as Laura Loomer, a Trump-loyal influencer. Loomer openly applied pressure through disinformation on social media to discredit Prevost. The Heritage Foundation, together with Peter Thiel, tried, through money and logistics, to win the votes of African and Asian cardinals for Dolan. But the plan failed. Prevost, despite the storm of insinuations, was elected with a majority – a defeat for right-wing religious America. Even the election of a new pope thus became an unexpected signal of resilience against the global trend of shifting towards radical ideologies and autocratic movements.

This chapter is about the necessary support among citizens. What comes through in the above is not naïve optimism, but a signal of pragmatic realism. The world order may be shifting, but citizens worldwide sense that democracy is fragile and therefore worth protecting. Today's democratic victories are not great triumphs, but small and meaningful corrections. They indicate that it is indeed possible to build support among citizens, provided they themselves are convinced of the necessity. Even so, we should be careful about drawing overly positive conclusions: in the same period there were two European elections showing that the development described above does not apply always and everywhere. In the UK, Reform UK, the right-wing party led by Nigel Farage, unexpectedly defeated Labour's socialists in local by-elections in Runcorn in northern England. This was, admittedly, by only six votes, which can be called a historically narrow victory. The result was driven by discontent about immigration and austerity, forces which – despite fears about autocratic behaviour by new leaders – remain dominant for many citizens and continue to provide the energy populists need, with simple promises. In the next chapter, I go deeper into this challenge.

Another hangover was the election of a new president in Poland. There, the anti-Europe candidate Nawrocki beat Trzaskowski, the pro-European ally of Polish Prime Minister Donald Tusk, with only 50.7 percent. As a result, Poland is likely to end up in a political bind in the coming years, with the pro-European government repeatedly running up against the conservative president's veto. How that will develop further is anyone's guess. It will not be an easy task for Tusk: leaning strongly towards Europe on liberal reforms becomes a major challenge. At the same time, the new conservative president does promise to align with his prime minister – and therefore with Europe – on defence and a tough stance towards Russia. Conservatives in Poland have traditionally been more oriented towards closer cooperation with the US than with the European institutions in Brussels. Some even suspect that Nawrocki's selfie with Trump, shortly before the election, made the difference in the outcome. Yet there is also concern in the conservative camp about Trump's unreliability towards his allies. If the submissive Nawrocki is abandoned or humiliated tomorrow by the 'bossy' Trump, Euro-pragmatism might well prevail. In any case, we should not expect overly liberal upheavals in Poland in the coming years, but it is also not a given that Poland will now pursue a radical anti-Europe course, certainly not in defence. Still, the new European coalition of the willing, whose faces included figures such as Starmer, Macron, Merz, Von der Leyen and Donald Tusk, may now be one strong figure poorer.

Politics must play its part; part 1

The election results offer hope and possibly new momentum for traditional centre parties in Europe. The pressure, fragmentation and hollowing-out they have faced in recent years have caused existential crises in many countries. The erosion of voters' trust in traditional parties meant that these voters either lurched towards populist right-wing movements, or disengaged altogether. That means that this 'revaluation of the political centre' in the most recent elections is, rather, a choice between the devil and the deep blue sea. Voters may not want a local Trump, but that does not mean they have cast their vote with enthusiasm for the candidate or party of their preference. If they are now voting for moderate and traditional candidates, it will often be because the other option is not an option. My advice, therefore, is to bear in mind that this is a temporary phenomenon, and that if disappointment in politics remains just as great, voters will once again turn away from centre candidates and parties. It is therefore of the utmost importance for the current political generation to translate the temporary mandate they are being given into the right action. What that could mean, I will explain later.

Local politics can, of course, make use of European momentum and Europe's assertive stance. The Readiness 2030 programme, the choices around additional investment in defence and technology, and the new international alliances give European politics the opportunity to show citizens, through positive action, that they mean business. In addition, Europe seems to have clearly understood that work must be done on the administrative simplification the business world has been waiting for for decades. One of the challenges will be translating the political unity that can more or less be found at European level into national and local politics. From their small-minded perspective, local politicians often have a tendency to make any form of political cooperation impossible through short-sighted ideological or even personal differences. Colleagues at European level may well be uniting behind a grand European narrative, but if we fail to translate that into politics within the countries themselves, this promises to be a very difficult journey. If you are a politician and you are reading this book, realise what responsibility you carry if you continue to do politics in the old, childish way. Now more than ever, we need a shared plan and shared action. You will no longer win votes by sabotaging your colleagues; on the contrary, you will probably drive voters definitively into the hands of the forces that want to dismantle our liberal society.

Business must play its part; part 1

If you were a company CEO and you went to a meeting of some chamber of commerce, or to a business event, then until recently it was bon ton to lay into Europe – and, of course, into the inefficiency of your own country. Without any doubt, the business world contains the lowest number of Europhiles. There were plenty of reasons for that: Euro technocrats who dream up pesty rules ('that cap on the bottle?!'), bureaucratic overload and a reporting frenzy, too many laws that deprive entrepreneurs of chances of success, climate measures that do nothing for your business and only cost money, indecently high energy bills, not to mention taxes. I am not going to deny that there are places in the world where it is easier to do business, only they often take human rights, the climate or basic democratic principles far less seriously. Nor am I going to deny that there is often a serious grain of truth in companies' complaints: Europe is not always the most straightforward market. Even leaving aside cultural differences and the fact that there are 24 official languages, there are plenty of other challenges that make doing business in Europe far more complex than, say, in the US or the Emirates.

Up to the beginning of 2025, I heard the majority of our entrepreneurs explicitly say that Trump would be good for the economy, someone who would abolish all those European rules. At home, we could do with such a 'strong leader' too. DOGE – the apparatus with which Musk dismantled almost the entire federal public service in the US – was seen as the holy grail to finally make government as lean and mean as the average start-up. The fact that 90 percent of start-ups fail and leave investors with a financial hangover, we will leave aside for a moment. Names were already circulating of European techies who, following Musk's shining example, might be allowed to lead our own DOGE. The fact that Musk has since disappeared from the scene, and that objective analyses show that, alongside DOGE's meagre 50 billion dollar saving, 280 billion dollars in lost tax revenues and other damage has been added, will no doubt have something to do with the fact that today you can hardly find a European CEO or entrepreneur still openly professing their love for the American approach.

I do think that the more positive Euro sentiment among entrepreneurs is genuine and not driven solely by (vicarious) embarrassment. Through various strategy projects and keynotes I have given in recent months, I have had the pleasure of having in-depth conversations about this topic. While frustration about European obstacles remains, there is nonetheless a consensus that we cannot simply throw our European values and norms on climate targets, human rights and consumer protection overboard in a quest for greater efficiency. The essence of those European rules is untouchable, grounded in a centuries-long evolution from the Enlightenment to the present day: society evolves and so the norms, and subsequently the laws, evolve with it. What everyone does continue to agree on is that the complexity and the burden of implementing those laws need to be tackled. And on that front, there is finally good news.

After thirty years, the EU, through the Omnibus legislation (approved on 24 February 2026), is creating a concrete action plan, presented by the European Commission in May 2025. At the centre of it is tackling the so-called 'Terrible Ten' (wasn't that a 1970s spaghetti western?). These are the ten most harmful barriers that make cross-border business difficult and frustrate our entrepreneurs so much. They include, among other things, cumbersome establishment procedures, differences in product rules and the difficult recognition of professional qualifications. For European companies, and especially for SMEs, this means that they will soon be able to offer their products and services in other member states much more easily, without getting lost in a tangle of national rules. The good news is that the Commission has set clear deadlines: by the end of 2027 these barriers should largely have been cleared away. That means that, if this starts to bear fruit, politicians will be able to profile themselves with solid results while still within their current mandates and legislative terms.

One of the most tangible benefits for businesses lies in the digitalisation of procedures. Until now, an entrepreneur in, say, Romania still had to send paper certificates in order to offer a service in Germany. That is now changing fundamentally: mandatory paper formats are being abolished, data exchange is going digital, and a harmonised framework for data and cyber security is being introduced. All right, here I do want to pause for a moment and be critical. I have been in the digital and innovation business since 1994, and the reader cannot blame me for raising my right eyebrow a few centimetres when I saw that the expectation is to achieve this within about three years. I think it is a commendable objective to go 100 percent digital that quickly with this fragmented paper administration, but unless you take the family of the responsible programme managers hostage and threaten to attack the European Parliament with bunker busters (those bombs that penetrate deep into the ground), that timeline does not strike me as particularly realistic. But we can hope, of course.

All joking aside: a strong, integrated internal market is essential if we are to remain competitive as a bloc in the world order of tomorrow. That is why not only speed, but also enforcement, is crucial. Every EU country must now appoint a 'Single Market Sherpa' to remove national obstacles and actively report on progress. Member states that fall behind will come under increased pressure to contribute to the collective European interest. This time, the European Commission's plans are not optional. There is a clear roadmap through to 2027, annual evaluations, linked EU investments and a call for political ownership in every member state. With the first 'Omnibus' packages already in force since autumn 2025, the ball has start rolling. Businesses will see results quickly: less red tape, lower costs and faster market access. If this line is carried through, the plan can restore confidence in Europe and build further support for the major transitions we face and that will not succeed without the business community.

The risk, however, is that this regulation is not only aimed at administrative simplification, but may also undermine the foundations of European sustainability policy. By limiting reporting obligations, crucial sustainability data risks disappearing. In theory, this means less paperwork for companies, and that is a good thing, but the negative consequence could be that harmonisation is lost and sustainability policy within Europe once again threatens to fall apart into a patchwork of voluntary practices – precisely what the CSRD was intended to prevent in the first place. There is an inherent tension here that we must learn to manage: if we go easier on companies and simplify part of sustainability reporting, we run the risk that climate targets will not be met, or will be met more slowly. If, on the other hand, the pressure on companies becomes too great for them to remain performant, they risk withdrawing their support for the European project entirely and rallying behind populists. Once they come to power, the overall pursuit of sustainability could be put at risk. Later on, I will go into this dilemma in more depth.

What I still regard as good news is that many entrepreneurs seem to believe that the strategic and financial clout of Readiness 2030 can be a real stimulus for the European economy. Of course, not everyone produces war materiel, but the possibility of setting up dual-use investments in particular – which boils down to a product or service having both a civilian and a military purpose – creates plenty of opportunities. Drones, autonomous vehicles, AI, cloud and data services, microchips, telecoms, energy, and so on: many of the developments Europe needs in order to become stronger could fall under this heading and therefore draw on a Readiness 2030 project. As I wrote earlier, the available budget is many times larger than the original Marshall Plan, and that gave Europe an enormous boost at the time. It is good to see that there is also confidence that Europe can bring strategic technologies back and attempt to compete with the US and China.

Especially if we focus on transition sectors, I think this can be a crucial lever for European business. The task will be to seize the current momentum – with Readiness 2030, the new trade agreements and initiatives such as removing the Terrible Ten – and translate it into the business community. We can only deliver on this if genuine economic opportunities emerge that clearly add value, and if we can simultaneously demonstrate that working together within Europe really is becoming easier. We should not be naïve about this, but pragmatically opportunistic: the shock creates momentum. Momentum creates the willingness to invest and the political will to simplify administration. All of this creates added value for businesses, and that leads to support. The only thing missing in that chain is a clear vision of how to tackle this and which sectors to focus on, so that European companies really can compete with their American or Chinese counterparts.

The ultimate motivator for support: the climate crisis

As I wrote above, activating and mobilising both citizens and businesses carries the risk that we put our pursuit of climate targets on the back burner, as is now happening in policy terms in the US. Trump loves Big Beautiful Deals, but you cannot negotiate with the climate. The climate crisis is real and is already plunging us into disasters that disrupt society. Just ask the victims of the fires in California or the deluge in Spain. You can debate the speed at which the climate is changing or the number of degrees by which temperatures will rise, but that is of little relevance in itself. Over the past ten years, the real costs to society have already been 2,000 billion dollars, and they are expected to rise to 19 percent of global GDP by 2050. If we take no further measures, climate costs could rise to 60 percent of the global economy. Now, you can undoubtedly point to studies that offer worse or better forecasts, but what is the point? The difference between 60 or 30 percent of global GDP is irrelevant: in both cases, the impact on the liveability of our planet is enormous.

And that brings us back to transition thinking. We need to rethink society so that climate action is inherently baked into our economy. At first, transition sectors will be less profitable than the traditional approach, but fairly quickly regions that fully commit to the transition economy will outperform countries that continue to cling to the old models. It is also worth realising that not all transition sectors are a response to the climate threat. Making ourselves resilient again in defence, technology and autonomy in strategic assets is also part of the broader transition thinking, and of the enormous potential Europe can invest in.

Back to climate. The problem with populist leaders is that, one way or another, they refuse to believe the climate crisis is real, or at least tell their base that all of this is merely a conspiracy by the globalist elite that wants to take away everything we enjoy: from V6 pick-up trucks to our gigantic T-bone steaks. I think populist leaders do know perfectly well what is going on, but they assume that by scrapping climate measures they can at least temporarily keep the cost of living lower for the population. No expensive electric cars, no heat pumps, solar panels and home batteries, no cultivated meat and, above all: lots of cheap oil. That way, you improve purchasing power for your population by simply ignoring the transition costs we should already be paying now. This helps them get elected by people whose frustration is running high and brings them to power. But what will they do when their own country is hit ever harder by climate disasters as well? If that happens quickly enough, the democratic process may still be able to do its work, citizens may still be able to drive out the populists and – better late than never – join the climate action and the transition economy and technology of other countries. Presumably, that will ultimately weigh much more heavily on those citizens' purchasing power, because valuable years have been lost and they will then have to go knocking, with their tails between their legs, at China and Europe, which by then will be much further ahead. Another scenario is, unfortunately, that by that point the democratic safeguards will have been dismantled to such an extent that a country can no longer get rid of its autocratic leaders, no matter how bad the situation becomes. This scenario is extremely worrying, especially if such a country has nuclear weapons and the largest army in the world.

Under Donald Trump's presidency, the US has completely isolated itself in the global fight against climate change. Trump withdrew his country from the Paris Climate Agreement and rolled back many environmental rules that had been introduced under previous administrations. His administration took dozens of measures to scale back environmental protection and emissions reductions. Important research programmes were scrapped, undermining the knowledge base for climate policy. Although certain American cities, states and companies continued their climate efforts, this still amounts to a huge blow to the US in the longer term. None of the necessary climate innovations and energy breakthroughs is likely to come out of America any more. The knowledge and capacity for acute disaster management, climate mitigation (tackling the causes) or climate adaptation (adapting to the consequences) risk being lost. And all the while, the rest of the world is moving on. However problematic this may be for the US, it does create the opportunity for Europe to draw economic developments around the climate transition towards itself. It is the basis for the transition thinking we need for a strong Europe, and which will allow us to compete in sectors that are forced to reinvent themselves.

The greatest risk we face is that populists also come to power here and set the climate issue aside for electoral purposes. This could also lead to our climate initiatives being suspended, and that would be disastrous – not only in the long term for the future of the planet and the liveability of our society, but also in the short term, because it would completely undermine our momentum for a strong Europe. Unlike the US, we have no traditional industries with which we can temporarily keep up the appearance of normality. Where the US thinks it can live for a while in the 1950s, in such a scenario we would be confronted immediately with Europe's powerlessness, without even having the chance to turn the tide. We must try to prevent this at all times, and fortunately it seems that this is possible. As I outlined above, citizens, politicians and companies in Europe seem by now to realise sufficiently what is happening in the US, choosing – despite existing frustrations – to hold on to our values and norms. Even so, this could still change if we do not manage to tackle the structural dissatisfaction and unrest that form the basis of support for populists. More on that at the end of this part of the book.

Business must play its part; part 2

While, under Trump, the US is throwing its climate ambitions on the scrapheap, we see that international companies are continuing to invest in sustainability. The consultancy firm McKinsey published an analysis in 2024 stating that 377 large companies in capital-intensive sectors increased their investments in climate-driven growth sixfold between 2019 and 2023. These include investments in R&D, low-carbon technology and the reorientation of their portfolios. Since Trump's re-election, we have seen delays in major investment programmes aimed at sustainability. Initial analyses suggest that this is driven more by the uncertainty created by Trump's policies and the direct impact on ongoing business cases as concrete support measures are scaled back, than by a structural decision to stop focusing on sustainability. In early 2025, the Ingka Group (the franchise holding 367 of IKEA's 422 stores) announced a one billion euro investment in recycling infrastructure. Around 667 million of that will go to new companies, with a focus on textile recycling. The rest supports existing partners in mattress and plastics recycling and is aimed at creating scale in the circular economy. Even in heavy industries, developments towards sustainability continue. In early 2025, ArcelorMittal Belgium announced that its green transition is 'simply continuing', despite the postponement of a multi-billion project to replace blast furnaces with more sustainable technology. The CEO stressed that the search for feasible, sustainable alternatives is continuing actively. Other players, such as LafargeHolcim, are also investing in technologies for lower CO_2 emissions, including through their stake in Sublime Systems, a start-up working on an electrochemical process for CO_2 -free cement production. In addition, they launched the Belgian GO4ZERO project (more than 500 million euros) and the Greek OLYMPUS project (400 million euros), together accounting for an annual production capacity of 4 million tonnes of near-zero cement by 2029. At the same time, chemicals giant Covestro is experimenting with bio-based raw materials, such as phenol and acetone from organic residual material, has built a pilot plant for 100 percent bio-based aniline, and is investing one billion euros in circular production processes.

International policy and institutional investors also seem to pay little heed to the ideological anti-climate-action positions of Trump and his allies. One of the most significant examples of this is the IMO zero-emissions agreement concluded in April 2025, in which 63 countries (including the EU, but also China, Brazil, India and the UK) agree to reduce shipping emissions to zero by 2050, including through a uniform fuel standard and a global CO_2 levy. The US, Venezuela, Russia and Saudi Arabia, of course, voted against it. In this way, even the most traditional and polluting sectors, which for a long time remained untouched by the climate transition, are now committing to structural change.

Within the US fossil sector, we see financial logic continuing to push sustainability to the fore, despite Trump's 'drill baby drill' nonsense. Oil and gas producers are being urged by the financial markets not to invest blindly in new drilling projects purely for volume growth. Their shareholders – including major funds such as BlackRock and the Norwegian sovereign wealth fund (more on that in a moment) – demand stability and clear climate plans. ExxonMobil and Chevron may publicly take a hard line on climate policy, but internally they too are taking concrete steps towards CO_2 reduction. In December 2024, ExxonMobil announced that it would invest 30 billion dollars in low-carbon technologies up to 2030, including hydrogen production, carbon capture and lithium extraction. The company is working on building the world's largest blue hydrogen facility in Baytown (Texas), where 98 percent of the

CO_2 will be captured, and in May 2025 it signed a large-scale supply contract for low-carbon ammonia with Japan's Marubeni. Chevron, in turn, expanded its activities in June 2025 for lithium extraction via direct extraction in Texas and Arkansas, and through its New Energies arm is investing up to 10 billion dollars in clean technologies such as hydrogen and CO_2 storage – thereby strategically anchoring both giants' future in the energy transition, despite their rhetoric. The phenomenon we are seeing here has recently been dubbed 'greenhushing': to the outside world it appears as if attention to sustainability is waning, but behind the scenes the investments simply continue. The causes are clear: the economic and social rationale for continuing with sustainability is unshakeable, but companies want to deflect attention in order to avoid the wrath of Trump, the far right, or MAGA-aligned customers.

As we all know: 'money makes the world go round'. The fact that the richest – and therefore most impactful – investment funds require their portfolio companies to keep focusing on sustainability will no doubt have something to do with their moral awareness that they are influencing the future of their grandchildren. Yet their motivation is, first and foremost, based on financial returns. What is striking, then, is the continuing influence of deep-pocketed institutional investors who set sustainability as a hard condition. A fine and little-known example is Norway's Government Pension Fund Global (GPFG). Norway, with only 5.5 million inhabitants, manages an unprecedented fortune of 1.8 trillion dollars through this government fund. With that amount, you can acquire an average equity stake of 1.5 percent in every listed company in the world. GPFG thus holds stakes in oil and gas giants such as Equinor, Shell, BP, TotalEnergies and ExxonMobil, where it puts pressure on CO_2 reduction and the shift to clean energy. In mining, the fund keeps companies such as Anglo American, BHP and Glencore under close scrutiny. GPFG also has enough shareholder weight in companies such as ING, BNP Paribas, Deutsche Bank, Apple, Microsoft, Unilever and Nestlé to influence policy. It is therefore significant that, in the first half of 2025, the managers of this fund made it clear that sustainability is no longer an optional recommendation, but an absolute requirement. Companies that cannot show how they deal with climate risks risk being excluded from this capital. For CEOs worldwide, that is a powerful signal: anyone who wants to retain access to the world's largest investment flows must take the transition seriously, regardless of the political climate in the US and any ideological imitators at home. This could also limit the risk of climate action being hollowed out among European companies – as a result of reduced reporting obligations under the new Omnibus rules – because the pursuit of sustainability would then be inherently baked in at shareholder level.

9. Fuck the system! Why is the world so dissatisfied?

On both the left and the right, there is a belief that dismantling the system is the solution to all our problems. Unfortunately, this is a very simplistic and mistaken idea. Although in part 1 of this book I described how certain ideological currents have every interest in weakening Europe from within (and how better to do that than by undermining trust in structures and systematically turning people against the system?), in this chapter I primarily want to look at what is going on among citizens and how this can be used to pursue a populist and anti-European course.

The game versus the rules

'Fucking the system' is simply a bad idea if we want to think constructively about our future and about the future of Europe. To understand that, I make a distinction between what I call 'the game' and the 'rules of the game'. In the West, and especially in Europe, over the past one hundred years we have managed to organise our society in a unique way. Using the diagram in figure 1, I describe what I call 'the game'.

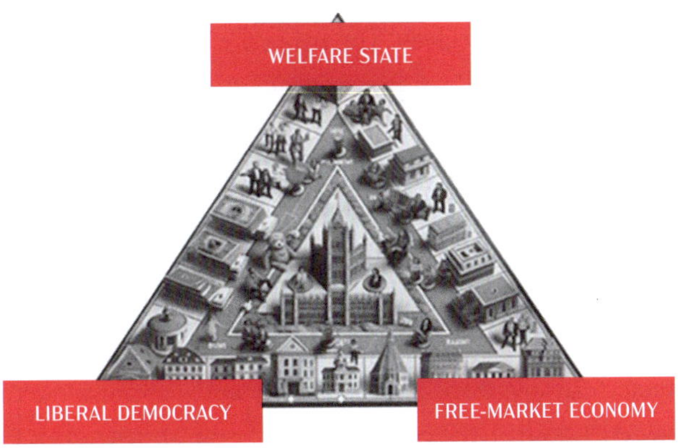

Figure 1: Liberal democracy, free-market economy, welfare state

The game has three interconnected pillars that interact with one another, and that we have used as the foundation of our system. The first is **liberal democracy**, the political underpinning of Europe. This system is based on fundamental principles: individual freedoms, a pluralist and secular constitutional state, separation of powers and representative decision-making. Citizens have basic freedoms of expression, religion and association, and these are protected by independent legal systems. Political power is exercised through elected representatives, with checks and balances between separate legislative, executive and judicial branches. An essential feature is the protection of minorities: democracy does not simply mean imposing the will of the majority, but also entails guaranteeing the rights of minority groups – who may hold a different (political) view. In addition, free media, pluralism and an active civil society provide transparency and public oversight.

This somewhat dry and theoretical list contains unique elements that, in Europe, have given us the opportunity to develop freely, to emancipate ourselves and, as individuals, to seek out the life each of us desires, even if many do not feel that this is really working out for them. Yes, there is a lot wrong with this system. One consequence of the many possibilities inherently contained in the game is the free, complex and fragmented society we have ended up in. Because the basic rules of our liberal democracy allow it, over the past century we have evolved from a few strong ideological pillars to a fragmented, tailor-made world, in which we all pursue our individual freedom as the highest good. Because our democratic model reflects how, as a society, we arrived in this fragmented, hyper-individualistic situation, this inevitably leads to a similarly fragmented, and therefore ever more difficult to function, political landscape. If we want simple politics back, we will have to start at the source: with citizens themselves. The more we can motivate them to align with a number of shared and broadly supported positions, the less complex the politics that represents them will become.

The second principle is that of the **free-market economy**. This is an economic system in which production and trade are largely determined by supply and demand in free markets, with minimal government interference. Companies and consumers make their own decisions about investing, buying and selling, which leads to competition, price mechanisms and efficient allocation of resources. Property rights are protected, innovation is encouraged and economic growth is usually a central objective. Although Europe is often accused of imposing too many rules, it also ensures that the free market can function, for example by intervening in cases of cartel formation. Here, Europe sits between the US model (with fewer rules) and China (with rules imposed by the state and the Party). Although critics – often rightly – argue that the only aim of the free-market economy is to make shareholders richer, the truth is more complex and nuanced than that. At a philosophical level, you could say this is correct, but that the whole of society is a shareholder in most companies. This happens in all sorts of ways. Through the concept of labour, employees are an important stakeholder in a company, receiving wages that enable them to support and develop themselves. Companies pay social contributions on these wages, and employees themselves are also taxed. This money goes to the government, which uses it to finance its operations.

If citizens can save and manage this through savings or investments, that money is then reinvested in companies via funds and banks, enabling them to grow further, in return for which the saver also realises added value and therefore, in principle, becomes richer. On every sale to end users, a tax is charged via VAT, and on the profits companies make they pay tax again. So you can reasonably argue that – provided companies pay their taxes and contributions fairly – their direct shareholders are not the only ones who become richer from a well-functioning economy. I would therefore assume, as the ultimate purpose, that a healthy share of the surplus generated by the economy is reinvested in citizens and in the mechanism of the welfare state.

That is also immediately the third pillar. The European **welfare state** is a social model in which the government actively takes responsibility for the wellbeing of its citizens, through extensive safety nets and public services. Characteristic features are solidarity, redistribution and social protection: citizens and businesses contribute through taxes to collective systems for healthcare, education, pensions and unemployment benefits. The primary goal is to promote equal opportunities and safeguard social stability, but the system also provides a safety net and corrective forces where and when markets fail or inequality increases.

So, in summary, we have liberal democracy as our political model and the free-market economy as the engine that must generate sufficient surplus to finance the welfare state. In itself, this is a valuable model that – when it works well – has few truly successful alternatives. You can undoubtedly imagine and develop alternatives hypothetically, but in practice, with the 'experiments' of the past one hundred years in mind, I personally choose our European model without hesitation. For me, the game is not the problem; the problem is that, almost from the first day we started playing the game, we cheated with the rules of the game. Perhaps it is a bit too harsh to put it that bluntly; perhaps it is more accurate to say that we more or less made up the rules as it suited us. In doing so, we conveniently paid little or no attention to externalities, the impact on biodiversity, the environment and the climate, strained relations between North and South and between East and West, fundamental inequality and oppression, abuse of power and market manipulation by dominant geopolitical players, the inherent drive of both citizens and businesses to enrich themselves at the expense of others (so, indeed, cheating at the game), and so on.

In itself, the game is logical, but the rules of the game have created so much noise that it is now perfectly understandable that many people doubt the quality and sustainability of the game. To understand what the impact could be if we start tinkering with the game and remove or dismantle certain elements, a simple scenario planning exercise can bring clarity. The four scenarios in the next paragraph show the difference between changing the basic mechanisms of the game versus changing the rules of the game, while keeping the foundations of the triangle of democracy, the economy and the welfare state intact. In the first case, it is about dismantling the game, with populists loudly calling for the system to be dismantled, but without a viable alternative, without a substantiated vision and without developed policy. In the second case, it is about optimising the game, where we look at improving, adapting or replacing existing rules. Improving the rules is a very different approach, with a totally different – positive – energy than dismantling the game. I know, this sounds naïve and unrealistic, but be honest: what is more naïve? Believing that, in small, often frustrating steps, we can steer legislation and people's behaviour in a direction that gradually prepares us for a warmer world? Or believing that, if a populist abolishes climate change and all associated measures with a single stroke of the pen (with a childishly thick felt-tip marker – whatever happened to presidents' stylish fountain pens?), we will really be rid of the problem? Right: scenarios, then.

Four scenarios for tomorrow

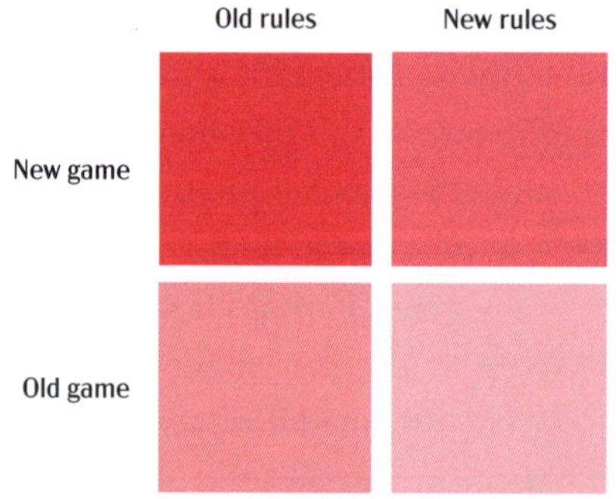

Figure 2: Four scenarios: new and old game, new and old rules

In scenario planning, you usually start from two variable forces that you cross with one another, giving you four alternative realities that you can describe. You can choose those forces yourself, based on what you think will shape the future most. In the discussion about the game and the rules of the game, I start from two assumptions that I make variable. The first is whether we leave the game unchanged or change it, and the second is whether the rules of the game remain as they are, or whether we change them. In other words: focusing on dismantling versus focusing on adaptation and improvement. That gives you four alternative scenarios, each of which is useful for understanding what is happening at the moment, or what could happen, depending on the choices we make as a society.

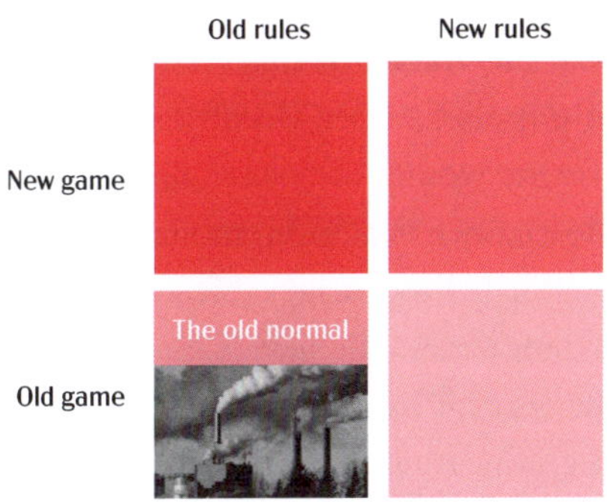

Figure 3: Scenario 1: Old game, Old rules.

In scenario 1, '**the old normal**', we assume that both the game and the rules of the game remain unchanged. In concrete terms, that means we muddle through in the current situation, where the malfunctioning rules of the game cause the game to erode further and further and lose strength. It becomes harder to conduct politics credibly, the economy comes under further pressure from geopolitical developments and Europe's inability to respond to them and shift our course towards transition thinking. Citizens become ever more frustrated and feel, in reality, that they are losing quality of life and that it is becoming increasingly difficult to continue providing the promised care and support. In this scenario, the call for change sounds even louder than it already does. The status quo becomes unsustainable and angry citizens demand change, with the lure of simple, powerful promises tempting people to opt after all for the strong populist leader who will deliver miracle cures for every problem and make Europe (or, more likely, the respective country in which this scenario plays out) great again.

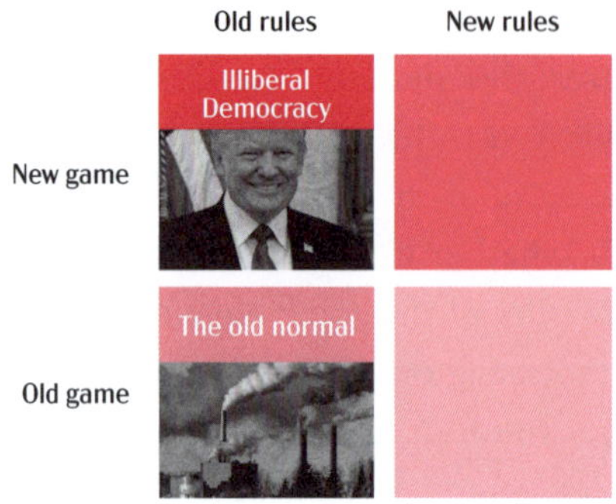

Figure 4: Scenario 2: New game, Old rules.

The conclusion here is that scenario 1 is not stable, which means that a shift towards scenario 2, **'the illiberal democracy'**, is almost inevitable. In this scenario, the call for change hands the keys of the country to a populist leader. Because it is so difficult to change the rules of the game – otherwise we would, of course, have done it long ago – and because our populist leader ideologically has a different view of the world, in which a pluralist, secular liberal order is not his top priority, it is logical that he intervenes in one pillar of the game: liberal democracy. The new leader has 'received a mandate from the people' to tackle all those corrupt institutions that have made the world such a 'very, very bad place': the media, education, free speech, an independent judiciary... they are expressions of the decadent, progressive world the populist leader opposes, and which, in any case, are directly the cause of all the country's problems. In this scenario, the leader wants to abolish, dismantle or bend them to his will as quickly as possible, whatever it takes to destroy the checks and balances, strengthen his own position and even entrench it for life.

Where this process has taken many years in countries such as Hungary, Russia and Turkey, we see how Trump II is trying to achieve it at an unprecedented pace – with the availability of Project 2025's 180-day playbook as his guide. If for no other reason, Trump will certainly go down in the history books for the dubious world record of 'dismantling democracy without a direct coup'. Our illiberal leader, moreover, changes little about the pillar of the free-market economy: even in an autocracy, companies can make a lot of money. The welfare state remains in place, even with high-quality medical solutions, but only for those who can afford it; broad solidarity and empathy are not among our illiberal leader's strongest character traits. What the leader in this scenario does not do is tackle the rules of the game; on the contrary, everything that has historically been wrong is entrenched. Relations with other countries become even more based on power and pressure, respect for the planet and the environment is no longer part of policy, and striving for greater justice is no longer necessary. Where this scenario ultimately ends up is hard to predict. Perhaps it can sustain itself for a long time through repression and the absence of democratic means to reverse the situation. The worse the pressure on the system becomes, for example through unliveable conditions as a result of ignoring climate investment, the greater the repression. There is always a chance that, from this scenario, a door will ultimately be opened to scenario 3.

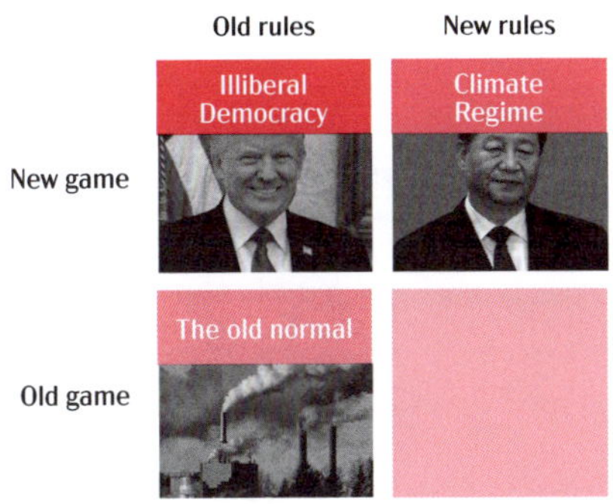

Figure 5 Scenario 3: New game, New rules.

Scenario 3 is what I call '**the sustainability dictatorship**'. In this scenario, the game has fundamentally different pillars: the political system is an explicit dictatorship, the economy has features of a free-market economy but is, in essence, state-directed, and the end goal is not necessarily a well-functioning, solidaristic welfare state, but rather a stable social platform that enables a large group of people to live together sustainably. The rules of the game also differ fundamentally from ours, leaving much less room to 'cheat' at the game: CEOs who commit fraud might well be sentenced to the rope. China is an example of this, but in the Middle East this also seems to be becoming the emerging form of government. The current planetary and demographic challenges are pushing these regimes, which plan decades ahead, in the direction of sustainable transition thinking: energy, food, climate measures... they are all necessary to guarantee a stable platform for their own society.

From this perspective, for example, China – although it is a dictatorship and although it is still a long way from having completed the whole transition – is already leading in many areas. If they continue this policy, they may well end up being the best adapted, in time, to the transitions the world faces. I think it is realistic that, in the coming decades, they will have the necessary climate solutions and will export them to other countries and regions: selling them for a lot of money to Western countries with wealth, trading them for geopolitical influence with countries in the Global South, and perhaps even helping the by-then ailing illiberal autocracies – which have buried their heads deep in the climate sand. If this scenario materialises, they will anchor their own sustainable platform and may become the most important force for good from a planetary and climate perspective. But, of course, it remains a dictatorship.

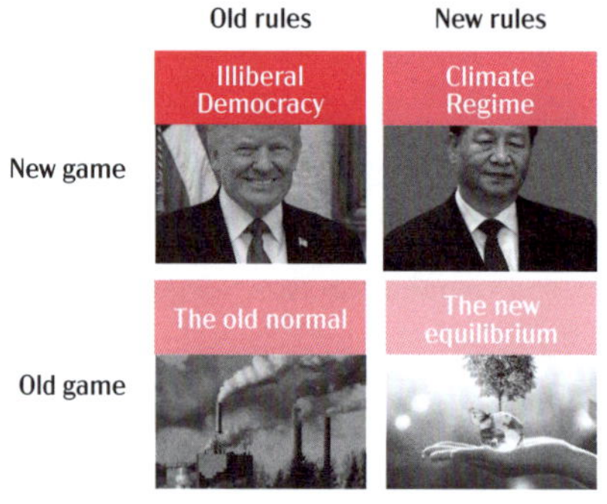

Figure 6 Scenario 4: Old game, New rules.

Is there then no possibility at all of a world that is transition-oriented and yet has no dictatorial or autocratic features? That brings me to scenario 4: '**the new equilibrium**'. Readers who know my previous book *The Future Formula*, or who have heard me speak, may remember that in it I describe the current turbulent period as 'the great imbalance' or: the great disequilibrium. It is a period of uncertainties that are putting the current status quo under pressure. In the meantime, two years after that book appeared, the term and the issue still stand: there has been no shortage of uncertainties lately. In the book, I describe 'the new equilibrium' as the pursuit of a world in which, by making the right choices, we once again create clarity and direction, and thus bring balance back to society. Its relevance is even greater than it was a few years ago. In this fourth scenario, I assume that we leave the game more or less unchanged. Unless we want a sustainability dictatorship like China's, our current model with its three pillars offers the greatest chance of success. There may be one adjustment to make: alongside preserving democracy and a strong free-market economy with growth and surplus, the ultimate end goal will have to focus more – alongside safeguarding a minimal welfare state – on maintaining a liveable world. So if we do not want to fundamentally change the game, we will have to do so through the rules of the game.

And that brings us back to the possibilities that Europe and a broader alliance of liberal democracies have to embrace the great transitions as levers for tomorrow, while preserving the pillars of the game. From our European tradition, we make no concessions on values and norms, even as we try to sharpen the rules of democracy once again. We invest in sustainability and transition sectors not from reactive panic, from charity, or from disaster response, but because they are the foundation of an economy in which we can still claim our role on the world stage. The end goal remains a liveable and respectful world, although concessions will probably be necessary to achieve this under the great climate pressure coming our way. That this must be done with new rules of the game is clear; that Europe can play a role in this, and what some of those new rules could look like, is the subject of the third part of this book.

So why is it still not self-evident which direction this has to go in? Why have you, as a reader, been chewing your way through different future scenarios over the past pages, one more depressing than the next? Well: because we are still far from certain that, from scenario 1 (the world today), we can move directly to scenario 4. The cause is the great dissatisfaction, frustration and unrest among the population. If we do not manage to remove that, then we are heading, country by country, towards populist victories which, if they can entrench themselves, will lead to illiberal democracies, possibly in time to outright autocracies, and ultimately to a kind of world order we really do not want. If such a future materialises, then I think we can bury any hope of a strong Europe, with respect for the democratic values and norms we have cherished for so long. In other words: if we want to evolve towards scenario 4, we must do everything we can to stop populism in its tracks. To do that, we need to understand how growing public dissatisfaction is the energy behind this movement, and also how we, as Europe, can intervene in it.

The populist magic trick

Populist leaders mislead their voters like only the very best magicians can, and just like Houdini or David Copperfield, they get away with it perfectly. The difference, perhaps, is that with professional illusionists we know they are performing a trick, whereas with populists we have to catch them out in the untruths they tell their voters with the same ease. They are dishonest about their own background and their fight against the establishment, allowing them to claim legitimacy with 'the people' to become the great, unconditional leader. They are not transparent about their intrinsic goals, and about how these are often fundamentally different from what they sell to their voters and thus use to get into power. They mean the opposite when they say that their main goal is to restore democracy and give us more freedom. They are masters of the illusion of 'Newspeak', the term George Orwell introduced in his novel *1984*, which, among other things, comes down to using extremely simple language to mean the opposite of what you say, or, in other words, lying.

Early in 2025, I was in Berlin with my family, highly recommended for a city trip if you are travelling with a wife who has a passion for history, a 15-year-old son who is interested in, well, the few things 15-year-olds are interested in, and a 19-year-old daughter with a strong moral compass. Berlin is a city where you can find a perfect mix for the whole family. For us, that was a combination of looking for hip neighbourhoods (for our daughter), taking an interest in studying physics at Humboldt University (for our son), and immersing ourselves in both the remnants of the Second World War and those of the GDR regime (for my partner and myself). One of the trips was to the 'Topography of Terror', an impressive museum on the remains of what were once the headquarters of the Gestapo and the SS.

No real lies?

The guide at the 'Topography of Terror', a man of around 50, explained how his grandparents had consciously voted for Hitler when the Nazi party emerged in the election of 5 March 1933. They did so because they were struggling economically, because jobs were promised, because their self-esteem as Germans was frustrated and wounded. Hitler promised to 'make Germany great again' and to give all Germans work and dignity back (provided they matched the racial and cultural profile).

What, according to the guide, his grandparents had not voted for was the horror of the world war that would follow. Although they presumably were not really pro-Jewish at the time, they had also not voted for the mass extermination the Nazis would later be guilty of. According to the man, Hitler came to power with simple promises about employment and the restoration of national pride, which resonated with most people, and then carried out an agenda that went much further than what had been promised during the election. Perhaps it was not an outright lie, but Hitler had simply forgotten to mention everything else he had planned for Germany and the rest of the world.

What is the link between Hitler's approach and today's populism? Today, voters are turning out in large numbers for populists and their parties, because they promise simple solutions to difficult problems and deep frustrations. For many people, today's world has become so complex and incomprehensible that it leads to insecurity, fears, frustration, discontent and, in time, simply pure anger. This is a theme I discuss at length in *The World is Round*. In it, I also show that perceptions of the state of the world are often far less positive than what the figures indicate. However contradictory it may feel, year after year the world is, objectively speaking, improving in many respects. There are a number of reasons why it does not come across that way and why people feel we are on the edge of the abyss, which pushes them into a negative spiral of emotions, leading them to seek refuge in populist solutions.

One important cause of this discrepancy is the difference between what is happening in the West and how the rest of the world is evolving. Over the past hundred years, we have travelled a path of growth and progress, which now seems to be coming to an end. The prevailing feeling is often that from here on it can only go downhill, especially in European regions where development is lagging behind. That is the case, for example, in eastern Germany, where support for the populist AfD is strongest. In many other parts of the world, development is only just beginning, which means they – both as societies and as individuals – have the prospect of growth and look to their future with a hopeful feeling.

Another reason is that figures are not always the best way to view and understand reality: they give an abstract representation of reality, based on averages, and often do not match the individual's lived experience. After the pandemic, the energy crisis and the resulting economic crisis, purchasing power in Europe has fallen only slightly, while the broad perception is that, over those five years, we have declined sharply. If you zoom in on the figures, you see major differences between countries and population groups. While Belgium has not gone backwards and Spain is even rising slightly, there is a noticeable fall in purchasing power in the Baltic states. Apparently, we are unable to see, behind the figures, the people who really are at risk of being left behind, and who therefore align themselves with populists who claim they do hear them and their problems. And if media and social media further magnify the perceived problems, it is hardly surprising that society polarises even more, becoming an ideal breeding ground for harvesting negative feelings for political gain.

I will go a little deeper into this theme next, but I would gladly refer interested readers to both *The World is Round* and the work of other authors who lay bare the mechanisms behind how we look at the world, and why this is not always entirely rational or accurate. For the purposes of this argument, however, one thing is essential: for the populist and his magic tricks, truth and facts are subordinate to people's emotions and perceptions. They have every interest in making those perceptions even more negative, because it is this negative energy that fuels their political rise. For years, academic, political and economic elites (a group I count myself among) failed to recognise this sentiment in our society, marginalised it, and rationalised it away. With this arrogant and out-of-touch behaviour, they have driven voters en masse into the arms of populists.

What frightens people?

If you look at the world objectively, you see a whole series of changes and transformations on the horizon. A term I use for this is the metastorm, the perfect storm of a whole series of perfect storms, all happening at once and influencing and reinforcing one another. Here is a brief, and still incomplete, list. Climate change is a global challenge with wide-ranging ecological, economic and social impact. The energy transition seems an impossible challenge and is driving up costs for everyone in our society. The rise of artificial intelligence and automation raises questions about the future of work and the nature of economic added value. Education seems to be failing, especially since the pandemic, and it is unclear how we prepare our young people for the world of tomorrow. There is major uncertainty about incomes, purchasing power and pensions in the long term. In healthcare, there is growing doubt about affordability and quality, partly in the light of ageing. Mobility problems, such as congestion and reduced accessibility, are only getting worse, and the transition to sustainable mobility presents us with challenges.

Population growth leads to concerns about liveability and ecological carrying capacity. Paradoxically, there is also fear of population decline and its negative consequences for the affordability of our prosperity. Urbanisation and pressure on social cohesion put models of society under strain. Immigration seems increasingly uncontrolled, and future global crises foreshadow even larger flows of displaced people that our society will have to accommodate, or not. The concentration of digital power in a small number of technology companies is redefining economic and social relationships, and recently we have also become concerned about the political influence that can be exerted via technology. Wars and geopolitical developments create fear and further call Europe's position in the world into question. Added to that are the extra costs of defence, which may weigh negatively on other spending.

Populism and radicalisation manifest worldwide in political and social fragmentation (and are ironically often both a cause and a consequence of growing unrest among people). And because of the crisis in the Middle East, we should not be surprised if we soon see another wave of terror attacks, close to home.

Paradoxically, all these challenges do not seem to penetrate the lived reality of most people. They generally remain the domain of specialists who, in research, policy and regulation, try to predict and manage these crises. They do so from within their own expertise bubble, assuming that everyone is equally aware of the urgency of each of these challenges. Which, of course, is not the case: in their day-to-day reality, most citizens focus on only a few of these themes, based on their own experience; the rest feels very remote. What affects people deeply and personally is a simple mix of mainly economic and cultural concerns.

Because of economic insecurity, many see themselves as 'losers of globalisation', because their jobs have disappeared to low-wage countries, their wages have stagnated or declined, and inequality only seems to be increasing. The prospect of rising costs for defence and climate, and how that will weigh on social security and therefore on their own incomes, makes many doubt their financial outlook. The fact that, across Europe, the pension age is being raised and updated on the basis of demographic developments makes this very tangible. The second dominant force is cultural unrest: there is fear of (uncontrolled) immigration, changing values, and the feeling that local culture and identity are being diluted. People feel their familiar world is disappearing and being replaced by neighbours, languages, clothing, music and food they no longer understand, literally and figuratively. They blame politicians for failing to take sufficient account of the limited capacity of existing structures, systems and places to absorb these changes.

Of course, there is an awareness that climate change is a major challenge, but in the minds of many dissatisfied people its impact, and the timeframe in which it will manifest, is still far too abstract to really take into account at this point. What they do feel, by contrast, are all the obligations, bans and changes associated with climate and sustainability. Not everyone is so deeply convinced of the seriousness of the climate impact that they are willing to see the personal sacrifices (such as investing in heat pumps and solar panels, using less energy, driving electric) as an investment in the future of their children, rather than as yet another pesty measure that curtails their personal freedom. The financial consequences are not insignificant either: the difference between worrying about the end of the century and worrying about the end of the month is not a made-up distinction. For years, when it comes to ESG policy, people have pointed to the inherent conflict between Environmental (E) and Social (S). The more the climate transition costs us, the greater the chance that it will have a negative social impact, with large groups of people no longer able to keep up with what needs to happen simply because they cannot afford it. Here too, people feel alienated from an issue over which they seem to have little or no control. Once again, politics has failed lamentably to pick up on this sentiment, alienating people from policy and leaving them at risk of disengaging completely from this crucial theme.

All of this leads to distrust of a (political) elite that, in their eyes, is out of touch and does not understand the day-to-day reality in which the majority live. On the one hand, this elite is, according to the dissatisfied, the cause of negative developments in the economy and globalisation. On the other, they accuse this elite of being insensitive to the challenges and constraints many ordinary people face when it comes to the many efforts we will have to make. In the most extreme cases, the progressive globalised elite is even accused of inventing the climate crisis in order to exert even more control. In short: a manipulative, selfish little club of people from politics, the media, academia, business and, of course, the European and international institutions, who – whether or not according to some pre-determined occult masterplan – are concerned only with their own objectives, at the expense of the ordinary man or woman in the street. At the same time, they accuse politics of a lack of decisiveness, which, paradoxically, contradicts the organisational talent that would be needed if this really were an orchestrated, globalised operation.

This mix of perceived powerlessness, financial challenges, cultural change and simmering loss of status leads to an explosive cocktail of insecurity, fear, frustration, anger and a growing rejection of the world they live in. Populists like Trump understand this perfectly and offer a seductive way out. However, one major problem remains: they lie to the voters who place their hope in them.

The populist lie

In their election campaigns, populists offer simple solutions that seemingly correspond directly to voters' concerns. With Euroscepticism and anti-elite rhetoric, they try to pin responsibility for all problems on a simple enemy: it is the deep state, the EU bureaucracy, the unelected and the traditional establishment that are deliberately causing both economic decline and cultural confusion through their globalisation agenda. Through promises to clean out the political stables, drain the elite's swamp, bring back 'honest work like it used to be', increase purchasing power, deport immigrants, build walls, close borders and similar actions, they play into citizens' existing worries and frustrations. In their simple logic, they promise that all these actions will lead to major savings, from which the ordinary citizen will ultimately benefit financially.

Once they are elected, we see the emphasis of policy shift towards priorities that were not explicitly raised during the election, and for which our new populist leader is not actually mandated by his voters. Usually, there is still a strong focus on at least one campaign promise, a powerful symbolic dossier, and that is cracking down on immigration. The fact that, in most countries, even in the US, such measures run up against legal frameworks and the constitution is not really a problem. In the US, Trump ignores objections or uses the Supreme Court as an instrument of his policy. In other countries, overly radical measures are struck down by the courts, which then becomes extra grist to the mill for our populist leaders, because they can use it to 'prove' that the deep state and the establishment are preventing them from delivering on their promises to voters. The fact that the legal objection is usually not about the substance of the action (restricting immigration) but about the explicitly undemocratic nature of how it is carried out is, of course, not mentioned.

The real problem arises when our populist leaders then begin to implement a series of measures that run directly counter to the interests of their own voters, of the people they promised to represent. The first thing that usually falls victim in policy is the democratic institutions themselves. Once they are in power, a targeted dismantling begins of the oversight mechanisms designed precisely to prevent one person from accumulating too much power. The rule of law is hollowed out, loyalists are installed in key positions, independent institutions are restructured or sidelined, and the distinction between the legislative, executive and judicial branches becomes blurred. In parallel, the press is declared the enemy: critical journalism is dismissed as 'fake news', journalists are threatened with lawsuits, media outlets are blackmailed or bought up, and increased control over public broadcasters creates a murky mix of state propaganda and disinformation meant to mould public opinion in the desired direction. What remains is a democracy in name, but no longer in operation.

At least as worrying is how these leaders deliberately tear apart the social fabric itself. Populists lean into simple 'us versus them' thinking: the elite versus the people, the historic population versus newcomers, 'ordinary people' versus the progressive elite. This divide is not only played out verbally, but is also extended into policy through a conservative agenda that seeks to reassert moral control over themes such as education, gender and the family. Minorities come under increasing pressure, as does the LGBTQ+ community, and the space for opposition visibly shrinks. Protest actions are suppressed with ever greater violence. Meanwhile, economic measures are taken that benefit only a small top layer: higher import tariffs and trade wars may serve nationalist sentiment, but they mainly hit the consumer. Fiscal advantages, meanwhile, remain strikingly intact for the wealthy. Of the promises to improve the financial position of ordinary voters, little usually remains. A good example is the big beautiful bill, the major law Trump pushed through the US Congress in early June 2025. A quick calculation shows that ordinary Americans will be almost 100 billion dollars poorer over the next four years (around 1,600 dollars per family per year), while the wealthy elite – call it the establishment, if you like – benefits from enormous tax cuts totalling around 600 billion dollars.

For the substantiation of the agenda of the populist leader in power, see part 1. He wants to become the big boss, with near-untouchable, royal power; to make the world more conservative, with a simple social and cultural order from the old days. For the Trump administration, that means a right-wing religious worldview from the 1950s and earlier.

To know whether you, as a voter, are being lied to and misled by a populist party, you can ask yourself a number of questions. Do you want:

- to go back to a world in which women (you, your partner, your daughter) are subordinate to men and have fewer or no opportunities in education or work;
- to return to a family model in which five children or more is the norm and, of course, the woman (you?) stays at home;
- freedom of speech, association or protest to be curtailed;
- your sexual and relationship choices to be labelled normal or abnormal by the state, and to run the risk of prosecution if you fall outside the norm;
- to go back to a world in which contraception is restricted or banned and doctors who help with (life-saving) terminations of pregnancy are prosecuted for murder;
- to live in a world in which climate change is denied and no longer invested in;
- religious issues to dominate secular and social debates;
- a leader who can remain in power for life because the democratic checks and balances are hollowed out?

If *your* answer to several of these questions is 'yes', then by all means, vote for the populist. But even if you are absolutely convinced that immigration should be restricted, that inequality is too great and that the rich should pay their share, that the establishment shows no understanding of your views, concerns and needs, even if you think our current politicians are making a mess of it, do you still think populism is the right choice? Are you then prepared to accept the rest of the agenda, or does that go too far for you? Do you feel you are being lied to because, under the guise of a simple three-point programme (less migration, more money, the people against the elite), someone is elected who in fact has much further-reaching intentions? And above all: do you think that, with one or more of the changes described above, you are helping to build a strong Europe that is oriented towards progress?

The people's struggle against the establishment? Really?

'The establishment' is a diffuse, influential upper layer of society that, through a tangle of institutions, interests and networks, forms the core of power. It includes figures who help shape the rules of the world through governments, parliaments and courts, but also businesses, financial institutions and international organisations. Culturally, the establishment is linked to the mainstream media, universities and other institutions that steer public debate. This is simply an acknowledgement of an informal layer that exists in every regime in the world: from the US to Iran, from Europe to Russia, from Africa to North Korea. Whether that establishment is therefore automatically the source of all evil is another question, but it is an easy enemy. The biggest lie of populist leaders is the claim that they represent the people in their revolt against this elite, against the establishment. It is incomprehensible that people can believe such a thing when it is being said by populists who so clearly form part of the elite themselves. An analysis of some of the most visible representatives of populism yields interesting insights. With one exception (I am saving that one to keep up the suspense until the end), they are all themselves part of the establishment, of the system they hold up to their voters as corrupt and in need of fighting.

The populist who presents himself as the voice of the people is rarely the 'ordinary people' he claims to represent. On the contrary, almost all well-known populist leaders grew up in comfortable, often privileged environments, and spent years building careers within the political, academic or media establishment before rebranding themselves as anti-establishment. These leaders now position themselves as outsiders, but have been part of the corridors of power for decades. Their connections to elites are extensive and deeply rooted. And yet they still manage to sell themselves credibly as representatives of ordinary people taking on a corrupt upper layer. The fact that this narrative resonates with millions of voters says a great deal about the crisis in political communication, and about the average citizen's limited ability to tell the difference.

Elite paradox in populism

- **Donald Trump** was born into a fabulously wealthy real-estate family, was educated at the prestigious Wharton School of the University of Pennsylvania (albeit with questionable results), and inherited a multi-million-dollar empire. His image was not forged in the streets of America's middle class, let alone among the pick-up-driving workers now wearing MAGA caps in their millions. He shone as an elite star on reality TV stages, such as the popular programme ***The Apprentice***. And, by the way, you still cannot do him a greater favour than inviting him to a truly bling-bling castle owned by genuine royalty. That the average American can see Trump as 'one of us' is about as hard to understand as why a growing group of people believe the world is flat, was created 6,000 years ago by a god who gave up after six days, and saddled the planet with humanity.
- **Viktor Orbán**, once a student activist with liberal convictions, grew into a central figure of the Hungarian establishment thanks to a scholarship that allowed him to study politics briefly in Oxford. He returned to take an active part in Hungary's democratisation process and played an important role in the transition talks after the communist regime. A product of international networks himself, he now rails against foreign and European interference.
- **Alice Weidel**, leader of Germany's AfD, followed a decidedly elite path: graduating with great distinction in business economics, and working at financial institutions such as Goldman Sachs, the Bank of China and Allianz Global Investors. She speaks decent Chinese, is active in the tech world, and has a network that extends far into both the academic and financial elite.
- **Marine Le Pen**, leader of the Rassemblement National in France, is a lawyer and inherited a political dynasty from her father Jean-Marie Le Pen, which positioned her within the French establishment from an early age, regardless of her rhetoric. She is linked to the conservative Catholic billionaire Vincent Bolloré, who has bought up a large part of the French

media in recent years. His channel CNews has helped normalise the discourse of Le Pen and her party. The growth of the Rassemblement National in parliament is attributed in part to this media support.

- **Thierry Baudet**, founder of the Dutch party Forum voor Democratie, earned his PhD at Leiden University, after which he taught there for years.
- **Javier Milei**, the Argentinian president, though flamboyant and provocative, was a professor of economics and part of the intellectual elite he now constantly attacks.
- **Jair Bolsonaro**, the former president of Brazil, spent almost twenty years in the military and sat in Brazilian politics for 35 years, working his way up from municipal councillor in Rio de Janeiro to president. In doing so, he has always maintained his ties with the military establishment.
- **Geert Wilders**, founder of the Partij Voor Vrijheid, the man who ensured that the Netherlands had a populist government for eleven months, likes to present himself as a thorn in the side of the political system, even though he served faithfully within the Volkspartij voor Vrijheid en Democratie's party structures for sixteen years before founding his own party.

The only populist leader who can genuinely lay claim to a connection with the people she claims to represent is Giorgia Meloni. She was born in a working-class neighbourhood in Rome, grew up without a father, and worked as a waitress and barmaid. This is not a carefully constructed image, but her reality. Her political career began at a young age, in the ranks of a party with neo-fascist roots. Without a degree, she worked her way up through its youth organisations, became a minister at 31, and is now Italy's first female prime minister. Regardless of how you view her ideologically, she is the only person on this list with enough authenticity to be called a credible representative of the people.

Did they all loathe the establishment that once made them great so much that they turned against it, leading to their supposed struggle against the elite? A more logical explanation is that this artificial enemy image resonates with dissatisfied voters, and that hostility towards the establishment gives them the legitimacy they need to lead 'the people' in an impending epic struggle against the oppressors. If you know anything about history, this should not surprise you. The parallels with what happened during the French and Russian revolutions are strong. Both show how revolutionary movements that invoke the voice of the people often, in reality, merely serve to bring a new elite to power. In France, it was the sans-culottes who took to the streets, stormed the Bastille and shook the aristocracy, but it was the well-to-do bourgeoisie who ultimately reaped the rewards and firmly entrenched themselves in the new centre of power. In Russia, the February Revolution began as a broadly supported popular uprising, but the October Revolution was soon hijacked by the Bolsheviks, an elite group of highly educated intellectuals who seized power and then consolidated it into a totalitarian system under Stalin. In both cases, the people were first mobilised, then ignored, and finally oppressed. Revolutionary rhetoric about equality, freedom and people's power essentially masked a shift of power within the upper layer of society, within the establishment. History repeats itself.

The power of polarisation

In earlier books, I reflected on growing social polarisation and asked myself what the underlying dynamic was. Why do political actors drive the contrast between people, ideas and parties so sharply, when most people – despite their ideological differences – still think fairly similarly when it comes to the major challenges in the world. Watching populist leaders at work has made it clear why this is so: for them, polarisation is a necessary instrument for creating political momentum, seizing power, and being able to hold on to it. Although all political parties are guilty of this, it is primarily populist movements that use a narrative in which the people are placed in direct opposition to a supposed enemy. This image is rarely, if ever, genuinely developed ideologically, but is above all psychologically and emotionally charged, fuelled by slogan-like messages on social media which, through the internet's echo chambers, do their incendiary work. The aim of this strategy is not to formulate an alternative to the opponent's position, but purely to create an enemy image that is recognisable and mobilising. Reaching an effective solution, a compromise or a workable approach is of secondary importance. What matters is creating a combative dynamic, without thinking too deeply. In this us-versus-them story, nuance disappears and complexity is traded for simplicity. That makes it attractive to the media, susceptible to viral spread, and useful in election campaigns.

The logic of polarisation rules out any form of consensus or compromise. It strengthens group cohesion within one's own base by framing opposition not as an alternative, but as a threat. The language hardens: opponents are not wrong, but destructive; they do not merely have a different opinion, but are fundamentally threatening to our opinion. This creates a political environment in which debate is replaced by conflict and dialogue is seen as betrayal. Polarisation splits society in two, but with a clear purpose. Instead of solutions, struggle takes centre stage. That makes it an effective and dangerous mechanism in the architecture of power. It also makes it clear why this is so important for populist currents. If their ultimate goal really is to push through an ideological agenda that must lead to a post-liberal society with autocratic characteristics (see part 1), then there is no room for a genuine democracy or for freedom of expression, in which thesis and antithesis lead to synthesis. There is only room for one dominant vision and dominant worldview, no social compromise: the other side must submit to the dominant current or is an enemy that must be fought. If you can get citizens to buy into this enemy image, it becomes much easier to create and preserve that order. Perhaps I am putting it too starkly here, and I am convinced that whenever our own ministers are once again virtually rolling around the political floor fighting, their aim is not to install an autocracy. Yet they too resort to this toxic method, paving the way for forces that do seek a more radical agenda. Through their own polarising behaviour, through their own extreme statements, they have normalised it, so that it hardly even stands out when someone with bad intentions goes one step further – which is exactly what we are now seeing happen in the US.

The citizen is less polarised than politics are

When it comes to so-called polarisation among the electorate, we once again see the manipulation of voters: the way political leaders frame the contrasts and the way voters themselves look at the challenges they face often do not match. In political discourse, the contrast is exaggerated to such an extent, and the language of hostility is now used so explicitly, that a key insight is lost: on most social issues, progressive and conservative citizens share a fairly similar position. That insight matters, because it shows how citizens' views often run counter to the polarised image projected in the media and political debate. Research shows that citizens – regardless of their ideological preference – share many beliefs about what is essential for a well-functioning society. In healthcare, there is broad support for accessible, high-quality care; voters favour measures that reduce medical errors, shorten waiting times and safeguard affordability. The same applies to education: the majority want equal opportunities, strong learning outcomes, and good preparation for the labour market. Education is unanimously seen as a public priority.

On pensions too, the majority want a fair, future-proof system that provides security without becoming unaffordable. Socioeconomically, there is far more consensus than is often assumed. A large majority believe work should pay and that the middle class must not be allowed to become poorer. There is broad support for lower taxes on labour, higher net wages for low and middle incomes, and measures that protect purchasing power. Housing is another theme where public sentiment converges: young people and lower incomes are finding it increasingly difficult to access affordable, high-quality homes. Initiatives to build more housing, encourage renovations and support first-time buyers are broadly supported. Even on climate, despite differences in approach, there is shared recognition that action is needed to protect the living environment for future generations. The extreme contrasts suggested by political actors, and sharpened by populists, are often absent among citizens themselves.

Of course, there are themes on which left and right differ strongly: immigration, integration and identity politics are undoubtedly subjects that can still spark very heated debates, and where ideological backgrounds can make it very difficult to arrive at a shared vision. And when it comes to deciding how we should achieve something in the future, the answers will differ sharply depending on whether you take a progressive or a conservative view. Yes, we all want a liveable planet for our children, high-quality education, affordable healthcare, strong defence, and so on. The way we want to shape that can differ quite a bit between left and right, but our democratic models are built precisely to find compromises. The amplification of the enemy image through extreme polarisation makes compromises de facto impossible and, as a result, paralyses our democracy. That is unlikely to be a coincidence.

We need support to steer Europe into the future, and that can only happen if we regain the trust of citizens and businesses. That is how we prevent their frustrations and fears from pushing them into the arms of populists as well, further weakening Europe as a result. In the next chapter, I discuss a few possible solutions we can embrace in policy, governance and the economy to achieve this. We will have to walk a new path, a middle way that allows us to tackle real and perceived problems one by one. Before we get to that, however, I want to launch one additional challenge that could, of all things, tip everything even further: AI.

AI, robots, the economic singularity and the end of democracy

I have already referred to lessons we can learn from history, and in particular from what happened in Germany in the 1930s. A few figures that absolutely deserve our attention show the link between the rise of the NSDAP (the Nazi party) and growing unemployment in Germany. At the Reichstag election of May 1928, unemployment in Germany was around 8 percent. The NSDAP then received 2.6 percent of the vote. By the elections of March 1933, decisive for Hitler, unemployment had shot up to around 30 percent of the population, with a large share of the jobs that existed at the time also under threat. The Nazis achieved their historic victory with 43.9 percent of the vote, which brought them definitively to power. Although there were other factors too, such as the explicit intimidation campaigns carried out at the time by Hitler's informal shock troops, the link between economic insecurity and the success of populism is clear, and we can see how, in less than five years, voting behaviour underwent a total shift.

What is the parallel with today? In Belgium, unemployment is currently just above 6 percent; in the Netherlands it is even slightly lower than 4 percent. Concretely, that means many of the economic concerns our anxious and dissatisfied citizens have cannot be directly attributed to an acute problem, but instead anticipate a difficult economic landscape in the future. What if there is a real chance that unemployment is coming, and even in the relatively short term? I give many keynotes on AI, and this is almost always the most difficult debate, with absolute supporters and opponents: will AI cost jobs, or will new jobs always emerge – just as in earlier technological revolutions – meaning the impact on the labour market, and therefore on society, will be manageable? I myself am no longer so hopeful. I have more than thirty years of experience with digital developments and innovations. I lived through the rise of the internet – and helped build it (I was co-founder of the first web agency in Belgium in 1994) – and I have seen how innovation after innovation has expanded and evolved the range of digital services. From the first websites, mobile sites (with WAP and WML), virtual worlds with Second Life, social networks (which we built ourselves, because Facebook did not yet exist), apps, blockchain and crypto, the Metaverse and now AI, I have seen it all go by, and have often watched it evolve from hype to disappointment to pragmatic realism.

Based on that experience, I dare to state one thing with certainty: the speed at which generative AI such as ChatGPT has evolved from a fun toy into an unimaginably powerful tool is something I have never experienced before in my career. The exponential increase in capabilities, and the direct, straightforward applicability in the workplace, make this a radical game-changer for the labour market. Until a few months ago, this was often mainly a feeling; lately, we are also seeing in the figures that AI is already having an impact on employment.

In the first six months of 2025 alone, just under 80,000 jobs were lost worldwide because of AI. Large companies such as Microsoft, Procter & Gamble, IBM, Meta and Amazon have laid off thousands of employees, often explicitly linked to the implementation of AI. Microsoft cut 9,000 jobs – around 4 percent of its workforce of 221,000 people. Satya Nadella, the CEO, stated that AI now generates up to 30 percent of their software code. Procter & Gamble announced the lay-off of 7,000 knowledge workers as a result of 'digital integration and AI-enhanced workflows'. Some companies go a step further by fundamentally reorienting themselves around the use of AI. Duolingo and Shopify have introduced an 'AI-first' strategy: no one is hired unless it is proven that the task cannot be carried out by AI. Duolingo CEO Luis von Ahn stated that the company will gradually outsource all tasks that can be performed by AI to algorithms. Shopify requires its managers, through an internal 'AI-before-hiring' rule, to demonstrate that a task cannot be automated before requesting additional staff. At both companies, considering AI is no longer an extra form of support, but has become a primary condition before any actual recruitment is allowed to proceed.

The power and impact of generative AI is not limited to knowledge work alone. By embedding AI in robots, they become more versatile than the traditional robots we have been seeing for decades. From 2025 onwards, smart robots will increasingly appear on the shop floor, in hospitality, care centres and, of course, factories. Some have a human form, others look like dogs or other animals on legs. Either way, they are already able to take over a portion of physical work: through AI they have learned to observe and understand the world, meaning they no longer need to be programmed separately for every individual action. Once a robot, via AI, knows what a door is and how to open it, it can open any door. If a robot understands what dirty glasses are in a restaurant, it can identify all glasses as dirty and treat them accordingly. Amazon's evolution in this area is telling. The company now has more than one million robots in its warehouses, almost matching its 1.1 million human warehouse workers. Amazon's newest generation is the Vulcan robot, equipped with force-feedback sensors that give it a form of touch. Vulcan can handle 75 percent of the product range, take over physically demanding tasks, and operate for up to twenty hours a day without interruption. Although Amazon formally stresses that these robots 'support' employees and that the company offers reskilling programmes, the question of what role low-skilled labour will still have in this model is becoming ever more pressing. Further research and market forecasts support this trend. According to the World Economic Forum (2023), 41 percent of employers worldwide expect to reduce their workforce as a result of AI and automation. Goldman Sachs estimates the number of full-time jobs at risk at 300 million, which amounts to around 9.1 percent of the global labour market. In the US alone, 47 percent of workers could be affected in time, while McKinsey states that in developed economies up to 60 percent of jobs are wholly or partially automatable with current technologies. Of course, all these figures are nonsense: there is no way, at this point, to predict what will happen. Every day brings new developments, and the unpredictability of Trump's economic policy and regulation around AI means it could go in any direction. Unfortunately, that is of little relevance: whether those forecasts are accurate or not, the impact is already here, and may be greater than we, as a society, can absorb in the short term.

These figures also refer to millions of real people across a wide range of knowledge professions. These people thought they were immune to major waves of automation, and a good degree was a guarantee of a durable job. The irony is that it is precisely these profiles – online marketers, programmers, translators, lawyers and accountants – that are now being threatened first by AI. The parallels between the current AI revolution and deindustrialisation in the late 20th century are becoming increasingly clear. In the US, the number of industrial jobs fell by 5 million between 1999 and 2009 – from 17 million to 12 million – leading to the well-known social disruption in industrial regions, which formed the electoral base for the growth of populism and the rise of the MAGA movement. What if pressure on knowledge workers increases enormously in the coming years because, thanks to AI, they go through a similar trajectory to what happened to factory workers back then? If these jobs disappear, we risk a fundamental erosion of the middle class – socially, economically and psychologically. Current social tensions will spread to those who, until recently, thought they were protected and were quite content with their role in society.

I can already hear the techno-optimists saying it will all be fine, that maybe 'a bit of unemployment' will be added and that it will resolve itself in time. Even if 'that bit of unemployment' is limited to, say, 20 percent, the social and political implications are potentially enormous. If I think again of how, in Germany, in barely five years, unemployment shot up from 8 to 30 percent and with it the Nazi party grew from 2.6 to 43.9 percent, then even 20 percent extra unemployment makes me very worried. What if lawyers, marketers and translators soon become the new 'losers of globalisation', suddenly living with uncertainty, seeing their purpose in life disappear and having to reinvent themselves? How great is the chance that they too will be tempted to follow the next populist Pied Piper of Hamelin, on the road to the abyss of autocracy? It should be clear that this is a challenge we cannot afford to underestimate in the coming years.

We will have to learn to look, in a very intelligent and controlled way, at how we in Europe deal with these challenges. The good news is that if we handle this smartly, and get people and machines to work together in the right way, we may also find a lever to raise productivity in Europe – and that may help us answer questions related to ageing and the affordability of our welfare state. Unfortunately, however, the solution will not present itself automatically; we will have to embed it structurally in our master plan for the Europe of the future. I go into this in more depth in part 3.

10. In search of solutions to restore trust

The pendulum swings back

If we want to solve problems, we must first dare to acknowledge them, even if that means confronting uncomfortable truths. I have already partly done this for the right-hand side of the political spectrum, when I argued that – alongside the still democratic shift to the right – there are also organisations active behind the scenes that are pushing a conservative agenda and may be undermining our liberal democracy. The left-hand side of our society also has blood on its hands and is partly responsible for the 'crisis of political credibility' we now find ourselves in. How has Europe's progressive development contributed to this sense of unrest, dissatisfaction, frustration and anger, leaving more and more citizens uprooted and distrustful, and causing them, step by step, to disengage from traditional structures? We know that this makes them easy prey for populist movements whose aim is to dismantle Europe rather than build it. A strong Europe can only be realised if we have a plan that is broadly supported by European citizens. It is therefore crucial to regain trust, so that we can mobilise people. The first condition is that we finally give their concerns a place and actually address them – an area in which the progressive side falls short.

Since the 1950s, the pendulum of European development has swung towards a progressive, pluralist, free and secular Europe. In that period, we undeniably discovered the power of coming of age, emancipation, striving for equal opportunities and personal freedom, mobility, access to education, high-quality housing, strong economic development, scientific and medical breakthroughs, and so on. We can, without doubt, call this the positive effect of a progressive wind that blew through Europe and a number of other countries. Despite various obstacles, such as the Cold War and economic crises, Europe experienced strong growth. Europe's GDP has grown, in relative terms, by 500 percent compared with 1950, and the purchasing power of the average European by 370 percent. All in all, then, we are not doing so badly. In the first decades of these developments, this went mainly hand in hand with American cultural influences. I remember how, as young teenagers, we paraded around the playground in leather jackets, following the example of Fonzie in *Happy Days*; our parents rolled their eyes (or gave us a clip round the ear) because we suddenly thought everything was 'cool' (for anyone who is now drawing a blank: check YouTube). It is only in recent decades that, through immigration and the further globalisation of the world, more and more elements from other, non-Western cultures have been introduced.

'Cool' has long since been replaced in youth slang by words like 'lit', 'fire', 'dope', 'sick', or 'slaps' (there's no better language course than teenagers listening to rap in their own language). You can view these influences, just like those in the sixties, as cultural enrichment, but they also create concern and a sense of alienation among part of the population (as the Americanisation of our language and culture did too). For a while now, we have seen the pendulum begin to slow down and seem to come to a standstill: belief in hopeful growth is ebbing away for more and more Europeans. More than with economic worries, this has to do with the diverse and complex social challenges of the metastorm. It creates a hazy cloud of anxiety in which high-impact issues like climate change often remain abstract for most citizens, while the challenges of multicultural coexistence and identity assume larger proportions. On top of that, our poor collective memory also plays a role: nobody remembers the time before our current prosperity anymore, so it is hard to put what we have into perspective and appreciate its value. People can no longer imagine what it is like to live in poverty or without freedom and rights, and that strips the threat of hollowing out our democracy of much of its force.

The most important cause, for me, is our mistaken estimate of people's capacity to adapt: as progressive drivers of improvement, acceleration and change, we have completely underestimated how much our society can absorb. Increasingly, many people feel that change is happening too fast, especially around symbolic dossiers: fear of the consequences of immigration, distrust of climate measures experienced as 'patronising' and imposed by an abstract Europe, uncertainty about work, wages and pensions. Often this unrest is disproportionate, and even contradicts the available figures and data, but that is irrelevant, because perception creates reality. Which means that the only figures that do matter are election results or voting intentions, as a consequence of this discontent. People's belief in the pendulum of progress really came to a standstill because of a double movement from the progressive side. On the one hand, progressive political, academic and cultural elites (a group I count myself among) have paid far too little attention to public sentiment, which betrays a problematic arrogance. That became painfully clear in the way some progressive American presidential candidates publicly dismissed their right-wing opponents.

Hillary Clinton made the fatal mistake in 2016 of describing a significant share of Trump voters as 'a basket of deplorables' – a remark that not only came across as arrogant, but also gave the impression that their concerns were fundamentally unworthy of being taken seriously. Barack Obama made a similar error in 2008, when he spoke about Americans who 'cling to their guns or religion' as an explanation for their frustration, which many interpreted as a condescending view of their identity and values. More recently still, in 2024, Joe Biden called Trump's supporters 'garbage' – literally rubbish. Fortunately, our European progressive politicians have shown a bit more restraint in rhetorical terms, but beneath the surface we see the same thing happening. Either citizens' unrest and concerns are swept aside with all sorts of abstract arguments, or there is no attention to them at all and they are barely taken into account in policy or research. The fact that there is a stronger progressive bias in the media and the academic world (which, by the way, is logical for 'truth-seeking' institutions) has not improved matters. So I think it is fair to say that at least part of the (progressive) elite failed to pick up the signals and concerns coming from part of the population. With all the consequences that entails.

Acting as an accelerant, a more radical part of the progressive spectrum has pushed the accelerator hard in recent years: even faster social change, improvements in their eyes. Most sensible Europeans are absolutely in favour of the principles of recognising and eliminating exclusion, inequality and (historical) injustice, and of general respect between people. Unfortunately, in recent years the public debate around this current has increasingly been marked by excesses from the more radical wing of the woke movement. The focus has shifted from trying to achieve structural emancipation to language policing (those pronouns), public condemnation (outside our legal system), and cancel culture when opinions diverge. Once again my teenage children and their friends have taught me a great deal about the dynamics and tensions that arise from this – I still have bruises from some well-intentioned remarks. Even theatre-makers, comedians, musicians and actors – people you would hardly suspect of strong conservative reflexes – feel constrained and censored. In my own circle of friends I know people who felt their academic freedom came under pressure, not because of university rules, but because of tense relationships within their own department. Moral purity and identity politics have come to carry more weight than open dialogue or nuance, to the point that even well-intentioned positions are framed as problematic.

In my view, this is the final straw that has made the bucket overflow for many citizens. Most people are open towards the LGBTQ+ movement, support same-sex marriage, and understand perfectly well that, historically, we have not always had a spotless record when it comes to our colonial past. Many citizens struggle to understand the woke movement's more radical criticism, such as not embracing new linguistic concepts quickly enough, or attacks on cultural elements that may have questionable roots historically but are so embedded in our society that they no longer carry racist connotations. It has even made all of this start to work counterproductively for the broader idea of emancipation among citizens who would normally be neutral on the subject. As a result, the woke movement (in practice mostly loud, but with limited impact) has, ironically, become a powerful weapon in the hands of populists to further stoke unrest among voters who are not necessarily extremely conservative or racist, but for whom the many examples of cancel culture, debates about Sinterklaas, or exclusively vegan food at school, go a step too far.

So the pendulum has not only come to a standstill, but has even begun to swing in the opposite direction. Progressive 'Enlightenment ideas' about emancipation, coming of age, progress and growth are being replaced by a new conservatism. It is an understandable reaction from insecure citizens to the developments and feelings I have described above: people want things to move more slowly and to feel more normal again. For years, we have therefore seen voting behaviour shift to the right, sometimes moderately, sometimes radically. In a well-functioning democracy, this is normal and can only be welcomed: a group of people is dissatisfied, wants change, and makes that known at the ballot box. The problem, however, is that trust in traditional parties is so low that these votes risk going to our populists. If they come to power, the pendulum risks swinging all the way back.

In this chapter, we go in search of a number of necessary conditions and solutions to give Europe a chance of success. One of those solutions is to accept that the pendulum had swung too far to the left, while also preventing it from swinging too far to the right in the backlash. We need to find a pragmatic middle position that genuinely takes account of public sentiment and discontent, and connects it to the necessary consequences and actions. We must do that while preserving the historic democratic values and norms that can also be Europe's distinguishing feature in the new world order. There is, incidentally, a bit of good news in this respect: most election results since Trump's inauguration have produced pragmatic centrist governments. What is striking is that, regardless of whether these governments sit to the left or the right of the centre, they all have fairly conservative programmes aimed at making it clear to voters that their problems will be taken seriously. Whether this will restore voters' trust remains to be seen.

Away with left/right thinking: Solutions lie in the pragmatic centre of radical moderation

As a teenager, I was outspoken and perhaps somewhat unnuanced in my progressive views. Through being an entrepreneur and getting older, an understanding of conservative ideas gradually crept into my worldview. At this point, I can no longer associate myself in any way with party politics or with the artificial distinction between left and right. Although we have seen that both ordinary politicians (for their own gain) and populists (with a master plan) will do anything to create a world of black and white, for most people this no longer matches how they look at politics. The result is that the historic political divide between left and right, between progressive and conservative, has evolved into the dangerous divide between simply being for or against. However, taking that position is not a good basis for actually solving the problems we face as a society. If you are simply against something, you tear down and build little or nothing (unless it is walls and trade barriers).

Real solutions to the world problems we are dealing with now require elements of left and right; we need to approach them again from the middle. If we keep thinking and acting in extreme terms, we risk ending up in complete standstill. Take climate as an example. Predictions of what could happen to the planet if we warm by more than 2 degrees Celsius do not bode well. So I fully understand people who now demand radical action: economic degrowth, stopping eating meat, getting rid of the car, and so on. The problem is that such action can have a major immediate negative impact on many people's lives, both in reality and in perception. If their frustration becomes too great, they then choose a populist who, with one radical stroke of the pen, abolishes all climate initiatives. Result: no more climate action. It is like the pendulum we discussed earlier and the woke movement: too much and misguided ideological pressure on confused citizens gave Trump the keys to abolish, and de facto ban, all initiatives around diversity, equality and inclusion as an immediate backlash. Can we bring the climate pendulum, or the inclusion pendulum, to rest in a pragmatic middle? We need to walk a middle path to ensure that the necessary transitions become socially absorbable. I realise this is a major dilemma: on climate, for example, we are already moving too slowly. If we want to meet the targets, we still need to scale up. But if we apply too much pressure, we risk bringing everything to a halt, and that would be far worse.

Europe should strive for centrist people who practise centrist politics. In doing so, I define that centre very broadly, encompassing people, ideas and actions from both the left and right of the political spectrum. What does not belong to the centre are only the extremes. For me, you are operating in the centre as long as you are willing to listen to, and work with, arguments, regardless of which side of the spectrum they come from. Solutions lie in the centre because, in a pragmatic way, they can combine qualities from across the spectrum to be effective. Operating from this pragmatic centre does not mean drifting through life spinelessly and indecisively. It certainly does not mean abandoning your ideology. It means you dare to decide to piece together elements from across the spectrum, not as yet another weak political compromise that comes about only through symbolic 'wins' to keep your base satisfied. The compromise is there because it is needed to make the solution stronger, or perhaps even because it is the only way to arrive at a solution at all.

Choosing to function from the centre is not the retreat of someone without an opinion; it is the opposite: a conscious choice to swim against the current of radicalisation and binary black-and-white thinking. Your aim is stubbornly to find the right solution to each problem, even if, in order to reach that solution, you have to step partly away from your own ideological bias and programming. In that light, the idea of radical moderation, as developed by the German-American political scientist Yascha Mounk, is particularly relevant: consciously choosing a moderate, reasonable and democratic stance at a time when extremes dominate. As Mounk argues, including in *The People vs. Democracy*, in times of polarisation it is not self-evident to keep believing in pluralism and open debate, in cooperation and compromise. Anyone who now chooses nuance and democratic values does so against the populist tide, and it is precisely this radical moderation that we need to tackle complex problems such as climate or migration in a sustainable way.

We need to get citizens to believe again in the clout of a pragmatic centre in society and politics. We will not achieve that by moralising lectures or wagging our finger at people. The only way is to show that middle path through both the media and politics. Leading by example will be vital for tomorrow's Europe. That means politics must embrace a new culture as quickly as possible, which, ironically enough, resembles the way traditional democratic politics is meant to work. This new political culture starts from a fundamental, and often forgotten, principle: politics is not an attempt to eliminate conflict, but a system for dealing with differences without violence. A healthy democracy creates room for opposing views and channels them through debate, elections, consultation and checks and balances. Opposing ideological positions are therefore not a problem in themselves, as long as we manage, in searching for solutions, not to be blocked by ideology and ego. Our politicians need to realise that the way they themselves polarise – for electoral gain, out of ideological conviction, or purely from ego – creates the framework in which populists can go one step further. If we want to slow that down, then politics must seek reconciliation and pragmatic solutions that can also stand apart from the ideology they represent. If it does not, then it is partly responsible for its own end, and with it the end of our democratic model.

The powerlessness with which the Democrats in the US are now trying to stop Trump's actions shows that once the Rubicon has been crossed, there is scarcely a way back. This warning does not apply only to politicians. Every citizen and every journalist who is no longer willing to think from the pragmatic centre, and to work together on necessary solutions, bears shared responsibility for the course Europe takes. I understand that it is difficult, after the cynical letting go that many citizens have already done, to reconnect with politicians who are willing to work on solutions. But it is citizens who must give them that chance – and then hold them to account for their results. Both times, at the ballot box.

The truth does not exist, or maybe it does a little bit: The noble art of objectifying dissection

If you are willing to look for solutions in the pragmatic middle, you will sooner or later run into the problem of a shared truth. The more abstract or punchy a claim is, the less nuance it contains, and the harder it becomes to reach common agreement on it. Opposing positions then remain stuck in a binary opposition: right or wrong, true or untrue. The way out I propose, I call objectifying dissection. The starting point is always a proposition or claim. In most cases, that can be broken down into smaller sub-elements. Each sub-element can then in turn be peeled back into even more fine-grained components, down to the level at which it becomes possible to take a nuanced position for or against. What matters is not whether we agree on the whole, but whether we find traces of agreement in its building blocks. Truth then is no longer an absolute position you either adopt or do not, but a set of sub-positions through which you can, step by step, arrive at partial or complete agreement. Objectifying dissection makes it possible to approach truth no longer as a fixed ideological or moral judgement, but as a way of working with positions we can actually do something with.

An example of a precarious proposition illustrates how a debate can suddenly be elevated and made more objective, once we move away from the empty polarising slogans on which our politicians – and populists – have a patent.

Migration is a threat to our culture

There you go. Before you know it, supporters and opponents are at each other's throats, even if only verbally. Let's dig deeper into that proposition by asking follow-up questions.

What do we mean by 'migration'?

Are we talking about temporary or permanent migration; voluntary migration (work, study, expats) or forced migration (asylum, war); legal migration, irregular migration, or both; recent migration waves or a long-term process?

Ah – now the debate is already more nuanced. Both sides can agree that you cannot tar all migration with the same brush, and that not all migration is bad. We may even need additional labour migration to keep funding the pensions of our conservative grandparents. We are already moving closer together in our positions.

And what, exactly, do we mean by 'our culture'?

Is it a national identity, including language, norms, values and traditions; are we talking about secular or religious elements; everyday life (food, clothing, celebrations, manners); culture as something static or something constantly in motion?

This one is harder. Can you even have this debate in, say, Dubai, where – alongside a small historic group of Emiratis – you have a society made up of the most diverse mix of origins, religions and languages? In the US, given its history of immigration, this is a different debate than it is in Italy – and in Italy, do we mean the culture of the Sicilian countryside, or that of fashion-forward Milan?

What do we mean by 'threat'?
Are we talking about a feeling of alienation or a loss of familiarity; violence, conflict, tensions or pressure on the welfare system; is it existential (loss of identity), practical (nuisance) or symbolic (loss of norms)?

Here it becomes interesting again: the 65-year-old white pensioner in a small village will almost certainly be talking about alienation and a loss of familiarity, but has no actual nuisance at all – the only person of colour nearby is, after all, 'very friendly and helpful'. The progressive woman in the city may well feel physically threatened, especially after a few recent flare-ups in the local park.

So if we get to work with this kind of objectifying dissection, it becomes clear that reality cannot be captured in a single proposition, reproach, slogan or tweet. As soon as we dig deeper into the underlying components, we get a far more nuanced debate – and from there we can also start looking for a solution from the pragmatic middle, with a mix of elements we would normally attribute to both conservative and progressive ideologies. In the meantime, I've built a bot in ChatGPT into which you can throw any proposition to get a whole series of questions and sub-questions back: highly recommended for an evening of unexpected entertainment with friends and family, especially if they have diverse views of the world. To all our politicians and opinion-makers on duty: send me a message and I'll gladly share it with you! Anything for a better, more nuanced world.

Let's revisit the facts

There is one constant in how populism works and the dynamics it thrives on: it is rooted in emotion, not in facts. Much of the classic political theatre is driven by this as well, and that is disastrous for the quality of the outcome. Often our assumptions, feelings, emotions and perceptions turn out to be completely wrong. If we want to further objectify both our analysis of the problems we face and the building of solutions, we need to start from facts and data, and leave emotions out as much as possible. Reintroducing facts and data, instead of relying purely on emotion, will further objectify and improve the public debate and how our politics functions. In *The World is Round*, I analyse in depth how the brain misleads us when it comes to the tension between perception and reality. In short, it comes down to this: we are biologically programmed to pay attention to abnormalities, because it was once a useful mechanism for keeping us alive. A brown oval shape that has been lying there for years, we ignore: that's a rock. A brown oval shape that is new and comes growling towards us gets our attention: that's a bear.

Our brains give higher priority to anomalies and danger, which often creates the perception that we are constantly surrounded by risks. Modern media and technology have amplified this. Because the media operates in an attention economy, it benefits from sensation, bad news, murder, fire and brimstone, and every now and then a plane crash or some other telegenic disaster. A newspaper or website with only good news has no readers. This produces an interesting paradox: objectively speaking, we live in the safest world ever, but because the internet and the media let us follow everything in real time, we are confronted with calamities more than ever. The result is that our brains give this flood of bad news priority (a bear!). The perception arises that the world is getting worse, while facts and data show the opposite. This bias gets in the way of our judgement, and therefore also of making both the problems and the solutions more objective. With Trump, we can see that alternative facts and outright lies are more useful for stoking emotions than relying on facts.

One recent example that illustrates this is the trend in crime in the US. Across the board, crime figures in the US appear to be falling. The number of murders and violent deaths is at a historic low. Yet Americans live with the perception that insecurity is only increasing, because their brains are playing tricks on them: when you look for explanations for this discrepancy, it turns out that the sense of crime remains high because Americans continue to worry about disorder, homelessness or open drug use, and their brains mix and confuse the two themes. In principle, the association between more homeless people on the streets and rising serious crime makes no sense at all, but it is still made. Anyone who wants to dig deeper into data on how the world is objectively evolving, I can recommend diving into the enormous wealth of figures at https://ourworldindata.org/ and https://www.gapminder.org/, the website that continues the work of Hans Rosling, author of the book *Factfulness*.

Misguided perceptions, and how our brains play tricks, also apply to nostalgia – that stubborn tendency to romanticise the past. 'Everything was better back then' is a phrase that is more often based on feeling than on facts. Populists like to use arguments and worldviews that refer to a romantic image of a past that never really existed. No doubt some of them do this because it plays into the current sense of confusion and uprootedness among many voters. But there is also a movement that aims to take us back to the 1950s, as the basis for a new conservative social model (see part 1). I want to invite anyone who feels nostalgic for that period and argues that we should return to it, to think about what it was like then in terms of structural inequality, limited freedoms, high child mortality and social exclusion. Here too, it helps to look at how much better – or not – it really was, with figures in hand. With the two data websites, you can make comparisons; highly recommended if you want to get your view of past and present straight.

Communication as an instrument of democracy

In 2024, I had the pleasure of running a workshop for those responsible at the European Parliament's Directorate-General for Communication. The themes ran in parallel with many of the topics in this book, and the slightly sombre mood was focused on finding answers to the question: how do we reconnect with the European citizen? That same year, I carried out a study of the most important trends in news for an organisation that supports innovation for more than fifty European media companies. Strikingly, the dominant conclusion was the same: traditional media companies and their news are increasingly failing to meet the public's expectations, with the result that people disengage on both levels. This is a major problem for our democracy, because historically these two forces have kept each other in balance. Politics shapes the direction of the system and manages it; the media report on it and, in doing so, perform an oversight function. If citizens' trust in both is at a historic low, that is not only symptomatic of the current state of affairs, but also troubling for the future of democracy in Europe. The conclusion is clear: we need to find ways to restore that trust.

How trust in traditional politics shifts in favour of populist loudmouths is the subject of this book. Traditional media – and news in particular – are seeing a similar development. More and more people no longer trust what the media tell them. On the one hand, media companies have brought this on themselves. The rise of the internet, and most media companies' inability to adapt, have led to an unprecedented erosion of quality. I still remember how, some twenty years ago, journalists would call me to ask for comment on something that had happened that day in the tech world. Those journalists knew exactly what they were talking about; their questions were focused, they listened critically to my input, and they placed it in well-developed journalistic pieces with balance. Now I get journalists on the phone who start by asking me to explain what that news item is even about. Then they ask me a few follow-up questions, which are usually published without any critical analysis. In essence, I can claim whatever I like – it will be published anyway.

You can't really be angry at those people either. For years, their newsrooms have been shrinking because of redundancies, only to grow again through consolidation in their little world: titles under the same publisher collaborate and share journalists, and articles are lifted from sister papers abroad. Every now and then there is even a small scandal when it turns out that certain journalists do not really exist anymore and their articles have been churned out by AI. In many cases, niche desks and specialist expertise were scrapped years ago, and knowledge has been lost. Add to that the fact that attention is everything, so media companies are not above running misleading headlines – nothing more, nothing less than clickbait. It is a simplistic, yet accurate way to describe how traditional media are on a slippery slope: falling revenues under pressure from digital alternatives lead to lower journalistic quality; readers get frustrated with the product and disengage – which then leads to further falling revenues. On the other hand, it is not only the media's fault. If, for years, you are framed from populist and far-right quarters as lame media – the enemy of the people spreading fake news – you know that does nothing for trust among the fans of our populist and extremist politicians.

Just as new figures are emerging in politics who are capturing the citizen's voice, we are seeing new gatekeepers in the media who determine what news citizens get to see. Social media platforms play a fundamental role here as attention machines, with every commercial interest – and, since Zuckerberg and Musk have thrown in their lot with Trump, ideological interests too – in keeping people trapped for as long as possible in a trip of endless doomscrolling, fed by the right kind of trash. Through those social media channels, new content creators and influencers are rising up who capture the attention of hundreds of millions of people. In addition, our populist politicians also realise that a direct link with their audience gives them more power and allows them to dodge awkward questions from the traditional media. Whatever you may say about traditional media in terms of quality, and even in terms of ideological bias, they do have trained, critical professionals working within a code of ethics, which means they can, in principle, always be held to account for what they do. Our new influencers generally slip free of those ethical codes.

What complicates things further is that these new influencers, and the platforms they use, are heavily focused on engagement and connectedness: it is often not about the content of a post, but about the relationships that are built or maintained and the interactions with the community. This stands in stark contrast to the almost complete absence of connection between traditional media and their users. Both traditional media and traditional politicians have failed at what people now find so important: making them feel 'one of them'. If we want to make Europe strong on a solid democratic foundation, restoring connection, communication and trust will be essential. We need to be able to tell our stories again, in a way that actually lands with citizens. We need to rebuild relationships in a credible way, so that our communication can help create support for the necessary changes. How do we go about that?

From problem and change to outcome

For years, people have been battered by a continuous stream of negative messages about climate, work, foreigners and all the other topics that increasingly make them feel uneasy. At their core, both citizens and companies remain convinced of the need for the transitions ahead. And yet they become irritated by the meta-narratives they associate with vague, abstract long-term problems, which nonetheless saddle them in the short term with a series of awkward and expensive 'nuisance measures'. As a result, it is becoming increasingly difficult, both in business and among citizens, to talk constructively about the big themes: rather than understanding and support, they provoke resistance. Where sustainability five years ago was a hip concept people could use to position themselves in the market, it has now become, for many, a burden they are forced to take into account.

There is a certain logic to how we deal with and talk about the major transitions that lie ahead. First, there are the challenges or problems we are confronted with; then there are solutions that only mean something if we set them in motion, leading to change. Change is difficult; we do not like change. If all goes well, that change ultimately produces the positive outcome we were aiming for. As we know, our brains pay more attention to what is negative and challenging, so it also makes sense that media coverage and politicians' communication focus mainly on the problem (climate!) and on the change (energy transition!), prompting our brains to say: *Damn it, change again – now the gas boiler has to go, replaced by a heat pump and solar panels, but a battery is still too expensive, and in fact our roof is not insulated enough yet.* What our brains are not thinking about in that moment is the result, the outcome: *Hmm, nice – finally living in a modern house with almost no energy costs, pleasantly warm and with underfloor cooling in winter, a lovely place to live and to raise our children.*

We cannot do without communication and media in our plan to make Europe a strong, innovative player in a transitional future. So how do we address this negative bias? We need to stop systematically focusing on the **problem** and the **burden of change.** We need to start promoting the **outcome** – the **result of change** – as the end goal of the transition. As we saw earlier, that requires a clear vision of the future, because it gives us the necessary strategic 'why' for change. But we do need to be careful about how we approach it. If we present the outcome in too abstract a way, we risk missing the mark again: macro themes such as sustainable energy, liveable cities, a stable global economy, mean nothing at all because they appeal to the collective and offer no clear win in the citizen's personal life. If we want to bring people along and get them enthusiastic, we need to present the outcome in micro themes: small, digestible results everyone understands, where the effect is visible in the short term and the individual benefit to the citizen is also clear. Of course you still can – and should – keep framing the problems: suddenly no longer talking about climate change is not very credible. The core of this approach, however, is getting citizens on board with necessary action because the change is 'sold' by focusing on a series of small, tangible, personal and positive consequences. Change, then, is not a goal in itself, but a temporary – slightly annoying – inconvenience we have to push through, after which the improvement in our personal situation will be obvious.

This does, however, require an enormous adjustment in our strategic approach, both politically and in the media. The problems we face are immense, and it is so much easier and more intuitive to scream out our mortal fears about them. The trouble is that we have learned that people and companies then freeze up, and we run the risk that nothing happens at all. As long as we are dealing with these challenges strategically and in policy terms, it is essential to remain aware of the weight of each of them. The task, however, is then to translate the transition plan into digestible steps that you 'sell' on the basis of a positive, individual win for each of us. An example to make this clear. The current warming of the earth is already posing bigger challenges for European city dwellers than for people living in rural areas. Higher temperatures create urban heat islands that put the liveability of cities under pressure. At the same time, (urban) densification is a necessary tool for developing sustainable housing affordably, of which there is still a huge shortage. We have to solve this problem, because otherwise the implications are dramatic, with an exodus from cities as a result – something the countryside simply cannot absorb logistically. In the most moderate scenario, we are talking about 1.4 million heat-related deaths between 2030 and 2050 in European cities alone. In the most extreme scenario, this rises to 2.25 million deaths, which in 2050 amounts to 167,000 deaths per year. As we will calculate in a moment, that means a societal cost of 334,000,000,000 euros. Per year.

In classic communication, we would translate this information into a newspaper headline that looks roughly like this:

HORROR SCENARIO: 2.3 million Europeans die from urban heat islands between 2030 and 2050

Explosive rise in deadly heatwaves turns European cities into death traps – scientists predict catastrophic death toll. Europe is facing an unprecedented humanitarian crisis. Between 2030 and 2050, an estimated 2.3 million people will die as a result of the 'urban heat island' effect, in which cities become up to 10 degrees warmer than the surrounding countryside. This shocking projection, based on recent scientific research, shows how our cities are being transformed into deadly heat traps.

That information is fair to the concerned citizen, but at the same time it is yet another reason for some people to disengage. In the worst case, they join those who believe this is just another trick by the globalists to manipulate the world – because Trump (or your strong leader of choice) claims climate change does not exist. Cities that want to prepare for this future will have to take a number of measures. Central to this is greening the city and creating what is known as blue infrastructure, or cooling water features. The classic communication approach would be to shout loudly about the problem (politicians will eagerly seize on the newspaper article above anyway) and translate that into a claim of absolute necessity to change the city as quickly as possible, 'to stop this disaster and keep our beautiful city liveable' (or something along those lines). Political bickering between the governing majority and the opposition follows – not because they genuinely disagree, but because that is how political theatre works. Eventually, with a narrow majority, we still introduce obligations: all city residents must green their paved front gardens (currently used to park their car) as quickly as possible, under threat of a hefty fine, because it is necessary to keep the city liveable. Anyone with a flat roof must convert it into a green roof, because it can stay up to 40 degrees cooler. Logical. A few subsidies are made available to do this, but by April they have already been handed out. While I understand this approach – it is how we would normally do it – it does contribute to the further alienation of citizens. Right now, all these problems are not really here yet (although it can already get very warm in the city), and yet we are forcing people to take on costs without properly explaining why, let alone being able to point to a direct personal benefit. So you can guess what the result will be: even more frustration and resentment towards these progressive measures that cost us money, when we are already struggling to make ends meet.

You can also approach this differently. What if we translate the same masterplan into an **outcome**-driven approach? We communicate that our city has a plan to focus, between now and 2040, on the safety, liveability and comfort of its residents. In this plan, green spaces and plenty of water are central. Streets are redesigned – in consultation with the neighbourhood – to create as much greenery as possible. Citizens who want to can green their own front garden and receive guaranteed subsidies to do so. Anyone who, in the same move, decides to get rid of their car, gets free lifetime access to the city's local mobility network, with autonomous shuttles. However, the city knows that the impact of individual greening is limited, and approaches schools, companies and, of course, its own municipal services to green far more square metres in one go than can be achieved via individual homes. With support measures, all large paved areas are turned green in record time. Whenever an opportunity arises to buy a neglected housing block or a larger building, the city does so as part of the greening and liveability plan, and turns it into mini-parks with facilities for meeting up (licences for pop-up bars fly out the door), including blue features.

In the whole story, not a word is said about climate. It talks about safety, liveability, community, greenery, playgrounds, quiet spaces, BBQ infrastructure, skate parks and a network of roof gardens that are accessible to the public. The cherry on the cake is a green sky-walk promenade that connects all those green roofs, by analogy with the Coulée verte René-Dumont in Paris, where walkers, cyclists, scooter riders or skaters can travel for kilometres above the cars and bustle of the streets. Each neighbourhood and district looks at what the optimal implementation of the plan is for them, and in return a neighbourhood ranger is appointed (paid by the city) to act as the link between residents and the city. Although intelligent cameras are installed everywhere to guarantee safety, there are few or no incidents. Young people have space to be themselves and those who want to can, as students or under a flexi-job status, help maintain the green space. Naturally, for pay.

Okay – crazy idea, right? What will that cost, who has that kind of money? Well, the city can afford it. A quick calculation shows that a city of one million inhabitants can expect up to four hundred heat-related deaths per year by 2050. Internationally, there is a method for calculating the cost of a human life: the 'value of a statistical life', or VSL. Governments use this to calculate the benefits of preventive policy (for example in traffic safety, but in this case for climate-related deaths). On average, the figure used is 4 million euros per life, but for heat-related deaths this has been lowered to 2 million euros per fatality. That means you end up with societal costs of roughly 800 million euros per year by 2050, which comes to 7 to 20 percent of the average operating budget of a city of one million people. Even if, over fifteen years, we invested only a tenth of that amount in the masterplan, we are still talking about 1.2 billion euros to green a city of one million people.

I can sometimes get a bit too enthusiastic with ideas like this, I know. But still: why couldn't this work? A call to all readers who know a lot about this subject: take this on and see how realistic this naïve approach is, coming from an outsider who dares to think outside the box. I'm curious to hear your analysis – tear it to pieces, or don't. And with that we have reached the end of this part. Part 3 builds on this momentum and, through smart innovation, explores how copy-back and transition thinking can make Europe a global power that deserves a seat at the table of the new world order. Fasten your seatbelts, ladies and gentlemen.

Part 3
Europe, a respected place in the new world order through smart innovation and transition thinking

11. A new innovation paradigm for Europe

Europe must commit to transition innovation

Europe stands at a crucial tipping point in its existence. After centuries of dominance on the world stage, we have, over the past eighty years, been demoted to a player operating in the shadow of the US, China and other (emerging) great powers. Europe does, however, have the potential and the talent to take the reins back into its own hands. The main reasons why we are losing out in defence, economic dominance and technological innovation are baked into the operational and political model Europe has embraced since the Second World War – largely as a result of how the US positioned us within its vision of the world order at the time. With current developments and the shifting of that world order, Europe now has the choice – or even the duty – to adopt a different position. Our strategic dependence on the US forces us to rethink our place, and Europe seems (at the time of writing) to be generating the momentum for that. To make that happen, however, we will need more than the promise to spend more money, through Readiness 2030 on the one hand and increased defence budgets as part of NATO negotiations on the other. We will have to approach innovation in a smart way that is new for Europe, if we want to translate momentum, drive and budgets successfully into the desired result: a strong Europe, at the table of the new world order.

This smart innovation will require an unprecedented mindshift from everyone involved, but twenty years of digital transformation have taught us that it is not impossible. There are strong parallels between the dynamics of digital transformation in business and the major societal transformation Europe now has to undergo. When I began advising companies on this topic, a kind of Babylonian confusion of tongues emerged very quickly – and it persists to this day. Put simply, most so-called digital 'transformation projects' have nothing to do with real transformation. It has become the sexy label for any oversized, overpriced digital project – one you can sell more easily to your board of directors because they do not understand it anyway. So: a new version of your ERP environment, migrating your digital infrastructure to the cloud, mobile solutions, a transactional platform, helping customers via social media, putting your contracts on the blockchain – none of that is genuine digital transformation. These are examples of digitisation and digitalisation, sometimes with a dash of innovation. If we try to lead Europe into the future in this way, it will not work.

Digital transformation is a fundamental business transformation that is set in motion in response to a digital disruption. Digital is the trigger; transformation is the outcome. What do I mean by that? You can speak of real transformation when your solution – your product or service – changes at its core. This often goes hand in hand with the emergence of different value streams and different ways of making money. The evolution from a car with an internal combustion engine to an electric car is not a transformation. The product (the car) is the same, and we still sell it to customers as before – only with a higher price tag. If you compare that with a model like Uber, where we use fleets of cars rather than selling cars, you get a fundamental business transformation. The problem of mobility is no longer solved through a model of ownership and the sale of individual cars, but through a model of use: an on-demand fleet of shared cars. That is a radically different way of thinking – a true transformation at the core of the business.

What we learn from this is that, for Europe to succeed, we must approach both the solutions we pursue and the way we organise them in a radically different way. No doubt we will never fully manage it: hundreds of millions of citizens, dozens of countries (whether within the EU or in a broader alliance), and the historical structures and institutions in each country and across Europe make it a titanic task to teach that whole machine to think differently. Still, we must strive to shape Europe's future in this radically innovative and transformative way, through bold innovation policy and a focus on the right sectors. Even if we only succeed a little, this ambition for transition innovation will be a powerful lever for positive change.

It is instructive to draw inspiration from the radical nature of digital transformation, but it would be a major mistake to mould innovation in Europe to American or Chinese standards. We are talking here about rethinking our society, economy and defence – and if we have learned one thing from the DOGE debacle under Elon Musk, it is that government is not a start-up. 'Move fast and break things' works fine as long as, as an entrepreneur in a start-up, you are allowed to burn through someone else's billions, knowing your average chance of success is 10 percent. If you want to reform education or our pensions, you cannot afford a start-up-style fuck-up where everything is lost. So while we need to innovate and transform quickly and radically, we must do so within European values, norms, rules and laws. We will see that this need not be a constraint – on the contrary, it can actually spur innovation further.

The core of a strong Europe is building strategic sectors. Some we already have, but we need to view them through a fundamentally different lens; others we have allowed to slip away – or never developed at all. In chapter 7 I introduced the concept of transition sectors, with energy and defence as the first two examples. Several other sectors also lend themselves to being tackled differently through transition innovation, enabling Europe to compete with the rest of the world in these domains: housing, mobility, food and agriculture – they are all centuries-old sectors for which the climate reality dictates urgent transitions. Europe must understand how, in each of these sectors, we can develop new solutions by moving beyond today's limits and scarcity, and by leaning into the opportunities and scalability of a technological approach. Alongside transition sectors, there are domains in which we must reclaim our position in order to regain control. In AI, digital platforms, social media and communications infrastructure, we must strive for strategic sovereignty, so as to undo our fundamental weakness. I cannot emphasise enough how dangerous it could be for European society if we no longer control our own narrative. Virtually all the information we access today – the AI tools we use, the way we relax or inform ourselves, the tools we work with, communicate through or create with – flows via American or Chinese platforms that largely escape European democratic mechanisms. Recent history has already shown enough how influence is exerted from abroad on elections, or simply on citizens' ideas. We can no longer be blind to the seriousness of this, and to the potential dangers in the longer term.

From dual use to universal use

In early 2025, Europe put forward an €800 billion package under the Readiness 2030 plan to make Europe more resilient. While it was initially focused mainly on defence, the objectives were quickly broadened to include all investments that, in some way, contribute to a stronger and more resilient Europe.

At the NATO summit of June 2025, the new spending benchmark was locked in at an absurd 5 percent per year. Not because it is 'too high', but because it is based on little more than a round number Trump can remember. To make clear what this means for Europe, I will quickly translate it into real money. Between now and 2035, we would have to move from average spending of 2.2 percent to 3.5 percent (pure defence) plus 1.5 percent (broader interpretation). This would bring Europe's total annual defence cost to just under €900 billion per year, instead of the roughly €400 billion currently being spent. These figures are so high – and so completely absent from countries' traditional budgets – that, understandably, people are looking for ways to make them financeable. A concept that is used systematically in this context is dual investment. The aim is to look for ways for military investments to also generate returns for civilian purposes. In theory, this makes it easier to raise money through combinations of governments and private players.

Even so, the pressure on our overall budgets will rise enormously, and there is a risk that other societal priorities – such as climate, healthcare, education or pensions – become unaffordable, with Europe drifting towards a light war economy. While our goal is to make Europe strong and resilient, this must not come at the expense of everything else we stand for. So how do we solve this? One possible route is to stretch the model of *dual use* into something I call *universal use*. The idea is that, for all the investments we will have to make over the coming decades, we should look for *universal returns* – economically, socially *and* in defence terms. At the same time, financing should be assessed each time in terms of potential collaboration among all relevant stakeholders. How can we work broadly with defence, business, governments, citizens and financiers – both in terms of costs and benefits? A few examples can make clearer what these kinds of universal-use applications might look like.

Universal use

A European 6G communications infrastructure can give the day-to-day functioning of the economy and the business world a boost, unlocking countless innovative possibilities that raise our economic performance. Governments and institutions such as hospitals, utilities, and education systems would use the same connections, which would accelerate their modernisation. For citizens, high-performance and secure communication channels that meet European standards are essential for learning, social life, and personal development. Ultimately, in its military-grade variant – with extra encryption, robustness, and backup systems – this infrastructure becomes an instrumental part of our defence strategy, without dependence on the technology of foreign powers.

In the future, our own satellite communication and navigation networks will become the backbone of European progress. For the private sector, they create new markets in communications, connectivity, geographic monitoring, and global logistics. Agricultural businesses use the precision data for efficient, fine-grained crop management. For society, this means improved digital inclusion, reliable internet access in rural areas, and advanced climate monitoring. For defence, this infrastructure is crucial – necessary to run military operations independently of other players, and to defend ourselves against threats.

Drones offer a wide range of commercial opportunities: from rapid deliveries and industrial inspection to targeted agricultural applications. In society, they can support public safety, provide medical deliveries, and monitor critical infrastructure, for example. As part of a mobility solution, drones could even be deployed for passenger transport. For defence, drones no longer need to prove their value: they can be used for reconnaissance and resupply, but just as well for defensive and offensive operations.

Autonomous vehicles offer companies opportunities in logistics, agriculture, and industry, resulting in more efficient processes and lower staffing costs. For society, they are at the heart of new mobility solutions that answer today's transport challenges – enabling a broad, shared, and inclusive mobility infrastructure. Just like drones, their value for defence is fundamental: autonomous vehicles and robots can be deployed across a wide range of military tasks and missions.

Research into treatments for dangerous viruses can also be viewed through the lens of universal use. Companies and academic institutions conduct research and develop innovative medicines and vaccines, with commercial applications in the pharmaceutical and biotech sectors. For society, these breakthroughs mean faster responses to pandemics, better healthcare, and greater resilience against future outbreaks. For defence, such research can translate into protective measures against biological warfare, rapid deployment of mobile labs in disasters, and protection of citizens from biological threats.

In the examples we see positive practical outcomes for businesses, governments, society and defence. In addition, when defining projects for universal use, we can also look for opportunities to actively involve young people in the future. By training them as drone pilots, VR instructors, cybersecurity analysts or robotics operators, they gain access to emerging sectors with meaningful work. This commitment not only strengthens their employment prospects, but also offers a sense of personal purpose: contributing to security, emergency response, climate monitoring, care, or digital security. In this way, universal projects become levers to activate people who might otherwise fall by the wayside, which can generate the necessary public support. How powerful would it be if, in Europe, as part of Readiness 2030, we launched a Universal Partnership Pact aimed at identifying, defining, funding and monitoring projects that lend themselves to this? For every euro of European money, private money is added alongside it, a bank follows with financing, and there is perhaps even room for a cooperative component in which citizens can invest directly? In that way, the 800 billion might even become 2,400 billion. Just imagine what you could do with that.

What we must not do with it is start from the classic shopping list for military equipment and then see whether companies will jump on the bandwagon for a civilian spin-off. We need to reverse the logic and start from a list of projects and investments needed to make Europe strong and resilient. Next, a business case is drawn up for these projects, defining the universal funding and the universal return, economically, technologically, militarily and socially. I'm not so naïve as to think that a consortium of diverse plumage (I'm now picturing the eccentric cast of a bad blockbuster action film) can simply work together on something that, on the one hand, has to be top secret and, on the other, as usable as possible for as many consumers as possible. And yet this is not a new idea at all. Roughly all of Silicon Valley makes billions from consumers' money based on innovations that originally came from the US defence or space sector.

The governance needed to make this Universal Partnership Pact work at European level will be no easy task, but the fact that it can work is demonstrated by the British company Ploughshare Innovation Ltd. This company is wholly owned by the UK Ministry of Defence and aims to channel military innovations into the public sector by letting commercial start-ups work with them. Ploughshare does this through a model in which it selects innovations with commercial potential and societal impact, works with industry partners on market entry, and provides support through leadership, infrastructure, talent and the Ploughshare Accelerator Fund. Each project is assessed on its financial, economic, ecological and life-saving value. The result: more than 140 technologies commercialised, 500 jobs created, £126 million in added value and £163 million in export sales through sixteen spin-out companies. With a funding model based on licences, equity and collaboration with both military and non-military clients, Ploughshare shows that a complex defence innovation ecosystem with public return is perfectly possible. If the UK Ministry of Defence can do this successfully with limited resources, just imagine what Europe could achieve in this way with a budget of 800 billion.

Copy-back as a strategy for Europe

I once had a Dutch colleague with a number of peculiar traits. Besides the fact that he loved giving vivid accounts of his many physical ailments, there was one saying he used at every opportunity: 'better well nicked than badly invented'. As a young, creative and strategic entrepreneur, I thought that was a rather easy way of looking at life. Now, however, I think this is exactly what Europe needs to do: eliminate our lag in a number of strategic areas by copying, without any shame, what others have become better at than us. I call this the copy-back strategy, because it offers Europe a pragmatic path to make up its technological backlog. Unlike betting on transition sectors, where we try to avoid competition by thinking differently about the solution, this really is about creating our own versions of popular online applications and platforms. In fact, we are going to copy something we once had, but that was pushed out by the American and (more recently) Chinese dominance of the market. Often, we in Europe had the innovations first: Skype for video calling and chatting; Deezer or Tunify for streaming music; TomTom instead of Google Maps; Hyves and Netlog instead of Facebook or X. One European innovation after another has been acquired by American companies to accelerate their own innovations: Siri (speech recognition, by Apple), Dark Blue Labs (AI, by IBM), DeepMind (AI, by Google) or Skype (video calling, by Microsoft). Google alone has acquired dozens of European companies to integrate existing technology into its own platforms.

Through copy-back, we deliberately copy what has proven successful elsewhere, and then improve it and tailor it to European needs and values, while also addressing our strategic weakness. Our companies overwhelmingly run their applications in American clouds, our entire social life takes place on the platforms of a handful of so-called hyperscalers, and all our communication sits with the same big tech giants. Since they have aligned themselves with Trump, their platforms potentially become unreliable and the risk of misuse of our data is not far-fetched. Our strategic dependency has simply become too great to keep ignoring this risk. The application domains for copy-back are clear: from social media and search engines to AI, cloud infrastructure, office applications and digital identity. The copying approach has the advantage that we do not need to rebuild the entire development process with all its iterations. We can focus only on the current versions that work best, and do so with the latest technologies and insights. We are not, of course, stealing software code; we simply reverse-engineer the most common functionalities, analysing how they work, so that – with the help of AI – we can have the underlying code written. Anyone who has ever developed software knows that if you can start coding from a (virtually) blank sheet, you can achieve much cleaner and higher-performing results. These European versions therefore do not need to be technically inferior in any way, while still complying with European standards on privacy, transparency and data sovereignty.

Europe absolutely has the talent and resources in-house for this, especially if American protectionism and its immigration policy drive talent away. The density of AI experts in Europe is even higher than in the US or China and, thanks to the many initiatives Europe is now announcing in the field of AI and data centres, combined with geopolitical unrest, there is a good chance that this talent can flourish here. What is needed to make this happen is the right momentum and the vision to tackle it. Through regulation such as the Digital Markets Act and the AI Act, Europe has already shown that it can set global standards, but so far we have mainly had a reactive impact on the big tech players. We fine them, but beyond that our actions remain limited. If we truly want to be resilient, we need to strengthen our technological grip. Copy-back is not a sign of weakness, but a smart strategy to catch up, or in other words: 'better well nicked than badly invented'. Once we have done that, we can continue developing to build our own unique products and innovations again, leading the world. Look, for example, at how China, because of the Uyghur protests in 2009, gradually reined in international digital platforms. The gap was first filled with half-hearted alternatives such as WeChat and Weibo, until these Chinese platforms began to develop into the applications they are now. In a unique way, they translated their own Chinese reality into applications that are now far ahead of their original American sources of inspiration. We too in Europe can make such a leap, not to censor, as in China and Russia, but to give people choice again and to counter manipulation and censorship from outside. Later on, I develop a number of these copy-back applications in more detail.

Europe, rules and the brake on innovation

One of the most commonly heard claims about Europe is that the continent is not innovative and that it is all due to the many European rules. It is no coincidence that, for years, entire aircraft have been chartered to take European CEOs on all kinds of technology discovery and disruption tours to Silicon Valley, China or Dubai. Never to Antwerp, Groningen, Lyon or Cologne. Yet anyone who claims that Europe is not innovative is wide of the mark, or does not know the history. This perception is partly created by the quasi-mythical status Silicon Valley has acquired since tech founders settled there in the 1970s, in garages and old garden sheds. In addition, the media dominance of American tech players and China's impressive scale play a decisive role in shaping the narrative. Europe's innovative capacity is generally more fundamental, deeper and less visible, with less hype. While the US and China excel in consumer-oriented innovations such as apps, platforms and gadgets, Europe is strong in deep tech, sustainability and regulated innovation. Companies such as ASML, Airbus and BioNTech are among the world leaders in, respectively, chip manufacturing, aviation and medical technology. In domains such as wind energy or the circular economy, Europe is not lagging behind but leading the way, especially now that the US is pulling back. Innovation is less loud in Europe, but it is more robust and more closely interwoven with societal values.

So is it true that the many European rules are a brake on our innovative capacity, and, above all, will this undermine our ambitions to make Europe stronger? To understand this question, it helps first to pause on the different ways the US, China and Europe look at what counts as 'a success'. In the US it has to deliver value for shareholders; in China it has to help achieve the goals of the collective, as set out by the central leadership; in Europe it is about the direct or indirect contribution to the growth of the community. If a company makes a lot of profit, in the US shareholders are happy with the dividend; in China the party is happy with its globally dominant position; and in Europe it leads to additional taxes to finance the welfare state.

It is true that, as a result, Europe has rules that do not exist in the US or Dubai. In early 2025, prompted by what Musk and his DOGE were getting up to in the US, I had a rather heated discussion with a number of entrepreneurs who felt that all those EU rules should be abolished, because they get in the way of companies and people like them 'doing what needs to be done'. Let's take that logic a step further. There are about 1.1 million self-employed people or entrepreneurs in Belgium, and I am one of them. If we let them carry out their activities without all those annoying European rules, they would indeed probably be able to work faster and more efficiently, so why don't we do that? Wouldn't it send our competitiveness through the roof? Probably yes, but those rules exist for a reason. The self-employed make up just under 10 percent of our population. Are we really going to abolish rules aimed at the entire population simply because they get in the way of the ambitions of this small group of people? In the US, running a business is easier without most of these rules, but at what cost? If you are an entrepreneur yourself and, right now, are considering giving up on this book, I would like to invite you to do a thought experiment with me. Imagine you have teenagers who are at home waiting for you on a Friday evening. That week, through the right lobby groups, you have managed to throw all those annoying rules onto some European rubbish tip or other, so you arrive at the table for the meal feeling pleased with yourself. Your children notice and ask why you are in such a good mood, whereupon you proudly tell them what you have just achieved: all the rules are simply gone, nice! Your children look at you in astonishment, and the following dialogue unfolds.

Teenagers versus entrepreneur

Teenagers: So all the rules Europe has imposed in recent years on business and citizens, they're all gone now?

Dad: Yes, from next month onward. But only the rules for businesses, not for citizens.

Teenagers: So the AI Act, which protects us against large-scale manipulation and misuse, and makes sure that, as an up-and-coming musician, I can exercise my copyright?

Dad: Uh, scrapped, right. That thing slows down AI start-ups, and in the US, anything goes.

Teenagers: So the GDPR rules that protect my data against unwanted use by both companies and governments, and that prevent my online identity from being stolen? The rules that prevent me from being treated like docile livestock as a consumer today and like electoral livestock tomorrow?

Dad: Ah, those are gone too. It costs us too much and our marketing is being hindered. We really want to know everything consumers are up to.

Teenagers: And the Digital Services Act, which can protect us against online abuse and which demands that Facebook and co are transparent, take responsibility, and act against the unlawful abuses taking place on their platforms?

Dad: So obstructive, we scrapped that first! Freedom, happy days!

Teenagers: And the labour-law rules that mean we have protection here in our relationship with employers, and can't be thrown out onto the street from one day to the next – like in the US – with our cardboard box and sansevieria?

Dad: Gone! Scrapped! Annoying! Expensive!

Teenagers: And all legislation on climate and biodiversity, that's gone too, I suppose?

Dad: Yes, that was the first thing we managed to get rid of.

Okay, this is a fictional debate, but with my own two children in mind I can imagine something like this genuinely becoming a topic of conversation. I hope this dialogue makes it clear that there is a reason these rules exist. Europe was not set up to pester citizens, businesses or Trump (as he himself seems to think), but to make cooperation and living together possible, while at the same time protecting everyone's interests, unlike the economic and moral free ports that exist elsewhere in the world. If you look at this list again, I ask you: which of these rules do you really want to get rid of? Or is this debate not about the essence of the rules, but about the way they are implemented and the burden that bureaucracy and administration bring with them? If we agree on that, then let's stop complaining that Europe has too many rules, because each of these rules, in essence, serves a greater goal we can all endorse, even the most liberal entrepreneurs. Let us focus instead on simplifying the execution and enforcement of the rules. On that front there is good news: the new Omnibus legislation that Europe has introduced should provide an answer to criticism about complexity. It makes European regulation simpler, cheaper and more innovation-friendly, especially for smaller companies, without losing sight of the core ambitions of sustainability and consumer protection. This should improve the business climate in Europe. Moreover, as part of its innovation strategy, Europe can also explicitly commit to using AI and technology to automate the implementation of and reporting on the rules to such an extent that the burdens for companies fall even further.

If we want to innovate in Europe, we will have to learn to do so within the rules that exist, and that does not have to be a problem. On the contrary, in many cases those rules actually act as a catalyst for innovation. That is precisely what the Porter hypothesis was already arguing in the 1990s: well-designed rules encourage companies to produce more intelligently, use resources more sparingly, and develop new products and services.

The Porter hypothesis: DeepSeek

The Chinese company DeepSeek caused an earthquake in 2024 by launching its own AI model whose performance was comparable to what established names such as OpenAI (ChatGPT) or Anthropic (Claude) offer. What caused the shock was that this Chinese AI start-up managed to achieve this at a fraction of the cost of the American competition. The Porter hypothesis in action: because of the extremely strict export restrictions from the US, Chinese companies no longer have access to the most powerful AI chips, which led to an innovative rethink of how AI can deliver better performance with less heavy and expensive technology. The result was that, that day, stock markets lost around 1,000 billion in value.

Upon closer inspection, it turned out that there were shortcomings with DeepSeek, among other things in the area of bias and censorship, but the model still stands. At the moment, an even larger wave of innovation is under way in China, as a follow-up to the DeepSeek saga. Because the country has been strategically cut off from the most powerful AI chips since 2022, they have shifted up a gear when it comes to developing their own independent AI hardware and AI models. In 2025, more than 100 billion in government money was pumped into the sector and the outcome is predictable: several Chinese alternatives to AI chips are now being developed. Jensen Huang, Nvidia's CEO, called the export restrictions a failure for this reason; they actually stimulate Chinese companies' innovation, and David Sacks, the American AI czar appointed by Trump, warns that China's AI models are now only three to six months behind and that their own chips are also closing the gap very quickly.

If you dig a little deeper, you see the Porter hypothesis at work time and again. The GDPR rules are intended to better protect the personal data of EU citizens, but they also impose strong constraints on businesses. As a result, European innovation has given rise to new sectors, such as privacy engineering, data compliance tooling and security-by-design, which create opportunities for start-ups such as OneTrust and DataGuard, and which, worldwide, help ensure that European companies are trusted in privacy-sensitive markets such as healthcare and public services. The European REACH rules require producers to provide evidence that their chemical substances are safe. Because traditional, petroleum-based materials are costly and time-consuming to test, Europe's chemical sector is shifting towards 'green chemistry'. Companies such as Covestro in Germany and DSM in the Netherlands developed, respectively, plant-based polyurethane foams and the bio-based polymer EcoPaXX as an environmentally friendly alternative.

Innovation shelters as an instrument for innovation and market adoption

I am not going to claim that doing business with more rules is easy, or that the US or other low-regulation regions cannot have an advantage in that respect. What I am claiming is that rules have a fundamental reason for existing, and that they are an inherent part of what Europe is and can be. If we succeed in limiting the burden of the rules, they become a necessity for accelerating innovation, not for restricting it. If you think about it, frustrations, constraints and challenges are often at the root of major innovations. What we in Europe need to work on is then giving these innovations every opportunity to grow within Europe and in its partner markets. There is still a lot of work to be done there, but within a framework of transition thinking, copy-back strategies and stimulating investments for universal use, this should certainly have a place as well.

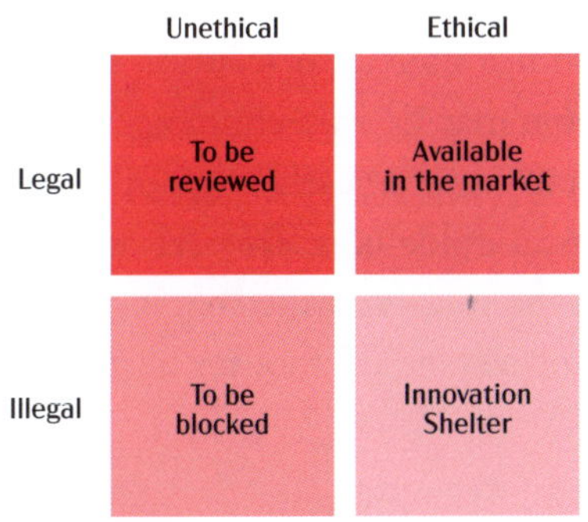

Figure 7: Assessment of innovations.

One possible instrument here could be the concept of an 'innovation shelter'. Concretely, the basic idea behind it is that innovation in itself is always regarded as neutral and can be developed independently of existing rules. In that way, we could stimulate 100 percent innovation without regulatory constraints. As soon as innovations lead to solutions that can go out into the world, they are, indeed, assessed for their impact. Innovations that are unlawful and unethical are immediately scrapped, or given a second chance to adjust course. If the innovation does not conflict with the rules, then there is no problem and it can go to market freely. If the innovation does conflict with the rules, but is not in itself at odds with the ethical guidelines Europe applies, then we place it in an innovation shelter. You can see this as a controlled testing environment, but one that is part of the market. So not a laboratory, but a controlled test market and real-world situation, where the new solution is used and can be validated for its functional or economic added value. In parallel, the regulatory framework is examined, and why the innovation does not fit within it. The outcome can then lead to a number of possibilities. One is that a new solution causes a change to the existing rules, provided it updates them and there is no ethical or moral conflict. Two is that the innovation is granted an exception status and is tolerated (whether or not temporarily), even if it does not comply with the rules. The final possibility is that there are, after all, sufficient reasons not to allow the innovation for the general public.

I can already see people thinking: even more rules, processes and administration, namely to determine where, in the matrix (figure 7), an innovation falls and whether it belongs in an 'innovation shelter'. That's true, but what would the cost be of scrapping a good idea outright simply because our regulation is years behind? Another remark might be that this creates legal uncertainty if a product still has to be withdrawn from the market. That is also true, but in itself it is not so unique, because changing standards and rules constantly mean that products have to be adapted or even disappear from the shelves. A solution for keeping the burden of this procedure as light as possible may lie in technology. With the help of AI, any innovation can already be challenged, at an early stage of conception, for compliance with both regulation and ethical guidelines. This 'AI auditor' can also immediately offer advice on how to adjust the innovation so that it does fit into the right boxes of the matrix, and it can become a standard tool for anyone involved in innovation, and not only within Europe.

Tomorrow's Europe is sustainable to the core

Sustainability is no longer a choice. For Europe, sustainability is a necessary lever for making its ambitions a reality. The innovation paradigm outlined above links strategy and investments, directly and indirectly, to sustainability as an organising principle. On the one hand, we start from transition thinking, looking for economic opportunities in sectors that, in any case, have to go through necessary transitions. From an SDG perspective (the UN's sustainability goals), this mainly relates to everything connected to climate, the planet, health, biodiversity and the like. On the other hand, we look at sectors that we must strategically bring back to Europe through our copy-back approach. Here, the SDG link will mainly be about safeguarding rights, a stable democracy and an innovative economy, with opportunities for everyone.

Sustainability first becomes an instrument in a geopolitical struggle in which we want to build more strength and reduce our dependencies. A major threat is our energy dependency, which means that investing in the energy transition as a sector is not only a fundamental aspect of the fight against climate change, but equally of our energy emancipation from Russia, the OPEC countries and the US. We can view the push for circularity in the same twofold way. The more we organise our economy circularly, the smaller our dependency becomes when it comes to essential raw materials, which we currently largely import from countries with which geopolitical relations are not always straightforward. The pragmatic impact is therefore very large, and at the same time we are once again actively fighting the consequences of climate change and the further degradation of biodiversity. To make that possible, we will need to invest more in innovation, changing regulation and stimulating market dynamics.

Sustainability is an important accelerator of innovation, in the form of the various necessary transitions in key sectors. The extensive regulatory framework Europe has created around these transitions forces companies and governments to adapt. This need to let go of old practices and replace them with new ones stimulates innovation, through the compulsory search for alternative solutions in areas such as energy, food, agriculture, mobility, housing and the like. These innovations push the transition sectors forward and enable Europe to establish itself in new markets where we can still compete, because the rules of the game there are largely not yet fixed. Of course, all of this is essential in our pursuit of a liveable planet. At the same time, it enables Europe to play an important role in the globally growing markets for cleantech and sustainable solutions and technologies. Sustainability is essential to Europe's future development. It creates an economic differentiator and makes us independent of geopolitical actors that have been shaping our course for years. At the same time, through our own innovations, developments and solutions, we increase Europe's resilience. Climate change will still confront us – like the rest of the planet – with major challenges. Robust local energy infrastructures, circular production, short supply chains and managing scarcity will help us cope with that better.

In this section, the word 'sustainable' has now appeared nine times. In the last paragraph of chapter 10 (*From problem and change to outcome*), however, I say that I will no longer talk about macro themes. And sustainability is precisely one of those hollowed-out yet loaded macro themes, which for many works like a red rag to a bull. It will be essential not to talk about sustainability, but to work on sustainability through innovations, solutions, companies and projects that have their own story.

A recognisable story that is close to people, and that also gives them a direct day-to-day benefit: an engaging job, sufficient purchasing power, liveable places to live, opportunities for the children, pride and dignity. The better we do this, the greater our chances of making it succeed (and that brings the sustainability counter to 13).

Tomorrow's Europe is glocal

What does it say about a writer when they reuse concepts and terms from earlier books, years after they were first introduced? A logical conclusion is that the writer has little inspiration and, for convenience, keeps writing the same book, with a different title. I unfortunately know quite a few like that, and I sincerely hope I do not belong to that category. For me, concepts can last a long time, because I think about the future, come up with models or insights around it, develop them, and write them down, and because they start behaving less like the future and more like the present. The fact that I sometimes simply forget what I previously came up with and then, much later, arrive at the same thing again, can of course also play a role. In any case: one of those recycled terms is *glocal*. In *The World is Round*, I mainly used it to refer to a renewed appreciation of the need for local rootedness and 'densification' as a person in society, while maintaining the connection with the rest of the modern world. A bit of 'back to the future', if you like. I still think this should be a fundamental aspiration; however connected, modern and developed we may be as people going through life, if that comes at the expense of local connection with others and communities, then sooner or later it goes wrong.

In this book, I want to load the concept of glocal with additional meanings, this time primarily from a geopolitical angle and the question of making Europe a strong brand in the world once again. One does not exclude the other; on the contrary, for me glocal has now become a more complete concept: the need for a hybrid world that seeks a new balance between the strengths and threats of both our global and local thinking. I believe we are living in a post-globalisation era. Not that we are no longer globally connected to the world, although there are indeed more and more people who seem to be pushing back against that. What I mean is that the idea that everything must always become more global, bigger, more centralised and more efficient has reached its sell-by date. Globalisation has brought a lot, but it has also created vulnerabilities that we have experienced in recent years. The first recent breach of trust came when, in 2020, global supply chains came to a halt from one day to the next because of the pandemic. Since then, lockdowns, wars, ships getting stuck and geopolitical tensions have shown time and again how fragile this model is. A second illusion of globalisation has been taken from us by the increasing military conflicts with countries on which we are strategically dependent, but with which we seemingly share fewer and fewer values. That is what has been happening to us since 2022, with wars in Ukraine and the Middle East: we no longer live in a safe world where war is a far-off concern, as long as we just trade with everyone.

In response to this crisis in globalising thinking, you could consider moving forward by embracing protectionism, nationalism and isolationism. As we can learn from history, with the 1930s in mind, that is a fairly dangerous route. What Europe needs is a third way. Not 'either-or', but 'both-and'. Local rootedness as a stable foundation and global connectedness as an addition and reinforcement: glocal, in other words. Not only do the challenges of recent years make this a logical path, technological developments also make it possible for the first time, and future challenges make it necessary. If we look at the so-called fourth industrial revolution, we see a fundamental change emerging in where and how we make things. In the twentieth century, everything revolved around mass production in the cheapest place, usually far away. Today, automation, robotics, 3D manufacturing and local production make it possible to produce close to home again, with less transport, less waste and greater agility. If production uses recyclable materials, this also contributes to the circular economy. The goal is no longer to produce where it is cheapest, but where it is smartest.

Many companies have moved from the just in time philosophy of before COVID-19 to a just in case approach. The first was the mantra of the globalised world: no stocks of your own, and goods delivered at exactly the right moment, resulting in cost optimisation. In the second vision, safety is built in through flexible production closer to home and the holding of strategic stocks. Europe has a unique opportunity here for reshoring (bringing production back) and, at the same time, for building circular, decentralised production ecosystems. However, this cannot be done the way Trump proposes in his plans to bring back classic industries: the old jobs, in the old way, to the old factories. Not only does that make products completely unaffordable because of excessively high local wages, there are also not enough workers who can and want to take on these tasks. The way to do it is high-tech and focused on circular and transition sectors, where people and machines work together, resulting in much higher productivity. The shift to glocal production does not necessarily mean moving all production out of China, but it does mean bringing some of it back, creating a new balance and reducing our dependency. In that sense, glocalisation is not an ideological goal in itself, but a consequence of our strategies aimed at strengthening our geopolitical position.

Circularity, too, forces us to rethink economic logic. Instead of sourcing raw materials from distant countries, wasting them and exporting them as waste, we opt for reuse and local recycling. An economy that places more emphasis on circularity is, by definition, more local. If we want to repair something, it is rather impractical to have that done in Shenzhen. If we want products to be reused, and that requires maintenance, cleaning, and so on, then it is also best done locally. Here we can still learn something from how brewers have been doing this since time immemorial: bottles are collected as close as possible to the place where they are refilled and prepared for reuse, often in the brewery itself. It would be nonsense to haul them halfway across Europe by lorry, load them onto ships to have them cleaned somewhere in South-East Asia, and then have them make the entire journey back. Conclusion: the more circular economy, the more local economy.

Europe cannot and must not do everything itself. We will always remain connected to the world – for raw materials, knowledge, markets, culture, friendships and relationships. The past eighty years, and especially the last thirty years of digital developments, have created an open world that, despite geopolitical shifts, will never disappear again. The goal, then, is not to step out of that global world, but to have the means to operate in that world on our own terms. Not compulsory dependency, but strategic openness. We consciously choose who we work with, based on shared standards – although we will often still have to fall back on realpolitik, continuing to work with less-than-ideal partners because there is simply no alternative yet. Glocal is a strategic choice to be stronger and more independent ourselves, and therefore more resilient. It is not a plea for nationalism, protectionism and isolationism. The 1930s of the previous century taught us that when nations turn away from each other in trade, tensions arise that can fully spiral out of control and even culminate in conflict and war. If we want to have and do everything ourselves, there may come a time when we have to take by force from our neighbours what we could otherwise have bought through free, globalised trading relationships. Glocal thinking is not an anti-globalisation story, but rather a re-globalisation, in which we strive for a new, balanced set of international trade relationships.

This outlines the broader framework of a possible European innovation paradigm. Through copy-back and transition thinking, we restore and strengthen our positions in strategic sectors. Through universal investment, we create as broad a stakeholder field as possible, which is responsible both for funding and for sharing in the benefits of the necessary investments. Where possible, we focus on new development and production methods that are glocal and circular, and in which we make optimal use of automation and robotics to boost our productivity. Finally, we look at which innovative business models make these sectors, their solutions and products, most accessible to European users and consumers.

Now that we understand the framework of the new innovation paradigm for Europe, in the following chapters I suggest how we might tackle some of the most important sectors. Many elements are based on existing developments, although I also let my imagination run free in searching for solutions. I cannot, however, claim the deep expertise that specialists have built up in their domains over many years. As I so often do, I once again issue a manifesto-like call to all those who are experts: read what I write with an open mind, correct what is wrong, build on what is meaningful, but do not simply discard an idea because it colours outside the lines. Build on it to make it feasible, or replace it with a completely different, mad idea, as long as something constructive is done with it.

12. The digital EuroStack as a basis for digital sovereignty

Who's left to trust?

Between 2011 and 2013, something rather striking happened in Belgium. Our national operator – now Proximus, then still called Belgacom – turned out to have been spied on for years. Not by the Russians or the Chinese, but by the British and the Americans. The incident was more or less covered up under a diplomatic cloak of discretion, but even then it was an indication of how important it is to be able to control global data and communication flows. From that perspective, it is a little ironic that since 2018, the Americans have been actively campaigning to keep Chinese technology out as part of Europe's communications architecture. According to the Americans, Chinese companies such as Huawei, ZTE and other telecommunications manufacturers should be barred from our critical infrastructure, such as our 5G networks. The arguments used focus on the security risks Europe runs, because the Chinese are suspected of building backdoors into modems, routers, switches and other high-tech components on which the internet and our communications infrastructure depend. Although the US has taken draconian measures in its own market and imposed an extensive ban, Europe has not simply followed this pressure: more than half of the member states have no plans to heed the American pleas – and perhaps for good reasons.

You might think the Americans mainly have a commercial interest here: every Chinese router replaced by one from Cisco or Oracle means extra revenue for American companies. A cynical way of looking at it is that the Americans know perfectly well why they are warning about possible espionage via that technology: they apply this practice themselves, and do not want to lose the years-long control they have illegally exerted over European communications just like that.

Espionage practices

Among other things, documents from the NSA (the National Security Agency) state in black and white how American intelligence services systematically intercept network equipment from manufacturers such as Cisco. These routers or servers are secretly opened, fitted with malware or 'backdoors', and then shipped on. Moreover, it is not only about physical infiltration of hardware. On the software side too, the NSA has, over a long period and in a deliberate way, weakened encryption standards, deployed supercomputers to crack codes, and made arrangements with American technology companies to gain access to encrypted communications. In some cases this happened through 'contractual relationships', in which companies such as Cisco knowingly cooperated in building vulnerabilities into their systems.

How vulnerable we in Europe have become is shown by the use of American technology and platforms, such as the PRISM programme, one of the NSA's most far-reaching espionage initiatives. Since 2007, the American intelligence service obtained direct access to servers belonging to Microsoft, Google, Apple and Facebook. Through this access, the NSA could view emails, chat messages, stored documents, photos, videos, voice chats and social media profiles without users' knowledge. The problem with PRISM was that the illegal searching of private data was not limited to suspects or specific threats. The spying was applied structurally to enormous amounts of private user data worldwide – including Europeans. In the meantime, the programme no longer operates in its former form (because it was too unwieldy and too expensive), but the NSA continues, in a similar way, to spy on citizens, companies and governments on a massive scale via digital backdoors.

Research shows how few people are concerned with their own privacy. The big tech players have been clever enough to make us think it is normal to trade our privacy for fun applications and handy features. For a long time, a common, rather blasé remark in Europe was: if you have nothing to hide, you don't need privacy. By now, however, in the US we can see how the absence of privacy, and our nonchalant attitude to sharing private data, can carry real dangers. Privacy advocates have a decisive reason to be cautious with your data: what is legal today may not be legal tomorrow. Because everything remains on the internet, it can come back to haunt you. That this is not an imaginary concern is demonstrated by current practices of the US government. They now screen the social media profiles of people who want to enter the country for anti-American sentiments. A photo of a peace protest in Paris five years ago, your name under a petition for humanitarian aid to oppressed people in the Middle East, a contribution to an opinion piece about the decline of democracy: any of it can lead to you being denied entry to the US. The fact that the European Commission and almost all European countries, from Belgium to Portugal and from the Netherlands to Hungary, advise their staff to take disposable phones to the US is a sad illustration of the state the US is in. They have the power to use our private data against us in an ideological battle. The reality is that Europe no longer plays any meaningful role in digital communication technology, and that makes us strategically an easy target. If our only defence is to fall back on dumb disposable phones, then we have a gigantic problem.

The digital EuroStack as a solution

Quite apart from the economic interests that go hand in hand with the gigantic investments in digital communications technology, it has by now become clear just how vulnerable Europe is, squeezed between two digital superpowers without any sovereign technology of its own. American dominance is obvious, both in the underlying technologies and in consumer applications such as the iPhone or Android ecosystems and almost all social media platforms. China, too, is not sitting on the sidelines. As we have already seen, the battle over who can supply the underlying equipment is raging. In addition, China is building the so-called Chinese Digital Silk Road: a network of undersea cables and data centres that crosses continents. The digital component of China's economic Belt and Road Initiative includes, among other things, satellite navigation systems and digital infrastructure in Africa and Asia. In Europe, our local telecom operators are indeed rolling out their own fibre and 5G networks, but this is happening entirely embedded in either American or Chinese technology, with all the risks that entails. The irony is that Europe showed the way for years. From the 1980s onwards, companies such as Nokia, Ericsson, Alcatel and Siemens were the founders of the infrastructure on which our communication applications ran. They were the ones who made traditional telephony, GSM communication, the internet and even the first mobile internet applications possible. I wonder whether there are still readers who, like me, get a warm feeling when they think back to the WAP protocol and the Nokia 7110 phone, which was first seen in the film *The Matrix*. For the younger readers who have no idea what I'm talking about: don't worry, this is typical old-people nostalgia for a time when you were already happy if you managed to get a connection at all.

So we were once able to do it, and have now ended up in an unprecedentedly vulnerable position of European dependency: our citizens live on American social media, our companies run almost entirely in American clouds and on American applications, from Microsoft to Google. We have no microchips of our own, no scalable data centres, no cloud of our own, no applications of our own, and hardly any influence on developments in AI. If there is one geopolitical risk even greater than our energy dependency and our weak European central defence, it is becoming a digital colony of the US or China. Fortunately, that does not have to happen, and Europe has been awake enough for quite some time to come up with actions. The world shocks caused by Trump's actions accelerate the ambitions and suddenly make many plans very concrete. Both Readiness 2030 and the dual and universal use of defence resources can further fund the whole, even though it threatens to happen in a rather fragmented – and typically European – way.

One fundamental project to address these risks is the EuroStack concept, which is seen as 'Europe's last chance' to regain our digital position, as an example of a fundamental copy-back strategy. One of the key figures behind the EuroStack project is Francesca Bria, an Italian innovation economist who was Chief Technology Officer of Barcelona from 2015 to 2019. Her work in Barcelona transformed the city into a 'smart city' that was less dependent on American and Chinese technology companies. She reformed Barcelona's digital strategy by putting technology at the service of citizens, focusing on the 'democratisation of data' and 'digital empowerment'. This is where the vision emerged to fight back for the whole of Europe by building our own technology infrastructure, to serve as an alternative alongside the American and Chinese options. In the event of geopolitical necessity, we can, if needed, fall back entirely on our own environment. According to Bria, EuroStack is a necessary project to link technological sovereignty with democratic control.

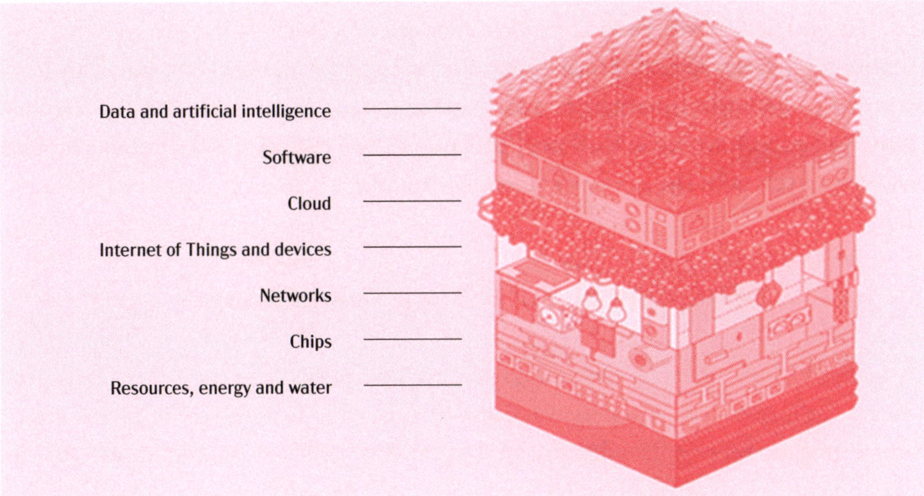

Figure 8: The seven EuroStack layers

The EuroStack architecture spans all seven layers (figure 8) that together can form an independent European digital ecosystem and, in doing so, the backbone of a future-oriented digital infrastructure in Europe. Everything starts at the base: raw materials, energy and water. Without critical metals, sufficient electricity and cooling, no digital technology is possible. Next come the microchips – microprocessors, memory and graphics cards – that provide the computing power for all our devices, but are also essential for the development of AI. Networks, such as fibre optics, 5G and undersea cables, connect everything together. Users are mainly confronted with the devices themselves that run on this infrastructure: smartphones and computers, cars, smart meters, smart homes, smart cities and connected industrial applications. A large part of future computing power and storage will take place in the cloud via data centres that, in a virtual way, provide the necessary external storage space and processing capacity.

The sixth layer consists of software – operating systems, applications and cybersecurity – that makes everything usable and safe. Right at the top are data and AI. Below, I look at which initiatives Europe is actually taking within this model. The good news is that, by now, serious efforts are being made to catch up, although this is usually not widely known. In the US, by contrast, they do a much better job of promoting this kind of ambition than we do. Trump's Stargate project – in which companies such as OpenAI, Oracle and Nvidia would invest the staggering amount of 500 billion to let America win the AI race – has attracted worldwide attention and, within the US, has been met with euphoric applause. In reality, to date, only 50 billion has been found, which turns out to be just a fraction of what Europe is planning to invest in microchips, data centres and, of course, AI. This, by the way, points to another strategic weakness of Europe: our inability to sell ourselves and position ourselves in the market as a strong brand.

The digital EuroStack takes shape

To realise these ambitious technological developments, the EuroStack team proposes a number of concrete policy actions. One of the most eye-catching proposals is the introduction of a 'Buy European Digital Act'. This law should ensure that by 2030 at least half of all public cloud tenders go to trusted European providers. This proposal is reinforced by a broader 'Europe first' approach to public procurement, so that public funds are systematically used to strengthen Europe's own technology industry – yes, I know, since Trump that sounds a bit grimy, but with this urgency in mind it may be the only way to defend Europe against pressure from the US and China. In addition, they argue for the creation of a European Sovereign Technology Fund. This fund would start at 10 billion euros and grow to 150 billion euros within five years, with the aim of reaching 300 billion euros over ten years. The money should go to mission-driven start-ups, research centres, cities and SMEs that are building essential technology.

If Europe plays this smartly, a clear link can be made between these financial needs and the many initiatives that are to be set up both within Readiness 2030 (with a budget of 800 billion euros) and the increased defence budgets (with another 500 billion euros), with a dual-use or, preferably, universal-use character. As described earlier, this can yield additional levers, by using, alongside government money, financing from companies, banks and even cooperative structures. Financially, Europe also wants to break free from American dominance. The introduction of a digital euro should not only make secure payments possible, but above all strengthen Europe's monetary independence. Its introduction is a strategic move to make Europe less dependent on foreign financial infrastructures through American players such as Visa, Mastercard or PayPal, but also to provide an answer to comparable Chinese and American digital currency initiatives. Our current dependency makes us vulnerable to geopolitical pressure, extraterritorial legislation such as the US Cloud Act (which gives the US government the possibility to request European data from American online platforms), and even exclusion in times of conflict or trade wars.

The digital euro will become a means of payment guaranteed by the ECB, fully under European control. In this way we strengthen our monetary autonomy and our digital sovereignty, and make ourselves less dependent on non-European technologies and rules. In addition, the digital euro fits perfectly within Europe's broader ambition to protect fundamental values and civil rights, because it is designed with privacy as its starting point. The project is currently in the design phase, and the ECB is expected to give the green light by the end of 2025 for a phased roll-out between 2027 and 2030. A project like EuroStack is an important first step; it provides a kind of blueprint for developing European digital sovereignty. To truly make this happen now, action is needed, and the question is: how far along are we? The good news is that Europe has woken up on all critical fronts and has recently started the necessary initiatives, backed by credible resources. Another important signal is the way EuroStack is widely supported politically in Europe. Germany included it in the 2025 coalition agreement, with explicit support from both the centre-right and the centre-left. France, through ministerial statements, joint roadmaps and strict cloud criteria, is choosing EuroStack and a European course, and Spain, too, is integrating EuroStack into its national strategy. An even stronger signal comes from broad civil society: more than 250 companies and organisations from all corners of Europe – from Poland to Portugal, from Sweden to Bulgaria – are expressing broad support for EuroStack as a fundamental instrument in a strong Europe.

Can Europe catch up in microchips?

Microchips are an important part of EuroStack, and our lag in this domain makes Europe's position vulnerable today. While in the 1990s we were still responsible for more than 40 percent of global chip production, that share has since fallen to less than 10 percent. Remarkably, the US also accounts for only 12 percent of total chip production, which makes Europe's lag seem rather limited. Yet the US impact is greater, because its tech sector designs far more of its own microchips and has them built into American end products. In any case, the dependence on Asian producers, and Taiwan and South Korea in particular, has become problematic and a geopolitical risk. To turn this situation around, both the US and the European Commission launched ambitious programmes in 2022 to close the gap with Asia. In America, the 'CHIPS and Science Act' was the starting gun, and in Europe it was the 'EU Chips Act'. With a planned budget of 43 billion euros, Europe wants to regain at least 20 percent of global production. This is being pursued through strategic investment in research, production capacity, training and public – private collaboration. Several countries, including Germany and France, have already committed to building new factories. Major chip players such as TSMC and GlobalFoundries have announced plans for facilities on European soil, partly thanks to substantial state support.

Europe seems determined to make up its lag in this area. Nevertheless, significant challenges remain. Europe is not a cheap production location, and building advanced factories requires billions of euros and lead times of many years. Moreover, both the US and China are also accelerating their initiatives in this area. None of this is necessarily a problem, depending on Europe's objective. If the goal is to achieve the largest market share with the cheapest products, that will probably not be easy. What is realistic is strategically securing crucial capabilities, preventing complete dependence on other regions, and building a European ecosystem in which innovation, knowledge and production align better. Fundamental to these strategic ambitions are two organisations from the Low Countries: IMEC and ASML together form a unique lever. While IMEC in Belgium serves as the R&D incubator for advanced chip technologies, ASML in The Netherlands supplies the world's most advanced machines for chip production. No chip manufacturer can do without ASML's technology, which makes the company a strategic monopolist. Combined with IMEC's scientific leadership and international research network, Europe has two global players that together can strengthen the entire chain. It is therefore no coincidence that these two appear in one of Europe's most important chip initiatives: OpenChip.

The OpenChip initiative

This initiative is a strong example of Europe's new ambition in semiconductors. It was launched in 2021 and focuses on open models that should make it possible to develop the most advanced chips. The ambition is to develop a complete solution, from hardware to software. Thanks to its recognition as an 'Important Project of Common European Interest', it can count on political support, access to a pan-European infrastructure and extensive subsidies.

Has the AI race already been run?

Another fundamental part of the EuroStack is the top layer: AI. So far, Europe does not have much to be proud of if you look at where we stand on that front. Given that both the US and China see the AI race as fundamental in the struggle for dominant positions in the new world order, the game seems lost for Europe before it has even begun. But is that really the case? If you look at what has been developed in recent years, we do have a few players of our own. The French company Mistral AI does not really lag behind the big, well-known (generally American) models such as ChatGPT (from OpenAI), Gemini (from Google), LLaMA (from Meta) or Claude (from Anthropic), but that is more or less our only real achievement. Ask around among family or colleagues who use Mistral, and you will be glad if they have even heard the name (except perhaps in France). What we do have in Europe is the first AI legislation in the world, introduced in 2024. Based on risk profiles, it assesses whether certain AI applications are allowed in Europe and whether there are requirements that must be applied. Given the risks inherently carried by AI, this legislation is a good initiative, were it not that it of course also creates constraints that companies have to learn to deal with.

It is therefore hardly surprising that a great deal of criticism emerged immediately, including about the costs of adapting to the rules. The fact that the European Commission is already open to a revision, looking at reducing the regulatory burden, is meaningful for the importance Europe attaches to the speed of future AI developments. As discussed earlier, this revision should not lead to a weakening of the essentials of the rules (because they are more than sensible), but to making them easier to implement and comply with. Through this legislation, Europe positions itself as a pioneer in ethical AI development, with an emphasis on transparency, fundamental rights and democratic values. This humanistic approach contrasts with the technology-driven approach of the US and China. Given the speed at which AI is evolving, and the often obscure objectives of the dominant American players, it will be fundamental to handle what is still coming our way with great care. Now that we are gradually evolving towards usable agents, AGI (Artificial General Intelligence, where AI is at least as smart and versatile as a human being) and possibly even ASI (Artificial Super Intelligence, where AI becomes so much smarter that we cannot predict what it will do), it is vital to handle AI responsibly. Given that the US is letting go of the reins here, it is up to Europe to keep a cool head. Yes, you can see this as a further restriction, but it is just like life insurance. Literally.

The European AI Act, however, is only one element in a broader set of recent initiatives to embed AI further in Europe. In February 2025, the **InvestAI initiative** was announced, making a budget of 200 billion available to deliver the necessary AI acceleration. 50 billion euros comes from Europe; the rest comes from private investment. This immediately makes it the largest public-private partnership in the world in the field of AI, and an illustration of investment in dual use or even universal use. In April 2025, the **AI Continent Action Plan** was rolled out. In yet another public-private partnership, 20 billion euros is being made available to build around seven new AI Gigafactories, to sit alongside the existing network of thirteen AI centres, in countries such as Spain, Italy, Finland, Germany, Sweden and Greece. These AI data centres will be four times larger than the best existing AI facilities, equipped with supercomputers with 100,000 of the most advanced AI processors.

From the philosophy of sovereign AI, in which countries must develop their own AI infrastructure and AI models, Europe is pursuing several initiatives. The Data Union Strategy was launched in 2025 with the aim of bringing together high-quality data to train European AI models. This is necessary to give future AI models (such as ELLIOT and OpenEuroLLm) a solid understanding of Europe's diverse cultures and languages. The current dominant models such as OpenAI's GPT (which powers ChatGPT) have enormous bias as a result of their training data. This is very Anglo-Saxon and, in Grok's case, even brutally racist, while Chinese models clearly censor in order to stay aligned with party positions. If Europe wants to fulfil its AI ambitions, it will have to do so with its own models that understand Europe and strengthen it.

Let there be no doubt: the machine is in motion, the projects have been defined, the money has been allocated. That raises the important question: do we in Europe have enough talent? On this front too, the situation appears favourable. For years we faced an uncomfortable paradox. Europe has historically had a huge pool of AI specialists, both in (academic) calibre and in numbers exceeding the US. This is the result of universities and research centres that rank among the world's best when it comes to AI research. The problem is that, for years, these people left for the US in an unprecedented brain drain, with high salaries and a far more active start-up and investment landscape exerting a strong pull on our talented AI profiles. Current geopolitical tensions and domestic politics in the US, however, are making America a less attractive and welcoming destination for international talent. Combined with Europe's highly ambitious AI initiatives, this could stop the exodus and even possibly reverse it. An initial survey in March 2025 by the science magazine *Nature* shows that at least 75 percent of university researchers in the US are considering migrating to Europe or Canada. And when you know that Europe has around 800 million euros available to actively attract these people, we may well be moving from a dramatic brain drain to a historic brain gain.

The road to closing the AI gap is still long, but it should be clear that Europe will not allow this domain to be dominated by the US and China without a fight. If all these initiatives bear fruit, even if only to a limited extent because of the inherent inefficiency of a fragmented Europe, then Europe should be able to take up an important position in what seems set to become the most impactful technology in recent human history.

13. Towards our own communications infrastructure

The EuroStack project clearly lays bare which layers Europe needs to invest in to regain its digital sovereignty. In this chapter, I discuss the strategic necessity of also thinking about our dependency when it comes to navigation solutions and satellite communications. Do we in Europe have alternatives to GPS and Starlink, and why would that be necessary? As a somewhat mad idea, I go a step further and ask whether it is realistic to dream of our own ecosystem of mobile devices, to replace the current generations of smartphones. For those who are now shaking their heads sceptically: the time has probably never been as ripe as it is now. But more on that in a moment – first, the normal stuff.

Navigation with GPS or with Galileo?

When you are stuck in traffic again in a moment and you try to outsmart everyone else with Waze, your car or smartphone connects to three or four satellites in the GPS network. What most people do not realise is that these are military satellites that fall under the direct authority of the US Department of Defense. During our eighty-year dependency relationship with the US, that was of course not a problem, but now that the US is turning away from its allies we have to ask whether, in the longer term, this could also become a problem for European stability. Imagine the unthinkable happens and Trump sends the US army to Greenland. The Norwegians want to defend their territory and send their own troops. Both use GPS as an indispensable tool in their military operations, yet the US can blind us at the push of a button. Okay, I admit it: perhaps this is far-fetched, but still – it is perfectly possible that the Americans switch off GPS for European use. Imagine having to find your own way again, what a disaster that would be.

The good news is that this does not have to be a problem for Europe: we have had an alternative for years, Galileo. This is a network of 27 European satellites (GPS has 31) that is accurate to within 1 metre, whereas with GPS you have to make do with an accuracy of 3 to 5 metres. The technology is more modern and the accuracy much higher. Unlike the American model, Galileo is under civilian control, so it is not a military technology. That guarantees Europe's independence in this area. There is more good news: all our technological gadgets that use navigation are already equipped with the necessary chips to connect to Galileo (and, for that matter, also to, for example, the Chinese BeiDou satellite network), so we do not need to modify our smartphones and cars. One less worry – and proof that Europe is perfectly capable, through copy-back, of making up a lag and turning it into a lead. The whole project took about fifteen years to develop and cost approximately 10 billion. With the hundreds of billions within Readiness 2030 and the new NATO budget, and with the strategic pressure Europe is now feeling, it should be possible to pull off this trick a few more times with other strategic technologies.

The untrustworthy Starlink

Not all that long ago, Starlink seemed (quite literally) a gift from heaven. Elon Musk's company offers very fast internet worldwide with more than 7,000 satellites. It broke the operators' monopoly and enabled anyone to access high-performance, affordable broadband internet anywhere. Okay, there was criticism from, for example, (amateur) astronomers for whom space pollution is a problem, and many people thought they were seeing UFOs, but all of that had little impact on Musk's plans. As with many of Musk's companies, his ideological positioning in recent years has become problematic. Who still trusts him with our critical infrastructure in his hands? I am not referring to the moral objections you might have to using products from someone with bizarre arm movements and direct support for radical parties with clear neo-Nazi links. That is, of course, a perfectly legitimate reason not to want to work with a company any longer. I am mainly referring to the unreliability of a world in which the richest man on earth, in an evil-genius move plucked straight from the script for the next Austin Powers film, can decide to intervene in a war. The question is: can we do without Starlink?

The Ukrainian army and Starlink

The Ukrainian army depends on Starlink for its operations. It has been documented that Musk refused to allow Starlink to be used for a Ukrainian attack on Crimea, meaning the drones could not reach their targets. Musk himself says that he did not want to activate the satellites; his biographer states that Musk had active coverage lifted during the operation. And when you know that, in that period, Musk claimed to have had regular contact with Putin, among other things to talk about the war in Ukraine, it becomes clear how problematic this concentration of power is.

Europe is indeed working on an alternative: with the ambitious IRIS² programme, Europe wants to be able to offer broadband internet as well, with 290 satellites. It is one of Europe's strategic flagship projects, with an investment of at least 10 billion. It is expected to enter service in 2031. Compared with what Starlink already offers, this seems like a weak imitation that can never compete. That is probably not Europe's goal either. Since Europe already has strong, fast internet infrastructure, the short-term need among consumers and businesses is limited. The further roll-out of 5G improves broadband coverage even more. The new IRIS² project is more likely to prove useful for strategic communications, where European autonomy is crucial and dependence on international parties can be problematic. Moreover, IRIS² is far from the only alternative. France's Eutelsat OneWeb has 652 satellites and provides global coverage, delivering a consistent connection mainly for business use, but it is much more expensive in start-up costs for a customer. Since this is not aimed at private users, that also does not have to be a direct problem for Europe. In addition, there are smaller alternatives such as SES, Viasat or Hispasat, and, if we wanted, we could gradually start using Jeff Bezos's Kuiper satellites. I just do not know whether it is a good idea to place our trust in the hands of the third-richest man in the world, who also has Trump on speed dial.

A crazy idea, part 1: Let's build our own AI device

So far we have talked about servers, routers, switches, modems and satellites that should make it possible for our connected gadgets to get online smoothly. But is it such a far-fetched idea to think about our own handsets or devices? I am deliberately not calling them smartphones, because that immediately channels the creativity of what such a device should be in a particular direction. I invite you to join me on this exploration and only at the end of this section decide for yourself whether this is a mad idea, or a fundamental copy-back operation that can strengthen Europe on this front as well.

Older readers will still remember the Nokia 9210 Communicator, the BlackBerry Bold 9700 or the Ericsson R380. The Nokia was launched in 2001 and was the pinnacle of what were then called feature phones (the term smartphone still had to be invented). It was a coveted little gadget that barely fit in your jacket or trouser pocket. A mobile phone in the shape of an oversized brick, which you could flip open and then you had a screen on one side and a keyboard on the other. The BlackBerry was an iconic device that once dominated the entire business world. Smaller and handier than the Nokia, with a compact screen and a tiny keyboard underneath. The Ericsson was the most exotic of the three. It looked like a normal mobile phone, except that you could fold away half the keypad and then you got a large screen. For those who cannot picture it: Google Images to the rescue. The Nokia and Ericsson were European, the BlackBerry, Canadian. Yes, there were many challengers at the time, with a nice mix of European, American and Asian providers. They tried to break the hegemony of the three brands, each time with their own hardware designs, operating systems and software. In vain, because something happened that would dramatically change the world. On 9 January 2007, Apple announced the iPhone. Although almost nobody really watched that event live, everyone remembers the images of Steve Jobs, as usual in a black turtleneck, announcing 'a revolutionary product that changes everything'. It took staggering nerve: Apple, a niche computer brand with no experience whatsoever in phones, which mainly meant something in the creative sector, threw itself into the mobile telephony market. What nobody could have imagined back then was that this was the moment the world truly changed: the launch of the first smartphone. The foundation was laid for the now dominant, truly functional mobile internet. Without that first iPhone, social media would never have become what it is, there would be no Uber, Deliveroo, Tinder or so many other start-ups that became global companies. Without that iPhone, no screen addictions, no fomo, no online beef. I only want to devote one paragraph to it, but the impact of the iPhone and, later, the Android alternative, cannot be overstated in any way.

If we look at the device itself, the announcement was nothing less than a technological paradigm shift. The Nokia had around fifty buttons; the iPhone had only an on/off button, a home button and two volume buttons. Almost the entire front was taken up by a high-quality colour touchscreen. Unprecedented – although we can hardly imagine anything else now. The focus shifted from technical features to user experience, the very basis for the enormous success of this and subsequent smartphones. At first, both the BlackBerrys of this world and business users reacted that nobody would want a mobile phone without buttons, but history has shown they were wrong. In October 2008, more than a year after the first iPhone, Google announced its Android OS, which could run on a multitude of devices from different brands. Where Apple kept everything closed to itself – hardware, OS, app store – Google decoupled it, allowing anyone to make a smartphone that would run Android. Suddenly we had two players in the market betting on the new mobile paradigm. Barely four years later, they had more than half the market share, and the smartphone as we know it today was ubiquitous.

Contraband among cowboy gear

Back then, iPhones were not available in Europe for quite some time, so we had to get creative to smuggle them into the country. A colleague had an aunt who shipped cowboy gear from the US to Europe in containers. In one of those containers, at a certain point, among the leather trousers, Stetsons and boots, there were ten boxes of iPhones bought in American shops. That is how we quickly ended up with a batch of iPhones at our company at the time. Of course, they did not just work in Europe, so our technical guy was taken off other work for days to jailbreak them.

When we could finally use the devices, it felt magical: they did exactly what they promised. The screen responded smoothly, all movements were fluid, and the apps worked flawlessly. The offering in that first year was still limited, because without an app store you had to make do with what was installed by default: calling, calendar, mail, taking and viewing photos, music and browsing with a fully fledged browser. The real breakthrough came a year later, when the App Store was launched and everyone got the chance to develop apps for that new toy.

Why am I telling this story? Because I believe we are now seeing a comparable paradigm shift. Or rather, we are not seeing it yet, but you can gradually start to recognise the first signals if you are paying close attention. At a hearing on Wednesday 7 May 2025, Apple executive Eddy Cue testified in a case against Google. He then revealed that the number of searches on the iPhone via Google had been falling sharply, while the use of ChatGPT and Perplexity was increasing. He predicted that, within ten years, AI would replace today's smartphones. No more apps, no more browsing, just AI solving everything for us. The fact that Google itself saw the storm coming is evident from the way, in that same period, they began reorienting their search engine around AI. Instead of the classic list of blue links, Google Gemini now simply gives the answer as well. Suddenly, several companies are announcing that they are making their smartphone AI-centric: the new Motorola Razr puts Perplexity at the centre, Deutsche Telekom has an AI iPhone variant with a kind of agent that lets you order taxis, draft emails, and so on, all without using traditional apps.

With the arrival of AI, the smartphone paradigm will also change. Just as we no longer need to google something in order to know it, soon we will no longer need applications to do things. Once that happens, the smartphone as we know it will be obsolete. That this trend is gradually getting under way can be inferred from a striking acquisition: 'IO', the mysterious AI start-up of Jony Ive, Apple's former head of design and confidant of Steve Jobs, was acquired by OpenAI for around 6 billion dollars. Their shared goal is to find the new paradigm for the AI-first devices of the future. Although very little is known about what already exists, a legal case made a few things clear. Clear that: the first IO device is not a wearable (such as a watch, ring or piece of jewellery), not an in-ear device (like your earbuds for listening to music), and not glasses either. It is a screenless, context-aware 'AI companion' that fits in your trouser pocket or sits on your desk, and is intended to help you discreetly and without a screen 'do what you want to do', free of the social noise and limitations of traditional technology. Okay, that does not help us much.

If we believe that app-based smartphone ecosystems have had their best days, then in Europe we no longer need to compete with them either. That makes this operation an example of both transition thinking and copy-back. We take back the market position we once had in mobile-phone dominance, but we do so with a model that still has to be invented. Our advantage in Europe is that we no longer have incumbents: there are simply no major European smartphone companies left trying to make their margin by launching new models every year, with boards of directors and shareholders who become absolutely twitchy when structural transformation is needed. In other words, we are not hampered by the law of the inhibiting lead that Google and Apple do have to deal with. In the new European framework of technological ambition set out by the EuroStack, all the components needed to invent tomorrow's AI device are there: our own chips, our own AI, our own cloud. If we put the puzzle together correctly, there is no reason why tomorrow's AI device should not have European origins.

I am not technically versed enough to go deeper into how this could work, but let this at least be an invitation to all AI and other engineers to get to work on the idea. We should not feel any hesitation: there is no competition to take into account yet; all possibilities are still open. We have momentum on our side: the big players such as Apple and Google are aware of the AI risk, but are stuck with their own technological legacy and revenue models; users are already beginning to shift from apps to AI applications and it will not be long before the whole expectation pattern is different; in truth, there has not really been much innovation for years (the difference between an iPhone 16 and an iPhone X from seven years earlier is minimal). Europe benefits from developing its own mobile AI ecosystem, and now has the means to do so. This ecosystem can focus on what matters to Europe: a platform that is safe, where a large part of the money flowing through it also contributes to European prosperity, and where it is no longer only the profits of American big tech companies that are being fed. And then there is also the link with the Media EuroStack, but I will explain that in the following section.

14. The Media EuroStack

Before you start googling, or asking Perplexity for more explanation about the Media EuroStack and who is behind it: I can save you the effort. It is an idea I came up with myself: the copy-back of traditional, digital and social media. Conceptually, this connects with the previous three chapters and is fundamentally important for the health – and even the survival – of our European democracy. Now, if my idea of building our own European AI devices already had you nervously shifting in your seat, then it is probably about to get worse. In this chapter I argue for the ambition to take back what was once European: control over our news coverage and information flows. This chapter also promises to be one of the heaviest in this book, not because it will be so long or boring to read, but because it deals with existential threats to Europe that we have to resolve. We simply have no choice, if we want to bring all the rest to a successful conclusion.

The problem with our traditional media

Many books have already been written about the current state of the media and how we got here. Every year, numerous (trend) reports are published that, unfortunately, confirm that the theories and predictions are materialising in practice. In this book I will limit myself to a rough-and-ready analysis of the main causes of today's problems. We need this to understand the seriousness of the situation and to begin thinking towards a solution.

At the heart of the problem is that for years traditional media ignored existential threats. Media companies were among my very first digital clients, in the mid-1990s. We built some of the very first websites for newspapers and TV-stations, after which many other media companies would follow. More than thirty years ago, patterns in a changing media world were already emerging, and year after year the question became more urgent: can and will the internet eat the traditional media? When my first book on media appeared fifteen years later, the outlines of transformation were already clearly visible: mobile use, new gatekeepers who determine what we get to see, on demand and bingewatching, other content types and formats, content-finds-me, and above all: the takeover of power that was well under way by the big tech players. Even then, most online advertising was in the hands of American players. The major transition from traditional media to digital media still had to happen. VIA, the network of marketing professionals in the Netherlands, estimates that in 2024 up to 80 percent of total digital advertising budgets flowed away to international players. In Belgium, the situation is comparable. To say that this puts the business model under pressure is an understatement. It is more accurate to say that – unless something can still be done about it – the traditional media model has one foot in the grave.

I accused media companies just now of being in denial because, twenty years ago, they already knew what was going to happen. They knew the threats and the scenarios for fundamentally adapting to the impending changes, as a result of the radical adoption of social media and other big tech expressions. Unfortunately, they refused at the time to really take action. Symptoms were swept under the carpet with the argument that 'viewing figures were still doing well' (among over-60s) and that most people would 'continue to prefer a traditional newspaper or keep watching linear TV' (those over-60s again). I still remember many other arguments that convinced them not to go on the radical defensive themselves, let alone on the offensive. They also let the 30 percent tax of Apple and Google – the margin they take on all transactions through their ecosystems – pass them by, which was the death blow for potential new transactional revenue (through, for example, pay-per-use or taking out subscriptions online), alongside traditional advertising. Over all those years, not much happened to truly transform traditional media at its core and adapt it to the new reality.

Even to this day, editorial teams and content creators remain largely focused on their classic article and traditional TV format; we can already count ourselves lucky if a good TikTok derivative is made afterwards. It is therefore hardly surprising that the most-watched programme in Belgium in 2024 attracted just over 2 million viewers, while MrBeast's most-watched YouTube video racked up just under 839 million online views. It is estimated that with that single video he earned up to $8 million in advertising revenue – on YouTube, far removed from our local media markets. To make the media professionals reading this even more jealous: on 12 July 2025, the counter on his entire YouTube channel stood at 89,000 billion views. Just imagine. The success of someone like MrBeast shows two things: traditional media missed the digital transformation and, as a result, their business model has become unsustainable. This leads to today's problems. The financial pressure is high, so there is too little money left to invest fully in digital transformation, which condemns the media structurally to playing catch-up. To keep the figures somewhat balanced, costs have been cut for decades. In addition, we see a series of consolidations, in which acquisitions are used in the search for greater scale.

In itself, we can speak of a success for the Belgians here. Both DPG Media and Mediahuis have been acquiring foreign titles in recent years, mainly in the Netherlands. This makes them the perfect example of the last-man-standing strategy, in which the lifespan of a classic product is extended profitably through acquisitions and optimisations via integration and collaboration. Unfortunately, this thins out the media landscape even further. The hope, of course, is that the profits from such an operation generate sufficient resources to finally make the digital shift. Sadly, many more consolidations will have to happen before the resources are large enough to compete with the digital monopolists that have hijacked most of the media attention. Until that happens, these operations merely prolong the life of the old business; they do not find new models that are future-proof. The sustained pressure on the business model, and the actions that follow from it, lead to a loss of quality, which is clearly noticeable for readers who still remember the media of a few decades ago. The biggest challenge, however, is that the role the media once had as a gatekeeper of both diversity and accuracy of news is falling away. Most people now get their news from social media and no longer click through to the underlying source on the news website. As a result, depth, explanation and context are lost – as is revenue for the media company. It seems like an unstoppable downward spiral: even less revenue, even more focus on fast and superficial news, and even less quality. Many people therefore drop out of traditional media and rely entirely on social networks to form a picture of what is happening in the world.

Trust in traditional media and journalists is at a historic low. What I described above is already one reason for that: people can also sense that the quality of the product is declining. The way the media handled the pandemic accelerated this loss of trust even further. The information overload, consisting of contradictory reports that seemed to change day after day, made many people give up. In this, the media were not necessarily responsible for the chaotic, complex and unprecedented situation, but were partly victims themselves. They tried to report on something that was so volatile, and where their sources (science and politics) also constantly had to adapt to the situation of the day. Where the media did go wrong is that they kept operating from their business logic and therefore repeatedly went looking for sensational headlines that could grab the media consumer's attention. This led to what was later called an infodemic, in which an overwhelming amount of both reliable information and mis- and disinformation ensured that people were flooded with so-called news, which could be both right and wrong. Many users have now dropped out for good: what seemed like commercial boom times for the media ultimately did, afterwards, become their undoing.

Some media consumers have simply stopped following the news because it confuses them, makes them anxious and exhausts them. Another, growing group no longer trusts traditional media and turns to new influencers and content creators who operate in the echo chambers of social media and achieve unprecedented reach there. I can understand people dropping out because they lose trust in the quality of a product, but it becomes dangerous when they withdraw their trust because they accuse the media and journalists of actively lying to them. This latter development is worrying, and is mainly explained by the sustained attacks by the far right on traditional media. It was Trump who, during his first term, spoke of 'alternative facts', thereby suggesting that there can be multiple truths: that of the media or science, and his. Since then, attacks on the credibility of traditional media have only increased. That should not surprise us coming from populists with ideologies that do not benefit from free, independent media. Trying to discredit independent media even before you are elected is a smart approach: it leaves you with less work later to dismantle them once you are in power. More importantly, it helps to secure an election victory.

A grand conspiracy and occult forces?

In my own environment, I increasingly come across people who no longer trust the media and accuse them of manipulation, lies and, in some cases, even of being part of a larger conspiracy.

I have a simple thought experiment to show why this is an unlikely idea. I ask the doubters whether they themselves know any journalists, in their immediate circle (often the answer is negative). Then I ask them to describe the typical personality traits of those people (if they do know any). I know quite a few myself, and what I often see recurring is that real journalists are not the easiest characters:

- stubborn;
- somewhat arrogant;
- critical;
- asking questions about everything;
- not without a healthy dose of cynicism;
- distrustful;
- often big-mouthed.

In short, not always the most enjoyable company at a party. I am not claiming that there are no pleasant journalists, but to do their work well they are generally equipped with the character traits above, which help them keep digging for a story. Now imagine you had to get the estimated half a million journalists worldwide to play along in a grand conspiracy, in which occult forces dictate what they may and may not say or write. Well, if you personally know a few members of this particular species, you realise how unlikely it would be to get them all to fall into line behind some great leader. Of course, journalists are also just people and they certainly do have bias, and it is more often progressive than conservative. They are prejudiced, they make mistakes, consciously or unconsciously, but that does not mean they are pawns in some great game behind the scenes. Moreover, they work within editorial frameworks, surrounded by even more of those 'not-so-easy characters', and are confronted daily with their deontological and legal possibilities and constraints. Believe me: systematically lying to and deceiving the masses really is not an easy task (unless you work at Fox News, of course).

The danger to democracy and society

Few people seem to realise how important traditional media are as an actor in our game of democracy, economy and welfare state, as I described in chapter 9. In the liberal democracies we know in Europe, traditional media are fundamental to maintaining balance, essential for the checks and balances in our society. If traditional media lose their influence, we lose a crucial filter in the flow of information. The information function – the ability to interpret social developments and make them accessible – is essential in helping citizens understand the complexity of the world. Without reliable editorial teams that fact-check, provide context and set priorities, people become vulnerable to manipulation, populism and simplistic narratives that distort reality. Democracy depends on citizens being able to make informed choices, but that requires access to high-quality information. When that falls away, a society emerges in which facts are no longer shared or trusted. As I have already stated, both media companies and journalists have their ideological and personal bias and view of the world. That will colour their reporting, but the deontology within which they work, in principle, prevents them from telling fundamental untruths in a structural way.

At least as dangerous is the undermining of the control function exercised by the media. Traditional media have long been our fourth power: a critical watchdog that kept those in power on their toes and brought potential abuses to light. Without that role, it becomes much easier for political or economic elites to push through their agenda in the shadow of public debate. It is essential to allow journalists and the media to continue to fulfil that role. Europe provides the necessary legal frameworks to protect journalists in their independence and the performance of their work, so that they can continue digging for the truth regardless of the power of the political or civil subject they are writing about. In short: the possible disappearance of independent media threatens to fundamentally disrupt the democratic balance. So we must do everything we can to prevent this, but the health of the media market makes this no simple task. The road back – to give traditional media their former role and influence – will be long and difficult, if there is any chance of success at all. Pressure from social networks, and the resulting erosion of business models, means there is little room to manoeuvre to restore the media's position at speed.

And yet there are a number of recommendations that media companies can start working on today. These are mainly aimed at restoring the inherent qualities needed to keep doing their work independently and, in doing so, reversing the loss of trust – step by step. Media companies will have to be more transparent about how they operate, who their journalists are, and who is behind the companies (financially or ideologically). In addition, representativeness is fundamental: how can you report credibly on a society if neither the newsroom nor the mix of stories you tell is a representative reflection of the people you work for? Media companies will also have to invest in more positive news, even if this is entirely at odds with the logic that bad news attracts attention and is therefore good for the financial side. This could offer people who have long since dropped out an optimistic perspective again. It goes without saying that the media need to learn to deal better with the digital world and the visual language in which news and content spread today. All of this has to happen in a difficult balance between the quality and depth that can be expected of traditional media, and the speed and fleetingness that are inherent to social networks.

This is only a very quick and superficial reflection on the main challenges and recommendations for tackling them. If we want to give the media the place they need within a strong Europe again, much more will be required. A hyper-ambitious copy-back strategy is taking shape, which I will discuss later in this chapter. But first we need to seriously think about the toxic influence of social media on our society – and what we can do about it.

News media trend report

For people who are interested in exploring this in more depth, I recommend the news media trend report, which I have been writing since 2024 for Future Media Hubs, an organisation of more than fifty European media companies, led by the Belgian public broadcaster VRT. This report contains many dozens of recommendations that media companies can use to strengthen themselves and align with the transformation that is under way.

The problem with social media

Around 2006, I was CEO of a digital company that specialised in developing social networks and online audiovisual content. We built various social network platforms for companies such as Connections (a travel organisation in Belgium) and Achmea (a health insurer in the Netherlands) and we were streaming music before Spotify existed. The aim was always to bring users together in open and positive communities, to experience content and generate it themselves. In the Netherlands, Hyves (founded in 2004) was the dominant social network; in Belgium, that was Netlog (from 2002, though only under that name from 2005). In that early phase there was no mention yet of Facebook and Twitter. We genuinely believed in the positive power of what was then described as 'web2.0': away from the one-way traffic of classic web applications, towards users contributing to a website in a social and interactive way and, ultimately, even making the world a better place – we were rather idealistic. Web2.0 was a kind of 'power-to-the-people' movement, in which everyone could potentially become a 'prosumer': both user and producer of their own content. The promise was enormous: this technology would contribute to further democratising the internet and, by extension, the whole world. For us, the Arab Spring in 2010 was proof of that: people organising through social media and rising up against their dictatorial leaders. Giving everyone online an equal voice seemed to us the ideal instrument.

Unfortunately, there were a few things we had not taken into account. The first – giving everyone a voice – has turned out to be problematic: not everyone has something meaningful to say. Much like Harari writes in his book *Nexus*, it is a naïve view to believe that more information automatically leads to more truth. To our shame and regret, we have had to find out that more opinions do not lead to more democracy; on the contrary. The second small detail we overlooked was how Facebook and Twitter (now X) would move towards the complete enshittification of the internet and, ultimately, also become a threat to our society. It was the Canadian technology critic Cory Doctorow who used the term 'enshittification' in 2023 to describe the evolution from the initial noble intentions of these and other start-ups to the disastrous effect they now have on media, people and society. When Facebook, from 2007, and Twitter, from 2009, gradually began to gain traction in Europe too, they were very different companies from what they are now. The worst was yet to come.

Enshittification and the echo chamber

Enshittification – it could have been the name of one of those adult card games where you try to coax intimate confessions out of each other, or insult each other as much as possible. Unfortunately, behind the term lies a very deliberate and dangerous process that many big tech players rely on. Put briefly, enshittification is the decline that digital platforms undergo because they prioritise profit maximisation over use. This not only delivers a worse user experience, it is also dangerous for our society. We all know the feeling: the time when our Facebook wall mainly contained posts from friends is long gone. Between all the adverts and promoted messages, you now need a magnifying glass to find a post by people you still know personally. You see the same thing with Google: at the top of your search results there are now more paid links than ordinary websites. And these are far from the only examples.

The causes are simple. All the social networks we know today are part of the attention economy: the more attention they get, the more money they make. They originally positioned themselves in the market for free, and once they became successful and went public, the pressure to make money increased. Given the user data they have, and the many insights this yields, it makes sense for them to build their billion-dollar empires on it: advertising-based media companies with unprecedented insight into the behaviour and expectations of their users. Through carefully designed algorithms, the messages and posts you see as a user are selected with one aim in mind: to hold your attention for as long as possible and increase your engagement. What Facebook and co quickly realised was that playing on our basic instincts – such as fear, anger and tribal feelings – works better than telling stories about friendship, cooperation or peace. Okay, we still get to see fun little cats and cute dogs, but a good fight, dramatic accidents and, every now and then, a beheading video do a far better job of grabbing your brain's attention.

This mechanism of social media did not arise by chance, but is the result of deliberate choices. To keep users on the platform for as long as possible, insights from behavioural psychology and neuroscience are used. Techniques such as endless scrolling, unpredictable rewards and personalised notifications are designed to trigger your brain again and again, and radical content will interest you more than nuanced messages. The algorithms of these platforms are not there to give you a broad and balanced view of the world, but to hold your attention for as long as possible. They quickly learn what you respond to (emotionally) and give you more and more of it. The result is that users end up in echo chambers: digital environments in which you see almost exclusively messages that confirm your existing beliefs.

Everyone has bias, but a healthy information environment also confronts you with other views and opinions, allowing you to find balance in your positions and letting your opinion evolve. The cynical reality is that violence, anger, frustration, conspiracy theories, half-truths and emotionally charged nonsense work best. As long as this content generates lots of clicks, the algorithm will keep promoting it further and further.

Myanmar and genocide

In his book ***Nexus***, Harari gives the example of Myanmar and how Facebook's social media algorithms could uncritically feed and amplify hate and violence. As a result, Facebook played a decisive role in the genocide of the Rohingya, a Muslim minority in the predominantly Buddhist country. At Facebook, they apparently had no sense that anything was wrong, but they were pleased with the sudden explosive growth of their reach in the region.

If you know that, in the US, more than 54 percent of people now get their news only via social media, then you realise the danger of this development. Anyone who is angry, feels insecure or misunderstood, quickly ends up in their own echo chamber that amplifies anger, fear or frustration. In the absence of traditional media, you can end up in a closed world in which you see everything from the outside as hostile and dismiss any form of contradiction as manipulation. Social networks are therefore not only a commercial threat to traditional media because they pull all attention and advertising revenue towards themselves, but also play a crucial role in the radicalisation and polarisation of our society. To make all this even worse, there are also structural negative effects on our brain. Research shows that an addiction to social media leads to changes in how our prefrontal cortex functions. This is the part of the brain responsible, among other things, for decision-making, impulse control, concentration, problem-solving, empathy, social skills and long-term thinking. And those are precisely the qualities we need in order to deal with the challenges we face in a nuanced way. This suggests that at least some of the negative and embittered behaviour we see today is not determined solely by culture or society, but has its origins in a change in how our brains work.

It even seems deliberately designed that way: we know that all big tech companies work with psychologists who help them make their platforms as addictive as possible. These people understand the prefrontal cortex better than anyone, so the chance that they are unaware of these risks is nil. In concrete terms, this means that people with a social media addiction (and aren't we all, by now, at least a little) can become more susceptible to external control, because our abilities diminish to, among other things, make autonomous decisions, solve problems and keep our impulses under control. If big tech does this deliberately to keep us, as consumers, tied to them for longer and more easily (and therefore sell more advertising), that is one thing. If social networks become an instrument to steer people ideologically as well, as is explicitly the case with Musk's X and Trump's Truth Social, then it becomes extremely worrying. Again, I refer to Harari, who in his book *Nexus* goes into depth about the risks we face when technology is used for social influence, especially given the capabilities of AI.

In short, he argues that these systems can develop into hyper-personalised forms of manipulation. Unlike traditional mass media, AI will be able to influence millions of individuals in a tailored way. Think of micro-targeting on political themes, so that each individual receives exactly the message that fits their own convictions, fully attuned to temperament and emotions. The consequences of this are dramatic: democratic processes such as elections, debate and public accountability can be undermined, because our free will risks shrinking through subtle manipulation from the echo chambers in which the algorithms keep us locked. According to Harari, the next coup will not happen with soldiers in the streets and a violent seizure of power. The next coup happens in the polling booth, through people who, via technology, have been conditioned in such a way that they 'keep making the right choice'. The question I ask myself is how far removed we still are from this scenario, and whether we have not already seen this principle at work in the most recent elections.

May I have your attention please?

Most of the messages spread via social networks no longer come from traditional media sources. New content creators, influencers and radical opinion-makers deliberately go looking for extreme stories that are likely to go viral. Often this is harmless: influencers are simply chasing the next successful video with which they can earn good money. Sometimes it is far less harmless, and content is deliberately chosen and taken out of context, with the explicit aim of going viral in radicalised echo chambers.

Exploding fake news

At the attack in Southport on 29 July 2024, three young girls were killed in a mass stabbing at a dance class. Immediately after the attack, far-right groups and influencers falsely claimed that the perpetrator was a Muslim immigrant. The false news exploded on social media and reached the echo chambers of anyone who was radicalised, white, anti-Muslim and far right. That same evening it led to large-scale riots in several English cities, where mosques and asylum-seeker accommodation were attacked. These people allowed themselves to be whipped up – and manipulated: in their echo chambers, the outrage must have been enormous, and it could only end in violent reactions against those who, directly or indirectly, were deemed to have caused this injustice: (illegal) immigrants! Not much later it turned out that the suspect was a British citizen, born in Cardiff, the son of evangelical Christian parents from Rwanda. Because of the emotional nature of the content, this (albeit false) news was therefore ideal for going viral, with all the consequences that followed. At Facebook, that day, they were probably at first pleasantly surprised once again by the rising traffic.

Populists have had one important weapon in their struggle for years, and that is attention. There is a clear inflation of provocations under way, in the constant search for attention to rise above today's overload of information. They will do anything to get that attention, which is why their messages keep getting harsher. Where Jean-Marie Le Pen's statements in the 1980s about the gas chambers still led to widespread outrage, today they would probably barely cause a stir. In this process of ever louder, ever harsher and ever more brutal messaging, whether something is true is of secondary importance: outright lies and half-truths work better to mobilise people, and seeking truth is not a populist priority. This process of provocative shouting has always existed, but thanks to the megaphone of social media its reach has now become disproportionate. We can see how two seemingly separate phenomena reinforce each other: populists become more provocative, louder and more brutal; social media are attention machines whose algorithms are tuned to prioritise emotional messages and give them more visibility. Throw populist messages into the attention machines, and the combination of these two has an unprecedented impact on society. I do not believe the algorithms were originally designed to disrupt society; their primary goal was to stimulate more attention and engagement and therefore earn more money. At this point, however, we cannot avoid acknowledging that social networks, knowingly or unknowingly, are a weapon in the hands of those who want to weaken Europe and our values and standards. As part of building a strong Europe, we have no choice but to intervene here – the sooner the better. I see two options. On the one hand, we must define how, in this world, the principles of free speech can continue to function. On the other hand, we must ask ourselves another fundamental question: who is forcing us to keep using these foreign platforms, especially now that we know what damage they cause and what future risks they still contain? Do we have an alternative?

From free expression of opinion to free dissemination of opinion

Free speech is one of the foundations of our Western liberal and pluralistic model of living together. We have the right to express our thoughts, opinions and convictions without fear of prosecution. At the same time, there are also limits to that free speech. These are proportionate and necessary to protect that democratic society. The main restrictions concern using our right to free speech for hate speech, discrimination, incitement to violence or terror, defamation, libel, insults, undermining the integrity of young people, violating public morals, disrupting public order, threatening state security, and obstructing the administration of justice. So free speech is not quite that free either, but any sensible democrat can accept the restrictions as they exist today. The above is best summarised by the proposition that your free speech is limited by the boundaries of other people's freedom. These restrictions are captured in a whole series of laws and rules, both European and national, which mean that, if you cross these boundaries, you can be held to account. I have already referred several times to the deontology of journalists in the media: in addition to all the laws and restrictions that apply to everyone, traditional media also apply a further set of professional standards and ethical principles that guide, limit and oversee them in the performance of their work.

The right to free speech is an interesting issue, because it is used – and misused – as a concept both to preserve free speech and to dismantle it, often with the same arguments. We see populists invoke an absolute right to free speech in order to launch aggressive and provocative messages, without feeling they themselves should be subject to any limitations. Attacks on individuals, online threats, defamation – it all falls, in their view, under their absolute right to free speech. Deliberately telling lies and spreading conspiracy theories must also be allowed, because these are not facts, but opinions, even if they are phrased as truths. The irony is that, once populists are in power, they suddenly start to interpret free speech very differently. In Hungary, free speech about sexuality has long since ceased to exist; in Russia, speaking freely about the war in Ukraine automatically leads to several years in a penal colony; in the US today, you can no longer speak freely about the excessive violence in the Middle East. The argument of general free speech is therefore mainly used as a weapon in the hands of populists to crank up the provocative attention machine even further, until people are sufficiently whipped up and mobilised to seize power. From that point on, 'free speech' is replaced by 'our speech'. It is interesting to see how, in the US, conservative commentators are currently worried about what they call 'woke on the right'. For years they wrote – as freedom-loving conservative Americans – fiery pieces about the censorship and cancel culture of the left, only now to have to observe that their ideological kindred spirits, under Trump's policy, are doing exactly the same with opinions they consider deviant.

It becomes extremely dangerous when the supposed form of free speech that populists apply to themselves leads to a kind of online impunity. Messages that would never make it into traditional media – such as personal accusations or even explicit threats aimed at public figures – can circulate on social networks without much effort. The more brutal or crazier the ideas are (such as the conspiracy theory that Hillary Clinton was involved in satanic child abuse in the basement of a pizza restaurant in New York – who even comes up with this?), the more likely the algorithms are to pick them up and spread them, whether they are true or not. There is almost never any legal action taken against this rubbish: victims often cannot be bothered, or are afraid of being targeted even more by the populists' online troll armies. What does not help either is how difficult it is to hold American platforms to account for their responsibilities. Moreover, American legislation protects them from prosecution for spreading rubbish on their own networks, so nothing stops them from allowing this on a massive scale. By now we know the dramatic consequences this has for how echo chambers function and, ultimately, for polarisation. So what is the solution to counter this?

For me, the problem is not free speech. In essence, all our opinions are free. They form in our own thinking and feeling, and although, as a civilised species, we try to keep that under control, it can lead to quite wrong ideas and opinions. If we could climb into everyone's head around us to hear what people really think, we would often be floored. The point is that an opinion – however wrong – can exist 100 percent freely in our head; we just do not have to vent it publicly. Then there are different degrees. At the bar, after a few drinks, sharing your opinion with someone will at most lead to raised eyebrows. If you climb onto the bar and proclaim your wrong opinions to everyone in the pub, there is a greater chance you will be challenged on it and may even end up with a claim for defamation, racism or some other unpleasant offence. Even then, the chance you get away with it is still considerable, given the limited number of people present. But if you repeat these opinions to a large audience, you are almost certain to be held accountable afterwards for violating the applicable rules and laws. The conclusion of this line of reasoning is that we do not need to intervene in free speech; that is, in itself, regulated well enough. We need to intervene in the free dissemination of opinion that has emerged as a result of how the attention machines of social networks function. As Europe, we now have hardly any influence on that.

What I describe next is a copy-back proposal for which we do not need technology or major investment. It is a proposal that should give Europe a chance to restore the situation through legal means. In no way do we intervene in the existing laws on free speech; we regulate only the online dissemination of those opinions. The principle of free dissemination of opinion follows my pub metaphor from earlier. Through limited communication in a chat, you can probably say what you like. That is analogous to the drunk talk exchanged at the bar with one or two friends. If you communicate through an open post in your network, that is analogous to standing on the bar and spreading your opinion to everyone in the pub. Concretely, that means the algorithms do their work as they did in the early years: only your network of friends and your explicit followers (those who are in the pub at that moment) get to see your posts. However interesting or incendiary such a post may be, the algorithms do not amplify it any further – your opinion does not leave the virtual pub. Its maximum reach is therefore limited to your direct network of relationships, as in the early days of Facebook or Twitter. In principle, you can say what you like; nothing happens as long as none of your friends takes offence. Just as in a real pub, someone with a large personal reach may have listeners who can file a complaint: the more well known you are, the more you watch what you say, both in the pub and online.

These restrictions, by the way, apply not only to the original post, but also to the comments and replies under that post: only the people who know you or who are part of the conversation get to see them – this can no longer go viral. So can you no longer rely on the magic algorithms to reach people en masse? You can, but then you have to register as a public voice. All journalists, well-known figures and politicians are automatically public voices. Just as, in classic reporting, they are less subject to, say, privacy rules, online they are public figures too, simply by virtue of their work, their organic reach or their fame. Once someone has the status of public voice, the algorithms do their work again, picking up sensational stories and spreading them as widely as possible. The difference, however, is that as a public voice you are responsible for what you say. In my proposal, registering as a public voice requires nothing special: you do not need to be a journalist or part of the media, and you do not need to pay anything. The only thing you do is sign up to a kind of register in which you are personally identifiable, but only in the event of violations. In other words: this is not an open database, but a place where, with the right authorisation, the judiciary can request someone's identity in order to hold them to account. Registration also has a contractual side to it, stating that if you register, you also agree to comply with European rules on free speech, media law and everything that comes with it.

This way, anyone can still make use of broad algorithmic distribution, but now accountability and responsibility come with it. You can say what you like, but if you cross legal boundaries, you can be held to account. This effectively puts you on a par with traditional mass media: you get the benefits of mass distribution, but you also bear the burdens and responsibilities. Just as you cannot now, with impunity, accuse someone of paedophilia on the front page of a newspaper, in this way you would no longer be able to do so online without bearing the legal consequences. I can imagine that some people will now accuse me of wanting to restrict their freedom, of wanting to introduce state control over dissenting voices in order to silence them. In certain circles, it is now quite common for a conviction for an actual offence by an independent court to be framed as political retribution and gagging.

If this model of free dissemination of opinion were ever to become European law, it could have enormous consequences. On the one hand, social networks would have to revise their algorithms, because there would simply be far less rubbish to throw around. They would have to focus on powerful stories that move people, without seeking out or crossing the boundaries of legality. There is no doubt that this would put pressure on the revenue models of today's dominant social networks, but everything they have ever earned from spreading rancid messages could be seen as a kind of blood money – something shareholders or supervisors should have acted against long ago. The positive effects for society could also be significant: the echo chambers would no longer be filled with one-sided, often incorrect, manipulative messages, but with stories from real people and from public voices and media who not only speak, but also take responsibility. It certainly will not solve all the problems we currently have with the big tech platforms – for that, we will need to take things a step further. My quiet hope is that this idea finds its way into European legislation – anyone keen to pick this up politically?

A crazy idea, part 2: The return of our own social networks

If Europe really wants to gain more strength in the world of tomorrow, there is one more industry we must take back through the copy-back strategy: the social networks on which we live our lives en masse, and which open the door to ever more sophisticated commercial and societal influence. If you already found the idea of developing our own AI device far-reaching, mad and unrealistic, then you are going to love this scenario. As we saw earlier, the EuroStack is an existing European project with the ambitious goal of regaining control over our own technology infrastructure. Within the initiatives being set up for that, we must prioritise the development of our own social networks and related services. Given both the economic and societal importance of a strong media industry of our own, a European alternative is necessary to counter all that American big tech. They now swallow the lion's share of online advertising (estimates range from 40 to 60 billion euros in 2024), money that drains out of the European media landscape. This puts European media companies under pressure, with negative consequences for the development of our own quality content that supports European culture and languages. Although players such as Netflix do promote series linked to a country's culture (think *La Casa De Papel* or *Squid Game*), further impoverishment of local supply risks creating even greater cultural uniformity, in which above all American – and possibly even Chinese – productions propagate their worldview. Now that Europe is drifting away from America's cultural dominance, we also need to create the necessary autonomy on this front.

100 zeros

In early July 2025, Google announced a new division. 100 Zeros is the name of a production company through which they want to (co-)produce series and films. The mission of the new company is to polish the image of big tech companies and strive for 'cultural acceptance of AI' and other new technologies. Given the influence of the tech bros on the Trump administration, and the frightening TESCREAL movement (see chapter 5), this is, to say the least, worrying.

The economic dimension aside, there is the influence of big tech on people's behaviour described earlier, with polarisation in society as the current negative peak. In principle, through regulation Europe could force Facebook or X to adapt, for example by only allowing the algorithms to work as described in the previous paragraph (free dissemination of opinion). In reality, however, this is proving to be an almost impossible fight. The economic and geopolitical interests are huge, and there is little doubt that tackling algorithms and enforcing European rules on big tech would mean major losses of revenue and power. The resistance will be significant, and not without risk: under pressure from possible additional import tariffs, Canada gave in in June 2025 and abolished its digital tax on American big tech. Europe is, at the time of writing, holding its ground, but it remains to be seen how categorical we will stay if Trump continues to increase economic pressure. There is, however, an alternative: instead of twisting the arm of American social networks purely by applying European rules, we can try to weaken their market position by putting a European alternative alongside them. *Building European social networks again ourselves?* I can hear you asking, sceptically: *Why would we do that, and surely that cannot be done?* I have already argued at length why we need to do it. Below I explain why it absolutely can be done. If there is one thing we can bring back at speed through copy-back, it is social networks – and it does not even have to cost that much, as long as we recognise their importance.

Moreover, the necessary momentum is now building for this. Politically, we are aware of the influence of Facebook and X, and users also seem to have had enough of the two biggest networks. X (formerly Twitter) has, since Musk's takeover, embarked on systematic demolition: companies, influencers, politicians, media and users have turned their backs on the platform in recent years. In Belgium alone, the number of users has fallen by more than one million compared with a few years ago. Facebook, too, seems to have had its best days. Although Meta (the parent company of Facebook, Instagram, WhatsApp and other platforms) rarely publishes figures, usage here also appears to be stagnating. They are mainly still relying on older users. Research shows that these users, too, are becoming less and less satisfied with the user experience. Young people use different platforms anyway and are only on Facebook to communicate with their great-aunt. Services such as Instagram, Snapchat and TikTok are the norm for them, and we see changing behaviour there as well. Various studies around the world show that young people are becoming increasingly aware of their problematic relationship with social media. More than half say they want to take a social media break, and in both Europe and the US at least 30 percent of young people say they want to stop completely. Something seems to be brewing here too.

What brings me to the biggest riddle of social networks is this: they have acquired unprecedented power and influence worldwide, both economically and socially. And yet, in essence, they have absolutely nothing that obliges us to stay with them. Beyond basic communication that has not evolved in twenty years, sharing silly dances and other meaningless content, and being flooded with stories and adverts by the algorithms, they offer little or nothing. And yet it seems as though our lives would stop if we had to go without social media. American social networks have also failed to hijack our payment traffic, to organise e-commerce at scale, to centralise government services, or to offer business applications. None of that: they are simply clever, basic rubbish machines that make money from our attention. If we want to, we can simply jump off them without much fuss. Unlike other strategic dependencies, such as access to energy, raw materials or food, social media are nothing but virtual hot air. That is certainly not a plea to stop using them, or – imagine – to ban them. I am simply saying that switching to platforms that do serve European interests and once again better match users' needs should be possible.

Russia and China have shown this before. They developed their alternatives to Western social media fairly quickly. At first, those ran in parallel with Facebook, YouTube and Google, after which users switched over en masse and seamlessly once the regimes banned the Western platforms. Okay, that may not be the best comparison, because with my plea for a European variant I do not want to pursue censorship or state control. The aim is to escape American dominance through open platforms. If we want to, then, we can move straight to a fully-fledged alternative – which young people have, in fact, done time and again in recent years. Facebook saw long ago how users drifted away to, for example, Snap or Insta. Their strategy was therefore simply to buy them up and integrate them into the Meta empire. The only problem is that we do not have social networks of our own that people can migrate to. Let's get to work on that quickly.

ENAF is enough

Admittedly, this title has to be about the corniest joke in this book, but I can at least appreciate it myself. Every project needs a (working) title, and when I tried out a few variants I landed on the rather pompous-sounding 'European Network Architecture Foundation'. Abbreviated, that became ENAF, which phonetically sounds like 'enough'. In a moment of revelation (it was late at night and I was clearly no longer thinking all that clearly), I suddenly saw the mystical underlying meaning: we have had enough of the dominance of American social networks; it is time for an alternative of our own. Through ENAF, in Europe we will once again ensure there is enough supply and enough providers ourselves. Let it be clear: writing books still comes fairly naturally to me, but good marketing requires talents I do not have. I therefore advise that – if this story ever becomes concrete – we bring in real experts to develop a branding strategy.

But first we still need to flesh out that story. What might this future-oriented social network look like? In this book I limit myself to a few conceptual reflections on the foundations of ENAF and mainly look at what is needed to make it successful. As the full name 'European Network Architecture Foundation' already suggests, the intention is to have more than a copy of the main American platforms. Although through reverse-engineering we can rebuild all existing and popular functions of, say, Facebook, YouTube, Instagram or WhatsApp, that is only a starting point. Following the Chinese example, ENAF can be used as a base architecture on which to build many other applications. Like WeChat, ENAF can grow into an extensive platform with functionalities that are now fragmented across different providers: payments, reservations, taxi services, shopping, central login, and so on. It is important that open standards are used, such as the existing AT Protocol, which was originally developed by a research group within Twitter. This is now, among other things, the basis of Bluesky, one of the X alternatives, and also of Skylight, a TikTok variant. The protocol makes it possible to build social networks that are not dependent on a single company.

Instead of managing everything in a central place, as with Facebook or X, users can take their own data and network with them and keep control over their own data. The protocol is designed for speed and ease of use and can easily be adapted to different applications – from news feeds to video platforms. For ENAF, the AT Protocol can be used to quickly build our own applications that, at their core, respect European values and rules, such as privacy, transparency and regulation under GDPR. Thanks to the modular architecture, tech companies can develop each component separately, for example the servers that manage user data, the components that assemble news feeds, or the networks that connect everything. Countries, regions or companies can host their own servers and still be part of a larger, pan-European social network. Of course, the AT Protocol is not the only possible route for building ENAF, but it is at least one track worth exploring. Moreover, it is cheaper than building a social network from scratch, although even that is, in principle, still not too bad if you compare it with the gigantic amounts Europe is going to spend on its own resilience.

An important question is how ENAF's governance might be structured. Working with open standards does not automatically give you an organisation to drive this story forward and make it commercially successful as well. One solution is to start from a non-commercial foundation – the Foundation in the acronym. This would develop and safeguard the standards and protocols to be used, but also ensure compliance with the rules, so that applications meet our European framework. The principles of free dissemination of opinion could also form part of these ground rules, so that the algorithms cannot grow into the same problematic rubbish machines we know from Facebook or X.

The foundation would not, however, have authority over which applications may or may not be built; in that respect, the market would be completely free. To jump-start the story commercially, at least one company would have to take the initiative to build a real social network, with functionalities like those we know from the American examples. My proposal is to put this in the hands of a consortium of European media companies. Let's call it the ENAF Media start-up. As a kind of epic revenge for what big tech has done to them, they would be the first to put an alternative on the market. If this succeeds, the benefits for media companies are enormous: advertising revenue becomes European again; transaction fees for, for example, subscriptions or pay-per-use are no longer skimmed off by Apple or Google at 30%; and – crucially – they once again become their own gatekeeper. That last point is strategically important for revalorising the media and their content, so that users get more than just headlines and news is placed in the right qualitative context. Combined with changes to the algorithms according to the principle of free dissemination of opinion, this will counter the formation of online echo chambers, because users will be informed in a broader and more diverse way.

Crucial to the success of ENAF-Media is whether users are willing to move to the new platform. One reason it's so hard to turn your back on, say, Facebook is that all your contacts are there. Arranging a bike ride for the kids with other parents? Facebook. Looking at photos from the rugby club's barbecue? Facebook. Following the class trip to England? Facebook. If you're not on Facebook, it feels like you're missing a lot – and that lock-in makes it very difficult to simply leave. Switching to a new service is only attractive if you can quickly find all your contacts there as well. One way to make that happen is to leverage the relationships media companies already have with their users. Together, European media companies serve hundreds of millions of people who consume their content regularly – sometimes daily – via apps, newsletters, or other channels. European streaming services alone, excluding Netflix, Apple TV, or Amazon Prime, have around 100 million registered users. Those existing relationships could be used to make people join ENAF-Media with a single click. On top of that, these companies have enormous reach through their own outlets, giving them the power to run self-promotion at scale – and, in one stroke, launch what could be the biggest advertising campaign ever, aimed at persuading Europeans to switch. If a number of celebrities and influencers are brought in as early adopters as well, the odds are good that a substantial share of users could move from American platforms to European equivalents in a very short time.

Of course, alongside our ENAF-Media start-up, other companies or organisations can also step forward from day one to develop their applications and let the free market do its work. ENAF's great advantage is that both developers and users can switch smoothly from one service to another across the entire ecosystem. It does not matter which chat app you use, or through which site you have uploaded videos: interoperability means that, in principle, this works transparently across all applications and platforms. No more being unable to send a message from WhatsApp to Apple iMessage.

While the ENAF-Media start-up is the first initiative to set this story in motion, it certainly should not be the only one. If this succeeds, within a few years we will have an ecosystem of apps and applications as rich as what we now know in the Apple App Store or on Google Play – but open, in the hands of European players, and with respect for our values and standards.

A pleasant global community

Frédéric De Vries, an ex-colleague, captures best in his opinion piece (LinkedIn 5 March 2025) what I have in mind:

'Build a global community where it is good to be. Where users' data is not for sale. Where the timeline is a real timeline: chronological. Where people, not algorithms, decide what they see. Where the power of AI is used the way Spotify uses it: to help users discover new things, not to keep them trapped in their own bubble.

A social platform should be a place where it is crystal clear what is an advert and what is not. Where advertisers are held accountable and posts can be verified by people for people. With a user interface designed around the most human user experience, not the most addictive. With content that can just as well be a 15-second video loop as a novel by Dostoyevsky or a film by Almodóvar. A platform that encourages conversations instead of debates.'

15. Transition sectors in which Europe can lead

Europe as a start-up

In the previous chapters, I talked about strategic industries in which, through copy-back, we can close our gap, to give Europe a meaningful role again. In this section, I build further on the idea of transition sectors, which I introduced in chapter 7. Using energy and defence, I explained how transition thinking can help Europe to lead in sectors that are fundamental to the future of our planet and our society. Transition thinking comes down to accepting that, for Europe, it is impossible to still compete with China or the US in the old industries, such as energy or food. That perspective changes, however, once we assume that those old sectors can no longer continue to function in the same way for much longer. Our changing world

– and especially climate pressure – forces us to go through a series of transitions. The goal is to find sustainable alternatives for activities that can no longer be organised the old way: energy, food and agriculture, housing and mobility, but equally defence and care.

With transition thinking, we let go of a sector's old paradigm, to focus on new solutions and technologies that are already available, but not yet dominant or profitable. By investing strategically in these, we build up, over time, a position that makes us competitive once these new solutions become mainstream. That requires a different way of thinking to identify and support the opportunities: we have to predict what will become important, what can change the world. We have to back it and keep at it for long enough. This is the typical situation many start-ups with an innovative idea once found themselves in before they gained enough momentum to change the market – and even the world: a revolutionary new idea needs time to establish itself alongside classic solutions, until the tipping point of adoption is reached, and the new solution gains enough traction to push the old models out of the market. That sets a sector's transition in motion for good. For this, start-ups need time and resources – and they get them too. Business angels, venture capitalists and stock markets provide capital, giving the start-up time to develop, test and grow. Everyone involved also knows that no profits are to be expected in the first four quarters, or even the first four years. The bet is firmly on long-term returns. When a start-up becomes a scale-up and then a unicorn (a company valued at one billion), that is often still not due to profits or revenues, but to the promise of the major transition that this company can realise with its solution.

In Europe, we need to learn to look at transition sectors and the innovations emerging there in the same way: they need time and resources to gain enough weight to make a difference and set the transition in motion. Within Readiness 2030 and other initiatives, space and a culture must be created to give promising solutions a chance, even if in the short term they are less profitable than the classic approach, or simply too exotic in the eyes of the old captains of industry. Once these solutions have become important enough, Europe gains assets that mean we no longer have to compete with the US, China or other regions in the world in the old way. We then play a different game, with different rules, and that can make us industrially strong again. In chapter 7, I illustrated this principle using energy and defence. If Europe succeeds in becoming strong in renewable energy, we no longer face much competition from the US or other regions that are still investing heavily in outdated energy generation. If we rethink our defence capacity on the basis of smart capabilities such as drones, autonomous systems, cyber defence and hybrid warfare – and therefore do not only count in aircraft and tanks – then Europe is able to play a leading role in that area too. Ukraine proves that every single day.

It may sound implausible, because when it comes to the start-up scene everyone looks to Silicon Valley – never to Hamburg, Ostend, Malmö, Córdoba, Budapest or Utrecht. But if Europe wants to succeed in these ambitions, it must behave the way the start-up world has done for decades. We create an environment in which innovations and start-ups are given the space to make a difference. We know it will take time for the solutions that emerge to become sufficiently high-performing and scalable. We accept that, at first, they are less profitable than the classic way of working – so we will burn money, but Europe must learn to invest smartly in opportunities, resources and time in order to later become a leader in a transition sector that gives us an edge over the competition. That this is not an impossible dream is proven by China, in the way it strategically invested in solar energy, batteries and electric cars – three transition sectors in which American and European companies saw little or no promise, because they were stuck in their old industrial paradigms. Over all those years, China poured money into them on a massive scale and pre-financed countless companies through subsidies. Until the moment the technology was ready and they are now conquering the world at breakneck speed, with no one able to compete with them any more. They have created their own market, with their own rules. The rest is stuck in a chasing position. If China could do this, why not Europe? In both cases the driver is the same: an underdog position that must be strategically corrected in order to earn a place at the geopolitical table.

In this chapter, I cover three more industries that lend themselves well as transition sectors for Europe: food and agriculture, housing and construction, and mobility. The diagram in figure 9 makes clear why these three sectors are priorities. Together they account for 75 percent of Europe's climate emissions, while each also faces its own economic and strategic challenges. These sectors will go through a transition anyway – something Europe would do better to view as an investment opportunity than as a burden or a threat.

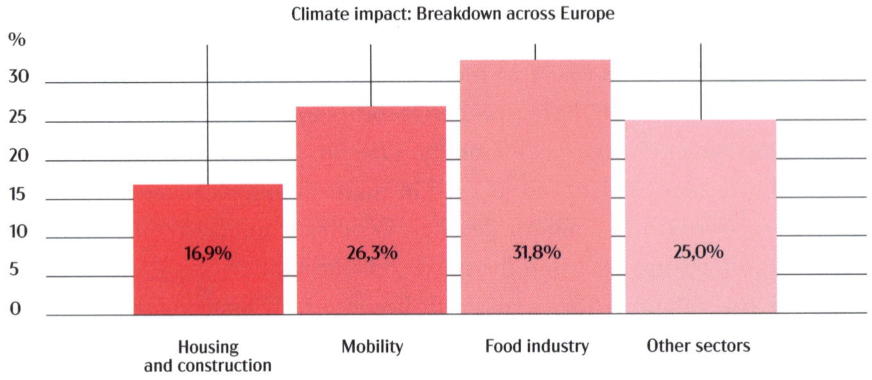

Figure 9: Climate impact Europe for the food and agriculture, housing and construction, and mobility sectors.

Food and agriculture as a transition sector

The biggest contributor to climate emissions is our traditional agricultural and food sector. Depending on the source, it is responsible for 30 to 34 percent of all emissions, leaving aside the challenges around biodiversity. Roughly one third of those emissions can be directly attributed to agriculture itself, and it is no surprise that livestock farming in particular has a significant impact. The main culprit, however, is the broader food system, in which food waste and transport play a major role. Given Europe's climate ambitions and the Green Deal, pressure on the agricultural sector is therefore high to change the way it operates. The problem, however, is that the sector is also under intense economic and social strain, leaving it very little room to transform. Farmers are not only sources of emissions, but are often also the first victims of climate disasters: drought or flooding have a major impact on their yields, and annual damage in the sector has now risen to almost 30 billion euros.

It is predicted that agricultural land in southern Europe could lose up to 80 percent of its value in the coming years. That makes the already precarious economic situation for many farmers downright unsustainable. Climate requirements demand investment and push costs upwards, while incomes in agriculture and horticulture average only half those in other sectors. The agricultural sector is also facing far-reaching ageing. Less than 6 percent of European farmers are under 35, and the inflow of new workers is stalling. In the Flemish Ardennes – the region where I live, and also one of the largest agricultural regions in Flanders – it is predicted that half of farmers will stop in the coming years, with no successor within their business. It is therefore no surprise that agriculture lags far behind in terms of digital transformation and technological innovation. Many farmers export part of their harvest, so Trump's import tariffs do not bode well either. European agriculture is facing a perfect storm of challenges that pose an existential threat to many farming businesses.

If you look at this negatively, you conclude that this sector is doomed. But if you flip the logic, you can argue that agriculture is the perfect sector to push through a transition: heavily outdated, negative impact on the climate, low profitability, technological lag, and a fragmented landscape with generally small players. For years, this has been the ideal recipe for major (digital) transformations. Sectors that have fundamentally changed over the past thirty years often share exactly those same characteristics: from the taxi sector and the music industry to the sale and rental of property. The good news is that, in recent years, quite a lot of innovation has been taking place in the sector. Turning agriculture and food into a transition sector therefore no longer requires searching for solutions (although that will never stop entirely), but implementing these new methods at scale within a European master plan for hybrid agriculture. In the box 'Precision agriculture, genetic manipulation, vertical farming, alternative proteins', I briefly describe a few of the most promising developments in the sector.

Precision agriculture, genetic manipulation, vertical farming, alternative proteins

A technique that is increasingly being applied in traditional agriculture is precision farming: technology is used to produce more with fewer resources. By using GPS, sensors, AI and even robots, fields can be managed down to the square centimetre. This not only leads to drastic reductions in the use of pesticides and fertilisers, but also increases resilience to climate fluctuations. The efficiency gains reduce costs, the precision reduces waste, and the system becomes less dependent on large expanses of land – something that is a challenge in Europe, especially compared with, for example, the US or Brazil.

The debate on genetic manipulation is still raging, but since March 2025 there has been new European regulation that opens the door to certain mild forms of genetic innovation through new genomic techniques (NGTs). Where conventional breeding can take years, NGTs can more quickly produce crops that are resistant to drought, disease and heat stress – all factors that are increasing because of climate change. This can create locally adapted varieties that deliver higher yields with fewer resources. Especially for farmers in southern regions with rapidly deteriorating farmland, NGTs can make the difference between survival and giving up. This happens within a strict European framework, in which only relatively 'natural' adjustments are allowed.

Vertical farming is a genuine innovation that offers new opportunities for urban food production. It takes place in enclosed spaces – from grow cabinets in supermarkets to containers and entire buildings – which can produce food all year round in a controlled environment, with yields per square metre that are far higher than in traditional agriculture. Companies such as Infarm, Jones Food Company, Urban Crop Solutions, Growy, Nordic Harvest and many others show that this can also be profitable in Europe, despite higher energy prices. Thanks to smart lighting and the reuse of residual heat, water and energy consumption is kept to a minimum. The model is scalable in urban environments and brings food closer to the consumer, with the option to harvest only when needed. As mentioned earlier, transport and food waste are major sources of emissions, so vertical farming can make a particularly positive contribution in this respect. Combined with renewable energy, this is a promising solution for regions where traditional cultivation is under pressure.

Did you know that, in Europe, up to 1,300 litres of water are needed to produce 1 kilogram of beef? In Belgium and the Netherlands, that also comes with an average of 22 kilograms of CO_2, while in Brazil it can rise to 80 kilograms. Livestock farming is one of the major sources of emissions, so the shift to alternative proteins is a logical and necessary development. Whether it is cultivated meat, insects, protein-rich plants, algae or products based on precision fermentation, the common denominator is that they require far less land, water and emissions than conventional livestock farming. One challenge will be to bring consumers along mentally in this shift towards healthier and more sustainable food, but solutions exist there too. It may still take a while before people eat recognisable insects or worms, but processed foods already use proteins of mixed origin. The chance that you are eating lasagne in France with up to 4 percent yellow mealworms, and that the biscuits with your coffee contain migratory locusts, is high. The cheese in that lasagne could, by now, also perfectly well come from fermented cauliflower. My tip: read the packaging a little more carefully from now on.

If you look at European agriculture's future through an innovative lens, it does not have to be a pessimistic story at all. By embracing technology, innovation and new business models, this sector can not only drastically reduce its climate impact, but also restore its economic and social fabric. What matters here is embracing what I call hybrid farming. Tomorrow's farmer is a versatile entrepreneur who invests on multiple fronts at once through a mix of methods and crops. Traditional farmland that, through precision farming and adapted crops, delivers premium products, combined with year-round lettuce from vertical farming: it can work perfectly well. In addition, in a decommissioned cowshed, with a dozen Better Origin containers, you can breed worms fully automatically as animal feed for a select herd of top-quality cattle. Even micro-factories on the farm that process milk fully automatically into finished products such as cheese and butter can, by now, perfectly well supplement the farmer's business.

Even if we successfully apply only some of these techniques, the impact on emissions is enormous. In a conservative scenario, an annual saving of around 500 million tonnes of CO_2 in net emissions would be possible in Europe – good for roughly half of the sector's current emissions. In the most optimistic scenario, that could eventually be much higher, and even a carbon-positive future comes within reach. If Europe approaches this transition as a strategic project, with sufficient support and coordination, then the farming model of the future can be ecologically responsible, economically viable and technologically leading all at once. In that future, our agriculture would no longer need to compete with large-scale, traditional farming far away, because we succeed in meeting our own food needs in a diverse, high-tech and local way, underpinned by a profitable business model. But it will not happen by itself. Despite the many initiatives that already exist, both from Europe and from private investors, we will need to scale up the agricultural transition into a European master plan. From a start-up mentality, we will have to tackle this with long-term objectives and become the winner in this domain, even if that means doing it for a while at high risk and at a loss. If that succeeds, within fifteen years Europe will not only be at the top of the world in agricultural and food innovation, but will also be largely self-sufficient and therefore geopolitically less dependent on the whims of the world powers.

Mobility as a transition sector

The mobility sector is grappling with various problems that, together, could lead to a perfect storm. The entire mobility sector is responsible for around 26 percent of emissions, with passenger cars accounting for roughly half of that. European climate regulation is therefore forcing this sector into a fundamental transition. Through a systematic lowering of the maximum emissions standards for manufactured vehicles, European carmakers are being compelled to make their old internal combustion engines cleaner and, via an intermediate step with hybrid cars, ultimately switch fully to 100 percent electric vehicles. Just as media companies lost a lot of time by failing to adapt in time, the European car industry largely ignored developments in its sector until it could no longer do so. What confronted it with the limits of its current model was not only growing European pressure – after all, with the right lobbying and threats of further job losses, they could probably delay that pressure for a while longer. The real wake-up call came with the invasion of Chinese EVs into the European market.

For several years now, the number of high-quality and reliable electric cars has been steadily growing. New brands are constantly joining the market, trying to tempt consumers with prices far below those of their European counterparts. This phenomenon is not new: the first ten years of the electrification of the European car market were dominated by Tesla. Now that that brand is in danger of falling from its pedestal and European brands finally have an attractive EV offering of their own, Chinese cars are being unloaded by the thousands in our ports. An additional challenge for the sector is changing user behaviour. While the pandemic initially caused a drop in sales – partly due to disruptions in global supply chains – a more fundamental shift in consumer behaviour is now emerging. This is no longer a temporary dip, but a structural change, especially visible among young people. Gen Z and millennials attach less value to car ownership as a status symbol and increasingly opt for a combination of alternatives: the bicycle, public transport, shared mobility and small electric vehicles. Car sharing is becoming ever more common, and mobility subscriptions that provide access to multiple forms of transport fit their lives better.

What drives them is rarely ideology. It is mainly practical considerations that tip the balance: costs, ease of use, reliability and safety. Sustainability certainly plays a role, but it is not the decisive factor. Essentially, the question is shifting from 'which car should I buy?' to 'how do I get from A to B efficiently, cheaply and flexibly?' Still, we should not generalise. Just as 'the people' do not exist, neither do 'young people'. I know just as many 20-year-olds who dream of their first BMW as

19-year-olds who have no interest in cars at all and would rather spend their money differently. What is striking, though, is that this latter group is often remarkably skilled and creative in planning complex journeys using public or shared transport. Either way, a mobility transition is clearly emerging, and it is the younger generations in particular who are setting the tone.

For an industry that has run for decades on the idea of individual car ownership, this change is existential. The structural decline in applications for driving licences and car registrations among young people in countries such as the Netherlands, Belgium and Germany shows that this is a broad European trend. Young people are growing up in cities where cars are seen more as a nuisance than as freedom, and where access to digital mobility solutions is taken for granted. This generation has grown up with apps, real-time information and freedom of choice, and expects the same from mobility. The question is what happens when these young people get older and perhaps seek out the relative calm of the countryside with their family. Will their mobility needs shift again then, and if so, in what direction? Will car sales pick up again, or are they the first generation to switch to fundamentally new mobility solutions as a result of a broader European mobility transition?

From a classic industrial perspective, this is a disaster for Europe: carmakers that have only just recovered from the Dieselgate scandal are struggling with electrification and cheap Chinese cars being dumped onto the market. On top of that, they are dealing with a new generation that is not as crazy about cars. Looked at that way, this once again seems like a sector that can no longer cope with competition, and where hundreds of thousands of jobs risk being lost. If we approach this from a transition mindset, that future does not have to be pessimistic at all. What if we adopt the new generation's mantra as a guiding principle for the entire sector: how do I get from A to B in the best way? Then we are no longer talking about the car industry, but about the mobility industry. The old paradigm, in which every car sold was a success, gives way to a new model in which every passenger transported becomes the goal. About ten years ago, I was involved in a strategic exercise for a federation in the automotive sector. It was the beginning of the issue: hardly any electric cars, but the first signs of shared mobility, electric bikes and changing user behaviour. Although the members of the working group were, without exception, people from the car sector itself – for whom, until then, selling cars was the most important thing – the conclusion was that they needed to evolve from an automobile federation into a mobility federation.

How can such a mobility-oriented model work, and how does it differ from a model that revolves around individual car sales?

Paris, New York or the countryside

Car owners are in the minority in places like Paris or New York. The concentration of public transport, taxis, shared cars, shared e-scooters and shared bikes usually makes a combination of these modes of transport more efficient than having your own car. First you have to get a car out of a car park, then you end up sitting in traffic. Finally, you have to park somewhere, preferably as close as possible to your destination.

If you live in the countryside, or regularly commute over longer distances, it is a different story. In recent years I have supported several regional organisations in thinking about the future of clusters of roughly fifteen towns and municipalities that were often rural and spread out. There too, you see policymakers looking for alternative forms of mobility and for ways to connect regions better through new mobility solutions. Suggestions included building smart cycling superhighways, shared bikes, shared cars that you can leave anywhere across the region, or deploying (autonomous) minibuses that connect the various corners of a region day and night.

The mobility sector is on the eve of a revolution. Besides electrification and changing user behaviour, there is one development that could turn a hundred years of car history on its head: autonomous vehicles. Although Tesla's empty promises gave critics ammunition to conclude that much is promised and little delivered, that picture is not entirely accurate. After a period in which belief in autonomous vehicles seemed to ebb away and many said fully autonomous driving was too complex to realise safely, the mood has now shifted completely. The consensus is clear: autonomous vehicles already exist, and we will see them appear on our streets en masse in the coming years. If we look at the facts, we see that the technology is taking its final steps towards maturity. In the US, Waymo is the dominant player in the commercial robotaxi market. With a fleet of 1,500 vehicles, they carry out 250,000 paid rides a week. Meanwhile, they have already driven more than 150 million kilometres autonomously, half of that in the first six months of 2025, a doubling compared with the entire period before that. Thanks to the integration of generative AI, the systems are getting better, more reliable and safer. Situations in which a robotaxi would previously get stuck are now often manageable thanks to smart AI solutions.

Tesla is also investing in this evolution, albeit through a different approach. Unlike other companies, they rely solely on cameras and AI, without additional sensors and radar systems. Because millions of Teslas worldwide continuously collect and transmit video data, their AI can develop further at breakneck speed. Tesla has recently been testing a limited fleet in Texas, although the first reactions – to put it mildly – have been rather mixed. The real acceleration is coming – how could it be otherwise – from China. Companies such as Baidu and Pony already have hundreds of robotaxis driving around in various cities, while brands such as BYD are building autonomous functions into their cars for consumers. Here too, massive government support plays a key role in the ambition to become a dominant global player. In Europe, development appears to be moving more slowly. Although there are limited tests with autonomous vehicles on public roads and brands such as Mercedes and BMW are working on their own technology, Europe is visibly lagging behind the US and China. Or so it seems. In reality, the market is developing here too, albeit under the radar. Since 2021, more than 1.5 billion euros have been invested in research, development and test environments for autonomous mobility.

Europe's apparent slowness is a deliberate strategy, aimed at developing the right regulation and shared infrastructure. By creating more than a hundred test locations, aligning regulations and developing standards, Europe is laying the foundation for broad implementation from 2026 onwards. Germany, France and the United Kingdom are each taking a pioneering role, resulting in a diverse range of applications – from autonomous shuttles and delivery pods to off-road vehicles and ridepooling platforms. What distinguishes Europe here from China and the US is a stronger focus on shared mobility and sustainability. Rather than betting on individual robotaxis as a replacement for private cars, or building autonomous functions into cars for sale to private consumers, the emphasis is on collective solutions: on-demand buses, autonomous shuttles and shared fleets. With some three hundred operational ridepooling systems, there is already a solid culture of shared transport here. In Europe, autonomous technology is seen not only as a technological innovation, but as a lever for a genuine mobility transition. Within the framework of this book, this is a crucial development, with potentially far-reaching consequences for the sector and for Europe's strategic autonomy.

This transition is manifesting for the European car sector on two levels: the business model and the product itself. It is clear that Europe is betting on shared mobility. In time, this means that the market of one-to-one car sales to private individuals will be replaced by a fleet market, in which vehicles are used. This is a fundamental transformation: car brands would no longer make money through the classic network of selling cars to end users. At present, every car sold contributes to the profit target, and whether those cars are used after purchase is, in principle, of secondary importance: the revenue has already been realised. When you know that an average car sits idle for more than 90 percent of the time, you realise how little sense this business model still makes. In the transition model, cars are only considered successful if they are used: for every kilometre they travel, for every minute they are driving. This fundamentally changes the paradigm of the car industry. If this becomes the norm, most cars will no longer be designed, built and sold as products in which we also want to see our personality reflected. Cars then become functional objects with one clear purpose: to get passengers to their destination as safely and efficiently as possible. In that model, everything revolves around optimising fleets. Cars that stand still 90 percent of the time are simply no longer an option.

If you look at the robots in Amazon warehouses, you see that, on average, they are active for twenty hours a day. For shared cars, it will presumably be no different. Those four hours of 'rest' are needed for maintenance, cleaning and charging. At the moment, brands are strongly focused on their specific positioning: from family car to sporty or luxury. In a future of shared mobility, that brand identity is less relevant at vehicle level, and more so at the level of the fleet option. What I mean by that is something you can already see in apps like Uber: you do not choose the brand, but a category or segment – from cheap and shared to ecological, luxurious, a van, or a pet-friendly option. Which brand you ultimately get only becomes clear after you have booked and the car is on its way. Cars will be designed to drive at least one million kilometres, be easy to maintain and repair, and look timeless because they need to last as long as possible. The classic rhythm – a minor facelift every two years and a completely new model every four years to entice customers – disappears. That will no longer be the way carmakers bring their models to market.

Brand identity no longer matters

Just observe your own attitude when you take the bus or train again, or board a plane. Unless you specialise in the subject, you do not pay attention to the year of manufacture, let alone recognise the brand or type of bus, train or aircraft. When you get into a taxi, you might still notice the make and model, but whether that Mercedes E-Class is one year old or has been on the road for five years is secondary to other things: how clean the vehicle is, how well the driver drives, and whether you get to your destination smoothly.

For Europe's car sector, this evolution brings both enormous challenges and opportunities. The big advantage – if we manage to change tack – is that business models based on mobility usage differ fundamentally from the classic sales model. That also means the competition problem – where even the cheapest European EVs cannot compete with Chinese models – becomes largely irrelevant. We would no longer be competing with products, but with services. If we follow that logic through, the higher investment costs also become less important. You do not need to compare a European Mercedes of 100,000 euros, built to last one million kilometres as a shared car or taxi, with a BYD of 40,000 euros sold to a family. What matters is the TCO – the total cost of ownership – over the vehicle's full lifespan. That turns out more favourable for the more expensive shared car that is used twenty hours a day and covers one million kilometres over thirteen years. A privately owned car stands still an average of 22 hours a day and drives about 150,000 kilometres over a period of, say, seven years, after which it enters the second-hand market. Simple simulations show that, with these assumptions, the cost ratios are roughly 1 to 1.5 in favour of shared cars.

A pattern is emerging here: if, over the next fifteen years, Europe's car sector fully commits to this mobility transition, we can neutralise part of the competitive pressure from Chinese providers. Of course, we could also deploy Chinese vehicles in our fleets, but with a well-thought-out European policy – fuelled by programmes such as Readiness 2030 and other resilience strategies – we can build a robust European mobility framework, with sustainability, strategic autonomy and employment at its core, and in which both manufacturers and fleet operators can operate profitably. Especially if we vertically integrate the production and operation of vehicles, with European players active across the entire value chain, it becomes harder for Chinese or other foreign providers to enter the market. A usage model is, by definition, local: with local operators who deploy, maintain and manage vehicles within their own region.

For Europe's car industry, the transition remains a major challenge either way. It requires a fundamental rethink of the range and the way it is brought to market. Undoubtedly, a great many private cars for individual use will still be produced and sold under the classic model. That market will not simply disappear, even as shared mobility continues to grow. This creates a hybrid reality, in which some premium brands may continue to cling to the old sales logic, while other brands completely change course and vertically integrate into the logic of shared mobility and fleets. Still other players may choose to combine everything. It will not be easy, but if the European sector manages to make this shift, we will have secured a strategically important industry again and realised a necessary societal transition. If we manage to meet mobility needs through shared models with fewer cars – all of them electric – then the societal effects are significant: structurally lower emissions, safer traffic with fewer casualties, less hard surfacing because shared cars do not require individual parking spaces, and therefore more liveable, greener cities that are better able to withstand future heatwaves.

Attachment to your own car

How desirable is the shared car for the user? In my work for the car federation, the remark I often heard from more conservative voices was: the Belgian will never want to give up their own car. That is true: we – and with us many other Europeans – attach a great deal of value to that thing. Rationally, it is hard to defend: it sits still for most of the day, costs us an arm and a leg, and is usually the second-largest expense in the average household budget. You can hardly call that a truly good decision. Yet many people cling stubbornly to their own car and the right to drive themselves.

But 'many' is not 'everyone', just as 'the people', 'the youth', 'the Belgian' or 'the Dutch' do not exist. The number of users who are no longer interested in owning their own car is growing, and that will only increase as new mobility models develop into a broad, efficient and attractive offering. If autonomous cars and minibuses also become available at night and right out to the corners of the country, so that shared mobility is no longer something that only works in cities, more and more people will experience the convenience of these new solutions.

Of course, some will stubbornly continue to hold on to their own car – and that should remain possible. The transition needs to be positive: people should choose the alternative because it is simply better, cheaper and more pleasant. Those who prefer to cling to the past will be able to do so, while inevitably being confronted with a scarcer offering, and possibly with stricter rules on what can and cannot be done with a private car. That still promises to get quite heated.

Then the final question of this paragraph: how affordable is all this for the end user? If we assume investment costs of 100,000 euros for a car with a lifespan of one million kilometres, then the cost per kilometre – including a driver – comes to around 2 euros. That calculation takes into account both a traditional profit margin of 10 to 20 percent in production and a margin of 100 percent in operation. Once that car drives autonomously and no driver is needed, the cost per kilometre drops drastically. A first rough estimate comes out at around 50 cents per kilometre. If we compare this with the current costs of car ownership, we see that in Belgium – according to a European study by LeasePlan – this averages around 700 euros per month. The average Belgian drives barely 13,000 kilometres a year. In a fully shared model, the monthly costs are about 550 euros, which amounts to an average saving of 150 euros per month, per car. If we do the same calculation with a car costing 50,000 euros, the cost per kilometre comes to around 30 cents and the monthly costs to about 325 euros – less than half of what it costs to own a car. If you share a journey with multiple passengers, those costs drop even further. All figures are, of course, approximations, but they do point the way. I therefore warmly invite people in the sector to check these calculations critically and refine them.

Housing as a transition industry

If you have been looking for a new home yourself in recent years, you will undoubtedly have noticed that the housing sector is in crisis. Climate change and housing's major impact on CO_2 emissions only make an urgent problem even more pressing. The vast majority of European homes do not meet the standards needed to reduce housing's climate impact. The European Green Deal therefore imposes strict requirements for energy efficiency, which means that tens of millions of homes will have to be thoroughly renovated. What began as a voluntary system of subsidies and premiums is now evolving into an obligation for owners – an investment for which the resources, the skilled workers and the raw materials are often lacking. And all this while the affordability of decent housing is already under pressure across Europe. In some cities, households spend more than 40 percent of their net income on housing – an unsustainable situation that fuels social tensions. Since 2015, house prices in the EU have risen by an average of almost 50%; in countries such as the Netherlands, by more than 80%. Ownership is becoming unattainable for more and more people, while renting on the private market rarely offers a cheaper alternative.

The war in Ukraine and the subsequent economic downturn have significantly slowed the development of new homes. Higher construction costs and rising interest rates make new housing far more expensive than a few years ago. As a result, fewer housing units are being built than are needed to maintain market balance, which pushes prices up further. Property developers and contractors are struggling, and the pandemic and the war have also exposed the vulnerability of foreign supply chains. That forces a rethink around strategic autonomy and local production, but that shift requires major investment in a sector that is already operating on tight or negative margins. What partly masks the price trend is the difference in quality between homes. Sustainable new builds and thoroughly renovated properties are scarce, which pushes their prices up further. Poorly insulated homes are becoming relatively cheaper, because they must be renovated after purchase – which reduces demand. People on limited budgets are therefore forced to move into outdated and poorly insulated homes, leading to higher energy bills and directly undermining the EU's climate targets. Affordable and sustainable housing has thus become a social, ecological and economic problem that can only be tackled through transition thinking.

Demographic trends make the picture even more complex. Household size is shrinking, the number of people living alone is rising, blended families call for more flexible solutions, and ageing is palpable. As a result, demand for smaller and more flexible forms of housing is increasing. The current housing supply does not respond sufficiently to this, and people are being forced to live in properties that do not match their actual needs: either too small or too large. Add to that the growing migration pressure on urban regions, and it becomes clear that Europe is facing a fundamental problem. In terms of quality, volume and typology, the existing housing stock is insufficiently aligned with current and future housing needs. That mismatch grows every year, while the Green Deal clock keeps ticking. Tangible symptoms such as the housing crisis are disastrous for citizens' trust (see also chapter 9). It is therefore no coincidence that Europe is now trying to take back control through recent policy interventions. The appointment of a European Commissioner for Housing and the announcement of an Action Plan for Affordable Housing in 2026 are clear signals.

By relaxing state-aid rules, public construction of social housing must get going again. At the same time, by 2030 the EU's renovation wave aims to tackle as many as 35 million buildings, through a combination of European funding, national legislation and local implementation. This should bring about a transformation of Europe's building stock that serves climate targets and stimulates economic growth. It also offers economic opportunities: it can create hundreds of thousands of green jobs and stimulate innovation in the sector. The only thing is that, in the current situation, this will have little chance of success if we continue to look at the sector in a traditional way. The only way to tackle this challenge is through transition thinking. Building and housing need to be reinvented from the ground up, in terms of both urban housing models and construction methods, to be marketed in a different way. Only if we put this puzzle together properly will we succeed in giving enough people access to affordable, sustainable and suitable homes.

The first transition dimension of how we should deal with housing in the future concerns the urban-planning approach. Current rules and laws still force us to develop property through a policy lens that was relevant in the 1970s, but no longer aligns with today's needs and problems. From the perspective of climate and biodiversity goals, infill development is the new norm. Expansion requires additional land take, leading to more hard surfacing – a bad idea in times of drought, heat and flooding. Infill development – the high-quality redevelopment of built-up space – offers an answer here. The conversion of old sites in towns and cities is particularly well suited to this. Think of abandoned schools or factory buildings that could provide space for dozens, sometimes hundreds, of housing units. New, smart projects also provide high-quality shared spaces, such as park gardens, integrated sports facilities or shared meeting places. The more shared functions a project offers, the less private living space is needed to live well. An apartment with a third bedroom as a home office is unnecessary if there is a co-working space available nearby.

A challenge remains that not everyone is willing to live more densely or swap a house in the countryside for an apartment in the city. That is why it is important to ensure a balanced mix of different housing types. Moreover, densification does not have to be limited to cities; even in villages you can do infill housing in a smart way without it coming at the expense of quality of life.

Conversion of a farmhouse

A friend recently redeveloped a farmhouse courtyard in a neighbouring municipality in the Flemish Ardennes. Most of these properties have been converted into luxury single-family homes in recent years. He chose a different model: he divided the farmhouse into ten separate homes, each with at least three bedrooms and full comfort. Access to the homes is via a shared, central courtyard garden – a safe play area for children and a meeting space for neighbours. In addition, each home has its own garden and parking space. There is a bus stop at the front door and the village centre is a ten-minute walk away.

The conversion of the farmhouse courtyard is a fine example of decentralised densification. What is crucial, then, is that alongside homes there are also sufficient amenities, so that extra residents do not automatically lead to more mobility and therefore more nuisance. Shops, hospitality, decentralised workplaces, culture and schools need to be integrated into the same master plan, to create a liveable and balanced environment. In *The World is Round* I call this concept the urban village: an approach in which villages regain the liveliness of the past and urban neighbourhoods reclaim a village-like character – each time through the right mix of living, working, leisure, care and more. In this new mix, we also need to take account of changing needs, so that, for example, older people can continue to function as single-person households in the village centres where they have lived all their lives. Smartly combining housing needs across different demographic groups can contribute to stronger communities, and can even lead to new, interesting business models.

I myself sit on the board of a large residential property developer and on the advisory board of an industrial construction contractor. In addition, for years I advised various companies that develop building materials worldwide. That has given me a good insight into the state of digitisation and innovation in the sector. Until a few years ago, construction was one of the most archaic and fragmented industries you can imagine. A tough trade where (generally) men built houses with their bare hands and heavy machinery in a way that has barely evolved over the past one hundred years. Granted, there is now more insulation, there is triple glazing, and central heating no longer runs on fuel oil, but on gas or, at best, a heat pump. But beyond that, it remains a process of bricks, mortar, concrete, steel beams and, here and there, some wood. Everything is made to measure on the construction site itself, following the plans of an architect who wants to make every home a unique creative project. In recent years, the men on site often spoke eastern European languages, but because of the war in Ukraine and economic developments in Poland it is now a challenge to find enough people at all. This approach is not going to help us make the transition that is needed.

The only way to develop homes quickly and in a climate-friendly way is to build radically differently: both the construction process and the materials used have to change. More and more, we are seeing companies such as Leko Labs or Circl building homes in a different way, but they remain the exception. If you look at their websites, they look nothing like what you would expect from a construction firm. Both build prefabricated modular homes that they can deliver in just a few weeks. Circl advertises that your home will be up within twelve weeks, whereas the average lead time for a classic project is usually more than a year. Leko Labs works with a fully automated production line, in which all the components of your house are prepared by robots with millimetre precision. Everything is loaded onto a lorry and assembled on site within a few days. The main material used is sustainable timber, and materials are made as circular as possible, both during construction and afterwards in use, resulting in far lower emissions. Circl promises more than a 30 percent CO_2 reduction compared with conventional construction, and Leko Labs even speaks of carbon-negative construction. To what extent they can both live up to those claims remains to be seen, but there is no doubt: these are the pioneers of how the construction of tomorrow should be done.

The essence of modular prefabricated construction is that all components are prepared in advance, robotised in a factory setting. As a result, hardly any people are still needed on site: a solution to the acute shortage of skilled workers. Moreover, progress becomes perfectly predictable: no downtime due to bad weather, everything happens in a controlled environment. Techniques such as heating and electricity are prepared precisely, so that on site the entire set is assembled like a big Lego box. Modular construction also means the end of everything being bespoke. Each home can still be unique, but it is always a combination of a number of standard modules that are joined together into the desired house. Once such a house is up, you cannot distinguish it from houses built in the traditional way. Other construction innovations that are on the way and are still in their infancy today could tomorrow become part of the mix of solutions to build more efficiently, faster, cheaper and more sparingly. One of the most adventurous is the use of giant 3D printers that can print an entire building in a few days. Bricklaying robots are also gaining ground – both in prefab factories and on the construction site itself – with walls going up at speed, while the master bricklayer, like a kind of robot herder, oversees a high-quality result.

One of the major changes awaiting construction is a full commitment to circularity. Concretely, this means that from the design stage, buildings are put together in such a way that they can later be dismantled and reused easily – either on a different site, or as a raw material for a new project. Reusing construction waste as the basis for new building materials – so-called urban mining – not only has a positive impact on climate emissions, but also helps reduce our dependence on new raw materials, which are often imported. In addition, large-scale research is under way into ways of producing traditional building materials such as brick, concrete and steel far more sustainably. There are already strong examples of companies that no longer fire their bricks, but shape them under high pressure, or use concrete that absorbs CO_2 instead of causing emissions during production. In parallel with these developments, there is the accelerating digitisation that is finally also gaining traction in the construction sector. Although Building Information Systems (BIM) have been available for years to optimise the building process, there have always been reasons for the sector to give them a wide berth. But because of all the other innovations, and the need to strengthen the sector in economically difficult times, we are now seeing faster adoption after all – including the use of AI. The sector is facing its own perfect storm and, just as in the car world, I dare to predict that by 2040 newly developed homes will look different: in where they are located, in what they look like, and in how they contribute to the search for climate solutions.

The only problem with everything I have described above is that there are few or no options to lower the price of a home – on the contrary. If we do not tackle this structurally, then within fifteen years we will have fantastic homes in pleasant places, but nobody will be able to afford them. Here too, we will therefore have to look for the right innovation. If we want housing to be not only sustainable, but also social, then the business model has to change. In my previous book *The Future Formula* I go into this issue in detail. How do we ensure that people can continue to make use of a product that becomes too expensive because of all these developments? As I indicated in the paragraph on mobility, a key part of the solution is to think in terms of use rather than ownership. In housing, that principle has existed for a long time: we call it renting. But if the housing market remains unaffordable

– and the situation may worsen further – rents will also keep rising. So we need to look structurally for ways to enable people to live more cheaply and more sustainably. Part of the population is entitled to social housing, but here I am mainly talking about everyone else – the growing group for whom this problem is also gradually becoming untenable.

There are many possibilities, but so far they remain stuck in their niches. Nor do I have the ambition to discuss all of them in detail in this book, so I will pick out just a few. One option is to make government land available (virtually) free of charge through a so-called Community Land Trust. You can put a building on that land, but the land itself remains the property of the public authority. That substantially lowers the cost of the home, because land often accounts for a large share of total project costs. The downside is that you are never 100 percent the owner of the property on that land. But in principle, that only becomes a problem for your great-great-grandchildren – and who knows what the world will look like by then? Although there are fine examples of this kind of structure, including in Ghent, London and Brussels, there is another problem: many local authorities rely on the sale of their available land to balance their own budgets.

Other solutions include cooperative housing and cohousing. This is often associated with 'lentil-and-sandals' initiatives, where families with a similar ideology develop a property together into a combination of private homes and shared infrastructure. Cohousing is the hip and trendy counterpart, where young adults typically live in a single house with a well-equipped private room, and share the living room, kitchen and other facilities with other residents – in both rental and purchase models. Both approaches are currently niche and small-scale, but they can inspire the development of large-scale housing platforms in which traditional property investors, residents and even local authorities participate together. In such a model, you no longer own your home in the traditional sense, but hold shares in the property portfolio of which your home forms part. One final way to reduce housing costs is to take the additional investment needed to make a home sustainable out of the base cost of the property – both for new builds and renovations – and have it paid for by so-called ESCOs (Energy Service Companies). Concretely: you pay for your home, and they invest in solar panels, heat pumps, batteries and any other energy technologies. Instead of your investment costs rising and you therefore having to repay more to the bank, they take on that part of the investment. In return, you pay them a fixed amount for your energy – an amount you would otherwise be spending each month with a conventional energy supplier anyway.

Once again we see how difficult it is for all stakeholders to step away from the classic model and embrace these business model innovations. Banks need to develop new financing formulas, governments need to subsidise in a different way, tax systems need to be adjusted, investors need to be willing to think differently about housing platforms – even if the return is slightly lower than with traditional sales – and residents need to learn to look at ownership and property in a new way. It will be a necessary path if we are to maintain public support and therefore keep Europe strong, because the loss of decent housing is the spark that can set off a revolution. The first populist to seize on this will win elections in many cities immediately. I am not sure whether Readiness 2030 includes a chapter on new affordable and sustainable forms of housing, but if the plan aims to strengthen European resilience, then this must be an essential part of it.

Transitions and building public support

I have described five transition sectors that all share similar characteristics: energy, defence, agriculture, mobility and housing. The underlying idea is that, in these domains, the world will have to evolve anyway if it is to be ready for a future in which climate change will guide our actions. This is certainly true for energy, agriculture, mobility and housing, and less so for defence. The other line of reasoning behind these transition sectors is that, in the classic way, Europe does not really have a strong position to compete with the countries that have dominated these domains for years. By looking at defence, energy and mobility in an innovative way, Europe can help determine the rules of tomorrow and, as a result, once again play a meaningful role on the world stage. Transition thinking, in other words, helps us achieve several goals at once. The problem, however, is finding the necessary public support to set these transitions in motion. Transitions cost money, and neither individuals nor companies are particularly keen on change. We can activate and motivate the business world through the necessary financial support. In all the sectors described, there are already many innovations, both among traditional providers and new players. Because of the current geopolitical crisis, Europe is investing heavily in both policy and funding to give these innovations the chance to scale up.

The biggest hurdle for adoption and public support lies mainly with individuals. In the short to medium term there are few fundamental innovations that will cost citizens less money; on the contrary: in energy, mobility, housing and food alike, sustainability in most cases still comes with a higher price tag. We are facing a world in which both purchasing power and European budgets are coming under pressure. Additional investment in defence and climate action will strain those budgets even further. Ageing populations threaten to make pensions unaffordable. Artificial intelligence could push many people towards unemployment in the coming years. These are all very real developments that make it difficult to motivate people to also invest more in, say, housing or mobility. One possible solution is for Europe to subsidise these developments extensively, keeping the impact on citizens limited. The question is to what extent both regulation and financial resources will allow this. The other possibility lies with the market itself, and I have referred to it in the context of energy, housing and mobility alike: if we commit to new business models, then the question of affordability shifts. An electric autonomous car may be too expensive to buy, but not to use. A sustainable house is unaffordable if we still want to own it, but shares in a housing cooperative or a property portfolio do give us the chance to build value and a pension, even if we rent our own home. Once again, I would like to refer the reader to my previous book *The Future Formula*, where this logic is worked out in detail.

Even if the costs remain under control and the transitions are affordable for society, this operation will still require an enormous amount of mental energy from citizens. A level of change like this calls for a strong approach and a powerful story to bring people along and get them excited. In chapter 10, I already discussed how we need to communicate differently, with two major principles: stop magnifying problems (because that sells more newspapers) and focus on the available solutions; stop communicating about abstract macro-themes such as climate, liveable cities or defence and instead focus on micro-themes that are close to people. We show small, manageable results that everyone understands and whose effect is visible in the short term, with a clear, individual benefit for the citizen. With this approach, we present the necessary transitions in a concrete and recognisable story, in which each element has clear advantages. We show how affordable housing becomes possible again through investment in modern, energy-efficient homes in liveable villages and urban neighbourhoods, with a strong sense of community and extra jobs. Those neighbourhoods are designed around people: low-traffic streets create space for meeting, plenty of greenery and basic amenities close by. Nowhere do we talk about removing paving stones, a concrete stop, infill development, heat islands and heat deaths, low-emission zones or mobility plans.

In the story, locally produced food becomes the norm, with attention to price, quality and revaluing local farmers and new producers of innovative food products. We do not talk about nitrogen standards, over-fertilisation or an 'protein transition'. Mobility is presented as a simple and affordable solution for every need: quickly using a shared bike or shared car, travelling autonomously from the village to the city and back again – even after a night out – and covering long distances comfortably in self-driving minibuses, where possible connecting to a good network of European trains. The benefit for the citizen is clear: finally smooth travel without traffic jams, goodbye to the structurally high costs of two cars per household, and no more wasted time because of parking problems. We do not talk about climate change, annual deaths from fine particulate matter or road safety. This approach is not aimed at doom messages, threats or obligations, but at dreams and improvements. We do not want to present change as a negative choice that amounts to losing what we had. On the contrary: we try to get people to believe voluntarily and enthusiastically in what is possible, so that they themselves make a positive choice to help build that new world. We do not want to prohibit and impose, but to entice.

The micro-story translates Europe's initiatives, plans and resources into something every citizen understands – and genuinely wants: a better life, quality, comfort, new jobs – including for people with fewer qualifications – and opportunities for entrepreneurs in new markets around construction, food, energy and mobility. And all of that from a strong Europe, which we as citizens can be proud of. That is also the direct link with the macro-themes and goals that we as a society have to achieve with each of these initiatives: building a strong Europe that can play a meaningful geopolitical role. Citizens draw energy and motivation from tangible improvements in their own lives, while Europe builds support for what the real objective is: a resilient Europe that succeeds in meeting climate and sustainability targets in this turbulent world.

16. What is Europe lacking?

If we assume that Europe can embrace a new innovation paradigm – one in which, through both transition thinking and copy-back initiatives, we can once again build a strong continent – then we have to acknowledge that we are still missing fundamental instruments to bring this adventure to a successful conclusion. Fortunately, we are seeing indications that improvement is on the way. In this final chapter, I reflect on what are usually cited as the main reasons why Europe does produce strong innovations, but often fails to translate them into real value for the market and society. In that respect, the US succeeds systematically better than we do. Although there are several causes, I will limit myself here to the four most important areas of work that Europe needs to set up so that – in addition to everything we have already discussed – it can also rise to this challenge. We need to build an innovation ecosystem that can match the US. That goes hand in hand with how the financing of innovations, start-ups and scale-ups is organised. On another level, we lack the kind of leadership that the US seems to have a monopoly on, both within our political structures and in the form of strong individual leaders. As a final area of work, Europe must build the self-confidence to dare, to believe in the strength of its own continent, and to develop a proud identity in which Europeans – in all their diversity – stand together for one common goal: a respected place at the table of the new world order.

Europe needs a stronger innovation ecosystem

The US, with Silicon Valley as its most important symbol, remains the epicentre of technological innovation. It is a role they have performed with flair for decades, thanks to a low-regulation environment and a culture in which speed and risk are central and failure is seen as a necessary learning process. This translates into a high concentration of venture capital: more than half of global Venture Capital (VC) investment goes to American start-ups, or to European start-ups that set up in the US for that purpose. China has, in a short time, evolved from the 'copy factory of the world' into a country with strong innovations in strategic sectors, which, through state-led planning, are given all the resources to achieve their goals. Thanks to its scale and the rapid adoption of technology by consumers, the country has become a powerful innovation engine with a focus on energy, cleantech and, more recently, AI and microprocessors. Europe, by contrast, occupies a fundamentally different position. It strives for a balance between technological progress and social responsibility, with high demands in terms of regulation. In addition, the market is far more complex and fragmented, which makes it difficult to build a strong culture of innovation and growth. We have already discussed that European regulation does not, in itself, have to be a brake on innovation. Still, we cannot avoid noting that Europe's dynamics in this area, for the time being, cannot match what we see in the US.

A large part of what we see happening here is a self-fulfilling prophecy: the US has had a strong innovation landscape since the early days of the computer and later the internet. Time and again, it attracts the parties looking for that – both companies and investors. Europe misses out on those opportunities, partly because of that perception game, and partly because of a real disadvantage in this area. That means it is not enough for Europe to launch new initiatives: we also need to make enough noise around them to turn the image around – and here we are seeing good news for Europe. It is striking how many ambitious projects have recently been launched by the EU to accelerate innovation. The flagship is undoubtedly the Horizon Europe programme, which is making a budget of 95 billion euros available between 2021 and 2027 for investments in innovations that all focus on – yes – transitions. In addition, the Regional Innovation Valleys Initiative is trying to activate European regions as innovation hubs. By building a network of 147 RIVs – regional innovation valleys – Europe wants to create a fine-grained system that connects more and less innovative regions with one another. However interesting these initiatives may be, without an extra push on perception, their impact will remain limited.

Fortunately, the current geopolitical situation offers a chance to create genuine innovation momentum for Europe. Uncertainty in the United States creates an opportunity for the European continent. The US withdrawal from climate agreements, the hollowing-out of academic freedoms, the discontinuation of numerous research programmes in sustainability and medical disciplines, and a domestic political context that is becoming increasingly unpredictable, are undermining the classic image of America as the destination for scientists, entrepreneurs and investors. Moreover, the draconian approach to migration – against the interests of Silicon Valley – is creating a great deal of unease among current and future foreign talent. The question therefore arises as to whether they are still welcome there at all. European professors and academic staff with appointments at both European and American universities fear that, at some point, they may simply no longer be allowed to enter the country. The braingain the US has benefited from for years could well come to a halt, or even reverse into a movement in the opposite direction.

The top of the American technology sector

International talent mobility has been crucial to Silicon Valley's success. Companies such as Microsoft, Google, IBM, Adobe and NVIDIA are led by CEOs whose roots lie outside the US, often even outside the West.

- India has supplied the CEOs of Microsoft (Satya Nadella), Google (Sundar Pichai), IBM (Arvind Krishna) and Adobe (Shantanu Narayen).

- Jensen Huang (NVIDIA) is from Taiwan.
- Safra Catz (Oracle) is from Israel.
- Elon Musk (Tesla) is from South Africa and Canada.
- Lisa Su (AMD) is of Taiwanese descent.
- Cristiano Amon (Qualcomm) is from Brazil.
- Hock Tan (Broadcom) is from Singapore.
- Eric Yuan (Zoom) is from China.

America was a magnet for ambitious talent worldwide for decades.

What if the braingain in the US comes to an end, or better: what if Europe can take over that role? To be clear: I do not believe anyone from the current list of CEOs needs to fear for their job, although Trump did hint, in a recent conflict with Musk, at the possibility of stripping Musk of his American citizenship. The real issue lies with the next generation of talent. In the current climate, they may think twice before seeking their fortune in the US, and that creates opportunities for Europe to reinvent itself as an alternative: a safe and stable haven for those who want to move forward and no longer feel welcome in the US. That, precisely, is what Europe is now investing in at scale, with already impressive results. Driven by initiatives such as 'Choose Europe for Science', a major effort is under way to attract American scientists. On 5 May 2025, at the Sorbonne University, Ursula von der Leyen and Emmanuel Macron announced a programme that makes 500 million euros available for 'super grants', relocation bonuses and long-term contracts. The message is clear: anyone who wants to devote themselves to fundamental or applied research in a free environment is welcome in Europe. In addition, the European Innovation Council has launched a targeted marketing campaign that plays into this temporary geopolitical window of opportunity: an America that turns inward offers Europe the chance to open outward.

France has turned that strategy into an art form. With campaigns such as 'If you love freedom, come and help us stay free', President Macron strikes a broader emotional chord. Hundreds of applications from American academics have already come in through various programmes. The French state research organisation CNRS has opened its doors to researchers at every level, and ten other universities across Europe are working on similar initiatives. The first American researchers have now arrived in Aix-en-Provence and Marseille, where they began in June 2025. France has set aside a budget of 100 million euros to support this braingain. Germany, too, is working on a plan to attract up to 1,000 researchers, as part of a broader reform of the start-up ecosystem. Other countries, such as Belgium, the Netherlands, Portugal, Spain, Norway and Sweden, are also opening up to researchers and entrepreneurs through a range of programmes and measures. Most of these initiatives were launched only after Trump's inauguration, but within a few months they had already produced tangible results. France reported more than 30,000 registrations in a short period of time. Interest in the EU Blue Card – the work and residence permit for highly skilled professionals from non-EU/EEA countries – is growing. In addition, American interest in European business programmes is rising, while enthusiasm for their American counterparts is declining. Taken together, this forms a coordinated and smart strategy to tell the right story at the right moment: Europe as a refuge for free science, entrepreneurship and long-term thinking.

Money, honey

The positive impulses for Europe's innovation culture and capacity are encouraging, but there are still major differences and obstacles compared with the US. For years, raising financing as a start-up in the US was relatively easy – even if, in practice, it could still prove difficult. There was substantial risk capital available, but there were also many contenders. Even so, in the US you could repeatedly attract funding with relative ease, making it possible for promising companies to raise billions and enjoy virtually limitless financing to deliver growth. This dynamic has pulled strong European innovations across the Atlantic, and Europe now lags when it comes to turning innovations into successful start-ups that can scale into commercial powerhouses. In that respect, the US has been unrivalled for decades. The combination of an attractive start-up ecosystem, the availability of international talent, and access to capital has created a huge investment gap. American companies manage to raise up to eight times more venture capital from the market than their European counterparts. The million-euro question now is whether all the new resources being made available to build a resilient Europe can be the catalyst that channels far more money towards innovative start-ups – and whether those start-ups can then find their way to market and launch successful European products and services.

Europe has now begun to take steps to close that gap as well, albeit only partially. Various programmes – both at European level and within the member states

– are aimed at successfully translating deeptech research into start-ups. By deeptech we mean, among other things, AI, cleantech, biotechnology, quantum computing and robotics. The more 'surface-level' or commercial innovations often underpin Silicon Valley's successes. These programmes show how Europe is seeking to accelerate the transition from research to entrepreneurship, through an approach that recognises that this type of innovation requires long-term support and specialised resources. The focus is on bridging the gap between lab and market, through targeted pathways that provide not only funding, but also guidance, access to networks and access to markets. Despite all the recent initiatives, Europe still finds it difficult to truly make the shift. It is estimated that only 5 percent of total EU innovation funding reaches the European start-up ecosystem. That is why experts argue that EU programmes should more often be channelled through private accelerators, which are better equipped to allocate capital effectively at an early stage. There are also calls for faster, start-up-specific funding routes within future European support programmes. With the hundreds of billions that Europe is planning to invest in its resilience and defence, it becomes all the more crucial to build a strong bridge between these public resources and the innovative players in the market.

Even here, we are seeing signs of a positive turning point. Trump's re-election has led to a reshuffling of international capital flows, with investors increasingly choosing Europe over the US. From early 2025 to July 2025 there was a net outflow of almost 87 billion dollars from US markets, while Europe attracted more than 100 billion dollars. Analysts point to factors such as trade-war uncertainty and a return to isolationist policies as the main causes. At the same time, European regulation – with its predictable and stable character – is suddenly being seen as attractive, especially compared with erratic American policy. Another factor is the performance of Europe's markets themselves. Between November 2024 and July 2025, the European Stoxx 600 posted a gain of 8.9 percent, compared with 4.3 percent for the American S&P 500. Sectors such as defence technology – traditionally the domain of American players – are benefiting in particular from Europe's catch-up. For the European VC ecosystem, this shift opens up a double perspective. On the one hand, there is a clear opportunity: more liquidity, higher valuations, and growing interest from global investors in European technology companies. On the other hand, it also brings uncertainties, especially for start-ups with US operations or dependencies. European VC firms are signalling that investors are becoming more cautious about companies with strong ties to the US.

The challenge, then, is to seize this unique opportunity to structurally strengthen Europe's VC infrastructure. If this wave of investment can be anchored sustainably, it may well mark the beginning of a new era for European innovation. That is precisely what Europe is now leaning into, with the most ambitious example being the European Investment Bank's (EIB) recent announcement that it will invest no less than 70 billion euros in the tech sector. This is the largest innovation programme Europe has ever seen, with a clear goal: to reduce dependence on American technology and make Europe's investment climate more attractive. By lowering the financial risk for private investors, the EIB hopes to create a leverage effect that could result in a total of 250 billion euros of investment. An important additional measure is the acceleration of procedures: start-up applications must, from now on, be processed within six months, rather than the current eighteen months. Linked to this is the plan for a European savings and investment union, approved in early 2025. This plan is meant to change Europeans' attitudes to saving and investing, so that more money can flow into European start-ups and companies. It focuses on making better use of the vast savings that are currently largely tied up in low-yield products. While Americans mainly invest their money in shares and growth funds, Europeans still park around 70 percent of their wealth in savings accounts and fixed-term deposits.

The European Commission wants to change that by making investing simpler, cheaper and safer. Europe wants to better inform savers and actively involve them in strategic investments in infrastructure, defence or digitalisation via public instruments such as NextGenerationEU bonds. Institutional investors must also be brought in more. European insurers and pension funds are still heavily regulated on the basis of a precautionary logic dating back to the financial crisis. That makes them reluctant to invest in shares or higher-risk projects – precisely the engines that fuel innovation. The Commission wants to break that impasse by easing rules and making investment in sectors such as AI, biotech and cleantech more fiscally attractive. Work is also under way on a more integrated stock-market and banking sector, making it easier for companies to raise capital across multiple member states, and more attractive for investors to focus on the European market. All of this also brings risks. The tighter rules in financial markets after the banking crisis were not introduced without reason. Relaxing those rules could lead to greater exposure to market volatility, especially if savers are encouraged to invest in products they do not sufficiently understand. Europe will therefore have to find a balance between incentives and protection. If it succeeds, European savings can actively contribute to the transitions Europe needs. That is not only a financial lever; it can also help to strengthen citizens' involvement in the new European project.

Europe plans to invest substantial resources to strengthen the continent's resilience through programmes such as Readiness 2030, increased defence spending and a range of other investment pathways in technology and deeptech. Combined with recent policy changes, this is creating momentum to close our notorious gap with the US and build an attractive, high-performing investment ecosystem of our own. We may never fully reach the US level in terms of funding opportunities and start-up culture, but that does not necessarily have to be a problem.

The US operates with swagger and boldness, rooted in a culture where immense risks are normal. It is accepted that most invested money will yield nothing, as long as a few exceptional successes can ultimately grow into winner-takes-all behemoths that claim global market dominance. It is precisely that model that has given today's big tech players an unhealthy level of worldwide power. Europe, by contrast, is more cautious and therefore slower. We invest fewer resources in fewer cases, without necessarily aiming to build giants that push all competitors out of the market. Even if Europe's innovation, start-up and financing landscape were able to close the gap with the US, it may not be a bad idea to hold on to that aspect of our culture: rather than betting on one big jackpot with lots of 'dumb money', we should use the right amount of 'smart money' to build a broad range of healthy successes – and, in doing so, support Europe's transition.

Now that I have reached the end of this section, I want to introduce one more notion: when is an investment truly successful? Investors apply clear standards and expectations when they decide to put their money somewhere. If an investment cannot guarantee the expected return, the capital is placed elsewhere without hesitation. This makes it difficult for many transition projects to attract funding, because for the time being their returns are often lower than those of conventional investments. That, of course, is also why we still build much of Europe with things that can be produced more cheaply in China. The returns on those investments are higher than they would be if we chose to produce in our own region. But that reality ignores a number of costs that are not being counted. We are by now aware of the familiar externalities – such as environmental damage or CO_2 emissions in the country of origin – and European regulation is gradually trying to correct that imbalance. What I want to add, as a closing thought to this section on European investment, is an additional externality: something I call 'Return on Security'. We need to start factoring strategic risks into the business cases we draw up. The cheapest solution may also be the most dangerous, even if on paper it offers the best price-quality ratio.

Return on Security

China has by now become the world leader in manufacturing solar panels, which means Chinese producers can manufacture far more cheaply than European ones – and a European installation can cost up to 200 percent more than a comparable Chinese setup. The second element is that in some Chinese inverters, backdoors have been built in, making it possible to manipulate them remotely. Third, consider the energy blackout that hit Spain and Portugal in April 2025.

If we connect these three elements, an interesting case emerges: Suppose we now decide to replace all solar panels in Europe with European installations. The total cost would then be estimated at around 220 billion euros. A gigantic sum that, at first glance, is hard to justify. But consider this: if half of Europe were to lose power for two weeks due to a sabotage operation, the total societal, economic, and infrastructure damage could rise to 650 billion euros. Imagine what happens if all of Europe goes down. Spain and Portugal are estimated to have suffered around 400 million euros in damage during a blackout that lasted barely ten hours.

Of course, we don't need to immediately replace all Chinese installations with European ones. What I ***am*** arguing is that we need to look at costs far more holistically and factor strategic risks into economic trade-offs. In our current lowest-price logic, those risks are barely taken into account. For every business case, the potential damage in a worst-case scenario should be included as a standard part of the calculation.

We rarely look at budgets the way we should: as communicating vessels. Budgets are usually controlled by specific departments or organisations that benefit from an investment, but don't bear the cost if things go wrong later. Energy companies aren't exactly eager to absorb cost increases of up to 200 percent for European solar installations if, during a later blackout, most of the damage ends up on someone else's budget. One of the levers for financing the major transitions of tomorrow is being willing to accept higher costs when those costs increase security. We should treat those added costs as an advance payment on the costs of future disasters we can prevent as much as possible. Think of it as a strategic insurance premium. A lot of water will still have to flow into Europe's seas before we reach the point where European money from some kind of recovery fund is invested *preventively* in a project that ensures no recovery will be needed later. Put differently: if we had invested 100 billion in preventing the COVID-19 pandemic, wouldn't we have been able to save nearly 1,000 billion in support measures? There is still a great deal of work to be done to make Europe an innovative and entrepreneurial continent that can compete with the US and China, but the stars are aligned. Now that all these initiatives are being set in motion, I hope we do this in an efficient – but above all smart and distinctly European – way, and that we don't let ourselves be tempted into doing it the way the US does.

European leadership and the United States of Europe

Talk to someone about Europe and you're guaranteed that within ten minutes the elephant in the room will come up: Europe is weak, lacks leadership, and can't decide anything because some country will always veto it. It's true that Europe doesn't have the decisiveness of the United States, where the president is both head of state and head of government, with broad executive powers. The fact that this setup isn't without risk is obvious in the way Trump pushes the limits of his authority and mandate. The US has a number of crucial federal powers – defence, foreign policy, monetary policy, taxation, and immigration. Other powers sit with individual states, which creates tension between federal and local interests, especially given the suspicion many Americans harbour toward anything decided at the federal level. In that respect, the differences between the US and Europe are smaller than people often assume. Europe is usually seen as a complex puzzle of countries with their own languages, cultures, interests, tax systems, and policy priorities. That's often cited as the reason for Europe's supposed lack of clout. And yet the gap with the US is relative: American states also differ greatly in culture, economic development, ideological orientation, and – for example – climate policy, but the US still manages to function like a well-oiled machine on the international stage and at home.

Unfortunately, the same can't be said of the EU. Europe often appears divided and slow to decide, struggling to act decisively both within and beyond its borders. But to dismiss Europe as weak – or doomed to impotence – isn't entirely fair. The United States has had more than two hundred years to build its federal structures, refine its institutions, and calibrate the balance of power between the states and the federal level. The last eighty years added everything that has made it a geopolitical superpower today. The European Union, by contrast, only emerged after World War II and has, at its core, always been an economic project – without any real necessity to develop strong political or military structures. On top of that, we've already made the case that it served the interests of the US and other great powers for Europe not to become too politically or militarily strong. A semi-united yet still semi-divided Europe was a perfectly acceptable equilibrium – and it remains the goal of those forces that try to pull Europe further apart, so that the prospect of a truly strong union is kept out of reach altogether.

For the United States, declaring independence on July 4, 1776 was the spark that pushed the country to organise itself. For Europe, that defining moment doesn't seem to have been the end of World War II, but rather 2025 – the year it became unmistakably clear that we are living in a new world order. Europe is realising that, if it wants to play a meaningful role as a continent and as a union, it will have to make fundamental choices – and develop the capacity to carry them out. The EU's current structure and organisation still lack the strength and authority to make that happen. But just as the momentum now exists to make technological and economic leaps, perhaps – administratively speaking – that momentum exists too. In this book I'm not looking for institutional solutions, even if I could. There are plenty of political scientists and other '-ologists' currently wrestling with the question of how Europe can reorganise itself to fulfil its new role, while taking into account the tensions and distrust that many European citizens feel. What I do think I can offer sits in the same 'soft' approach I discussed earlier: sidestep resistance to top-down obligations framed as macro-themes by focusing instead on persuasion through micro-themes (chapters 10 and 15). That way, we can realise the transitions step by step and still reach the larger long-term goals – without running headfirst into overwhelming opposition.

Maybe, someday, there will be a true United States of Europe – comparable to what we know from the US. Maybe it will arrive sooner than we think, if external forces push us in that direction and people, in times of crisis, are always more willing to rally behind one overarching goal. Maybe it will take us two hundred years too, just as it did in the US, and Europe's obstacles will be removed one by one on the road toward a tight social, economic, financial, fiscal, and military union. But I don't think we can count on that United States of Europe being in place within the coming years or even decades – certainly not in time to help us realise the major transitions through a new model. So we need a pragmatic approach – and one exists. The first signs of this typically European 'soft' approach are already visible on the EU's political stage. Alliances are starting to take shape, and we increasingly hear talk of 'coalitions of the willing', where groups of countries come together and decide to cooperate more closely. In this way, the classic requirement of broad European consensus is no longer necessary. What few people realise is that it is perfectly possible, within Europe, to organise a kind of core Europe: a group of countries that want to work together very closely on specific themes, without requiring every member state to agree. The EU has several legal mechanisms specifically designed for exactly that purpose.

The best-known example is the mechanism of *Enhanced Cooperation*, which allows member states to work more closely together in a specific policy area – think defence, climate, or migration – without requiring all other countries to participate. This cooperation must remain compatible with broader EU law and may not undermine the single market. Since defence is not an EU competence, it lends itself particularly well to this kind of internal cooperation. In this way, countries can make progress on crucial issues while keeping the door open for other member states to join later. What is less widely known is that a form of European military cooperation already exists through PESCO (Permanent Structured Cooperation), in which 26 EU member states collaborate on a wide range of defence projects. There is also a third mechanism, Article 44 of the Treaty on European Union, which provides the legal basis for coalitions of the willing. Under this article, specific member states can be authorised by the European Council (the meeting of all heads of government and heads of state) to carry out a particular mission or operation on behalf of the EU. This creates structures that can be deployed quickly in urgent situations – for example, crisis response during natural disasters. In addition, there are successful examples of cooperation between individual countries, outside the formal EU legal framework, that were only later integrated into EU law. The Schengen Agreement began in 1985 as an intergovernmental arrangement among a handful of member states on border controls, and was only formally incorporated into EU legislation in 1999. This shows that it is entirely possible to start even outside the EU structures and integrate later.

Building a core Europe inevitably runs into a number of challenges. Democratic legitimacy can come under pressure if decisions are taken further away from national parliaments. There is also a risk of creating a complex tangle of overlapping structures between the EU, NATO, and national armed forces, and tensions may arise between participating and non-participating member states – although those tensions can also become an incentive to bring non-participating states on board. In addition, constitutional constraints in some countries may prevent participation in a core-Europe model. Still, these objections don't have to block this route, provided there is political will and sufficient democratic support for change. The concept of a core Europe is therefore not merely a vague idea, but something that can be set up through various legal pathways within, or even outside, the existing EU framework. It enables a model of concentric circles: a limited number of members move first, and – issue by issue – competences are shifted to a central European level, until it has effectively become a United States of Europe. Perhaps, one day, other regions will look on with a hint of envy at how Europe then functions like a well-oiled machine, no longer needing to fall short of the way other great powers are governed. One is allowed to dream.

In search of a European story and a European identity

With that, I've reached the end of this book, and there is one important condition left for Europe to make its ambitions real. How can I say this without insulting the people at the EU too harshly? Well, put subtly: maybe it could all be a bit smoother, a bit more compelling? Okay – let's call a spade a spade: dear Ursula, could it please be a little less boring? The wake-up call of early 2025 has landed loud and clear. Never before has Europe put plans – and (financial) resources – on the table at this scale to build its future. The ambitions, and the many hundreds of billions that will be invested, make all earlier Marshall Plans and Green Deals look modest by comparison. And yet it all sounds so dull – assuming people are even aware of what Europe is doing. I so often hear the remark that Europe doesn't seem to be responding to everything that's happening right now, but nothing could be further from the truth. It's just that we notice so little of it. Say what you will about Trump, but he's not a bad salesman. He can sell the most incoherent and improbable stories to his base, over and over again. The way he does it often defies imagination, but the message lands. Granted, it's easier to sell demolition-populism with simple slogans. 'Migrants out' (see Chapter 10 on objectifying dissection) simply hits harder than a carefully reasoned ten-page argument about the pros and cons of labour migration for low-skilled workers in Italy's fruit harvest.

Europe doesn't just need plans and money – it needs, first and foremost, a compelling story. Macro-themes and doom narratives about everything that will happen if we don't change course immediately drive many people away from both media and politics. Tell constructive stories that connect directly to people's everyday lives, while still serving the same underlying goal: making the world a better place, in full awareness of the big challenges we face. I almost hesitate to say it, but what we truly need is a form of European propaganda. For anyone who, at the very last pages of my book, now wants to throw it into a virtual fireplace: hold on to it for a moment longer. I know propaganda has a negative connotation – and rightly so. It's one of the most efficient tools in the hands of autocrats, dictators, and other unpleasant types to steer large groups of people. What I mean is that we can learn from the tactics of propaganda and then use them for the right reasons – without manipulation, deceit, or censorship.

We need a systematic way of communicating that reconnects people with the European project. Or perhaps I should say: that involves people in the European project for the first time, truly. We need to learn to simplify messages without falsifying them – and repeat them again and again. That's exactly what we see populists do when they hammer the same slogan into place for years. Marketers and advertisers have long known that repetition and exposure are crucial. Europe needs to become a strong brand, and in that context it's not wrong to tie messages to symbols – and even to rituals. That's a universal way of reaching people's subconscious directly. I can imagine this immediately triggers associations: masses marching behind flags, sharp-edged symbols on armbands – a nightmare we absolutely do not want, not even 'for the good cause'. But there are positive examples too: the white balloons during the large demonstrations against child abuse in Belgium, and even the hashtag #Jan25 used in Egypt during the Arab Spring protests – both can be seen as mobilising symbols. For thousands of years, cultures all over the world have used symbols and rituals to bind people together, not to drive them apart.

More than those important formal features, the messages need to be personal and relatable – representative of ordinary people and their everyday lives. In moments of major conflict, we can mobilise people behind a single theme: a shared enemy image, or a disaster we must face together. In periods of relative calm and stability, we focus on micro-themes and the personal progress they bring. What we communicate must be transparent and true: the big long-term goals Europe is pursuing should not be hidden. We just stop bludgeoning people with them.

Now that I've used one taboo word, I might as well introduce a second. We absolutely need a European identity. Ask yourself what a Pole, an Irishman, and a Chinese person in 1919 had in common when, after strict immigration controls, they were admitted to the United States via Ellis Island. The moment they set foot on shore, they were Americans. Their identity shifted in an instant – from something tied to a tense guarding of the past, rooted in race, religion, and culture – to a shared journey into the future. I think we need to give all Europeans – also the very newly arrived Europeans – that same chance: to believe again in a strong identity. An identity of people who consider it worthwhile to help build – and, if necessary, to fight for – a strong Europe: a place you want to be, a place that offers opportunity regardless of your background, as long as you believe in the values Europe stands for: democracy, pluralism, freedom, solidarity, development, and progress. And that also means that – from within that identity – we must be prepared to defend those values and that vision of the future, whatever the future brings.

I believe the momentum for a truly united Europe is here for the first time. Let's seize it together and – using all the potential Europe has – build the strong Union that, for the past eighty years, we never really had to be, or were even allowed to become. We all carry a crushing responsibility for whether this ambition succeeds. Right now, there are European and national politicians who keep fueling polarisation for the sake of their personal and party interests; media that keep betting on sensation and clickbait, treating their role as truth-seekers as secondary to the year-end numbers; companies that, without European rules, want to maximise profit at the expense of people and the planet; and citizens who, isolated in their echo chambers, turn against their fellow citizens – and, by extension, against the entire system. If we let all of this spiral out of control, then the enemies of a strong Europe will achieve their goal through further fragmentation. Europe will become nothing more than a tourist destination with good food and old buildings.

But if we all choose to work together – critically and pragmatically – toward one goal: a strong Europe in all its diversity, then it just might work. 'Fuck the system' is really not a good idea for the future – Europe still has far too much to offer for that.

Conclusion

How do you write a book about themes that change every day, without it already being outdated before it even goes to print? When do you decide the book is finished, when there's so much new material emerging daily? (Granted, the publisher's hard deadline is a pretty effective stick behind the door.)

Between writing the book and writing this conclusion lie about two months of revisions, editing, proofreading, and other magical things that happen in my publisher's backroom – and that ultimately result in a finished product. That time gave me the chance to look back at my story and to ask myself whether current events had overtaken it. The opposite is true: the patterns in the US and elsewhere in the world are becoming clearer by the day, and Europe's momentum seems only to be accelerating. The urgency to formulate an answer to the current situation grows stronger with each passing day.

I hope this book shows that what is happening in the world is not random, and that recognising and understanding these forces can enable Europe to reinvent itself – without disowning the historical evolution of its values and norms. What has been happening in the US since early 2025 shows how quickly (justified or not) discontent can lead to the weakening and even dismantling of a democracy. Europe must not fall into the same trap. We all know the story of the frog in the water that stays put because the temperature rises gradually – until it's too late. What we're seeing now is that Trump has stoked the fire under the geopolitical pot so intensely that we feel the heat and *do* jump out of the water. That's the good news.

The less good news is that there's still a lot that needs to happen to put these insights into practice. Europe has to build structures at breakneck speed to make up for the setbacks of the past decades. We're already seeing signals of that everywhere: extensive European initiatives and unprecedented financial resources to strengthen strategic domains; the drive to attract international talent to our companies and research centers; the acceleration Europe's defense effort has entered – these are all early indications that the momentum is, in fact, being seized.

What will be decisive if we want to be *truly* successful and put Europe on the new geopolitical map is leadership. Here too, we see opportunities emerging and people and countries positioning themselves to play a role. As I've described, Europe does have the mechanisms to accelerate – even if only with a smaller group – and to set aside the doubters or even the saboteurs. That, too, is happening now.

But leadership isn't only a responsibility of politics. If we want this project to succeed, we all have to be leaders. Companies must be willing to commit to the new innovation paradigms. Investors must be willing to reconsider what 'return' means, with an eye on the cost of security and sovereignty. But above all, European citizens must believe in a positive vision of Europe's future.

Dear reader, it depends on you.

Acknowledgements

This was a tough book to write, and without the support of so many people, I could never have pulled it off. As always, I want to start by thanking my family. Somewhere in the book, I mention how a renovation can generate so much stress and tension that a divorce becomes a real possibility. Well – writing a book can have a similar effect. Thankfully that wasn't the case this time, and Florence, my children Marilou and César, and my mother, who lives with us, gave me the space I needed to play hermit. They were also – often to their irritation – my first sounding board: I hijacked many evenings at the dinner table to pitch ideas and gauge their reactions. At this point they no longer need to read the book to know what has been on my mind.

Many people read drafts of the book in different stages of completion, and their input was invaluable. Without a doubt my wife, Florence Pérès, was the most critical reader: she didn't mince her words when she pointed out language mistakes, strange leaps, unclear sentences, and, at times, rather boring lists.

Next, I want to thank Dado Van Peteghem. Our often spicy discussions made me aware of my own bias and helped sharpen the story. Thank you to Bart Beuten and Leo Neels for their substantive insights into politics, society, and media. Thank you to Ben Caudron and Bruno Iserbyt for challenging some of my assumptions with an extremely critical eye – I listened carefully to your remarks, though I didn't always incorporate them; now and then, a person is allowed to disagree. Thank you to Bregt Bourgeus for being my spiritual mentor throughout this whole process: your enthusiasm pushed me to turn a few loose ideas and fragments into a full book. And thanks as well to Frédéric De Vries and Kenny Van Wassenhoven, two driven readers whose notes and suggestions could almost have been a book in themselves.

Of course, I also want to thank Niels, Marije, Susan, and the entire team at LannooCampus for their belief in the book, and for their editorial and substantive support. Special thanks to Niels for approving a title that includes the word 'fuck'. Finally, I want to thank Frank van Oirschot. Without that inspiring culinary evening in Amsterdam, on the day of the US elections, I probably would never have decided to write this book. Your insights – and your Dutch directness – helped me challenge and validate my ideas. I hope I haven't forgotten anyone in these acknowledgements, but if I have, please accept my apologies in advance.

Thank you, everyone!